Visual Marketing
From Attention to Action

Marketing and Consumer Psychology Series
Curtis P. Haugtvedt, Ohio State University
Series Editor

Cele C. Otnes and Tina M. Lowrey
Contemporary Consumption Rituals: A Research Anthology

Gad Saad
Applications of Evolutionary Psychology in Consumer Behavior

Michel Wedel and Rik Pieters
Visual Marketing: From Attention to Action

Visual Marketing
From Attention to Action

Edited by

Michel Wedel
Rik Pieters

CRC Press
Taylor & Francis Group
Boca Raton London New York

CRC Press is an imprint of the
Taylor & Francis Group, an **informa** business

CRC Press
Taylor & Francis Group
6000 Broken Sound Parkway NW, Suite 300
Boca Raton, FL 33487-2742

First issued in paperback 2019

ISBN-13: 978-0-8058-6292-8 (hbk)
ISBN-13: 978-0-367-86667-9 (pbk)

Visit the Taylor & Francis Web site at
http://www.taylorandfrancis.com

and the LEA and Routledge Web site at
http://www.routledge.com

Preface

This book is the outgrowth of the Visual Marketing Conference that was organized at the University of Michigan in May 2005. It was sponsored by the Yaffe Center for Persuasive Communication and the University of Michigan Business School.

The Visual Marketing Conference was, to our knowledge, the first to have brought together leading scholars from psychology and marketing who work in areas related to visual aspects of marketing and consumer behavior. It was motivated by the idea that although visual processes are a central component of consumer behavior, they have been unduly neglected as a prime area of research in social psychology and marketing at the expense of cognitive-affective processes. This situation has rapidly changed in recent years, however, and the conference aimed to assimilate the research interests and efforts of leading researchers in visual marketing with the purpose of stimulating the transition of the visual marketing field to its next stage. The contributions to the conference showed once more that rather than being mere input or recording processes that translate the visual world "out there" into the affective-cognitive world "in here," visual processes play a central role in the mental stream, both consciously and unconsciously, and thereby directly implicate consumer behavior. The presentations also revealed that the practice of marketing presents a fertile testing ground and offers ample opportunity to study visual processes in real-life conditions.

Therefore, the time has now come to further establish visual marketing as a discipline with a focus on the central role of vision in consumer behavior. Establishing this field is pertinent because the amount and diversity of visual stimuli in the marketplace is growing at an ever more rapid pace, as are the needs of companies and professionals to better understand their impact on consumer behavior, and how these insights can be used to improve visual marketing efforts.

Each participant at the conference was invited because of his or her persistent pursuit of improved understanding of the role visual processes in consumer behavior, and because of his or her of significant contributions to it. Consequently, the presenters extensively engaged in critical discussion and mutual inspiration. We were fortunate that the invited researchers enthusiastically presented provocative empirical findings, models, and integrated frameworks based on their often long-standing research programs. We are very grateful for their contributions.

Our editors Anne Duffy and Rebecca Larsen at Psychology Press embraced the idea of publishing an edited volume based on the presentations at the Visual Marketing Conference. The authors had the task of being "thought-provoking" in reworking their conference presentations into the book chapters. The authors did more than we asked for. Each and every chapter in this volume is a gem of visions and new ideas based on outstanding research. To see this, one only needs to look.

Michel Wedel
University of Maryland

Rik Pieters
Tilburg University

Contributors

Eric T. Bradlow
Marketing Department
The Wharton School
University of Pennsylvania
Philadelphia, Pennsylvania

Monica S. Castelhano
Department of Psychology
University of Massachusetts
Amherst, Massachusetts

Pierre Chandon
Marketing Department
INSEAD
Fontainebleau, France

Hyejeung Cho
Marketing Department
College of Business
University of Texas at San Antonio
San Antonio, Texas

Eric Greenleaf
Marketing Department
Leonard N. Stern School of Business
New York University
New York, New York

J. Wesley Hutchinson
Marketing Department
The Wharton School
University of Pennsylvania
Philadelphia, Pennsylvania

Chris Janiszewski
Marketing Department
Warrington College of Business Administration
University of Florida
Gainesville, Florida

Aradhna Krishna
Ross School of Business
University of Michigan
Ann Arbor, Michigan

Edward F. McQuarrie
Marketing Department
Leavey School of Business
Santa Clara University
Santa Clara, California

Joan Meyers-Levy
Marketing/Logistics Management
Carlson School of Management
University of Minnesota
Minneapolis, Minnesota

Rik Pieters
Marketing Department
Faculty of Business and Economics
Tilburg University
Tilburg, The Netherlands

Priya Raghubir
Marketing Department
Haas School of Business
University of California at Berkeley
Berkeley, California

Keith Rayner
Department of Psychology
University of Massachusetts
Amherst, Massachusetts

Norbert Schwarz
Department of Psychology
Ross School of Business, and Institute for Social Research
University of Michigan
Ann Arbor, Michigan

Hyunjin Song
Department of Psychology
University of Michigan
Ann Arbor, Michigan

Nader T. Tavassoli
Marketing Department
London Business School
London, United Kingdom

Michel Wedel
Marketing Department
Robert H. Smith School of Business
University of Maryland
College Park, Maryland

Scott H. Young
Perception Research Services
Fort Lee, New Jersey

Rui (Juliet) Zhu
Marketing Department
Sauder School of Business
University of British Columbia
Vancouver, British Columbia, Canada

Series Foreword

The Marketing and Consumer Psychology book series was developed to serve as a bridge between basic research and practical applications. In this volume, *Visual Marketing*, Wedel and Pieters bring together internationally recognized experts to summarize, challenge, and stimulate further development in state-of-the-art knowledge regarding roles and influences of visual stimuli in attracting attention, as well as influences on visual stimuli on consumer memory, persuasion, product choice and other behaviors. The book chapters identify numerous and innovative practical applications as well as areas needing greater development to provide clearer answers to basic research and application oriented questions. This book will be of great interest to new and seasoned practitioners as well as young and established researchers.

Curtis P. Haugtvedt
Ohio State University

Contents

1

Introduction to Visual Marketing

Michel Wedel and Rik Pieters

The Emerging Visual Marketing Discipline

Visual marketing is widely recognized to be important in practice. As consumers, we are exposed to several hundreds of explicit advertisements daily on television, in newspapers, magazines, billboards, the yellow pages, retail feature ads, and on Internet sites. We experience even more implicit visual messages in the form of product packages in stores and at home. Point-of-purchase stimuli, such as store displays, shelf talkers and flyers, are omnipresent and commercial visual messages appear on the side of trucks, road signs, food wrappers in restaurants, on service provider uniforms, t-shirts, CDs and electronic devices. Often, these are part of corporate visual identity communication, ways in which companies organize to visually present themselves in a consistent manner. Visual aspects are also a key component of marketing collateral, which involves the use of visual aids to make sales effort more effective, after a prospective buyer has been identified. All this requires graphical design of the commercial visual stimuli in question. The basic elements of graphical design, as in many other areas of design, include shape, size, form, texture, lines, and color. But, the visual context in which products, brands, and ads are presented may affect consumers' reactions to them as well.

All this is part of what we term visual marketing; that is, the strategic utilization by firms of commercial and noncommercial visual signs and symbols to deliver desirable and/or useful messages and experiences to consumers. An important component of visual marketing is the actual design of the visual communication, including logo, packaging, and advertising design, and more recently web page design. If indeed "seeing is believing," and "believing is buying," it is important to manage what consumers see to maximize profit. This is increasingly recognized in business. A search for Visual Marketing on Google produced about 46 million hits in November 2006. Firms and consulting agencies in such diverse areas as web design, advertising, retail merchandising, store and mall design, packaging, and company image and identity development all associate themselves with visual marketing, many times even using "Visual Marketing" in their names.

But in spite of the prevalence of visual marketing in practice, and the large amounts of money invested in it, sound theoretical underpinnings have long been lacking or were not synthesized in marketing science, and thus its potential effectiveness was insufficiently reached. The body of theoretical knowledge backing visual marketing efforts is still limited and scattered. This situation is changing, with leading research groups in marketing and consumer behavior establishing this new field. Much can be gained from the emerging insights into the effects that brands, package designs, print and banner advertisements and other visual tools have on consumers' visual perception, and into the role that visual perception plays in shaping consumer behavior.

Theory development in visual marketing is situated at the intersection of vision science, cognitive psychology, and social psychology. Vision science is interdisciplinary itself and sometimes considered the most successful branch of cognitive science, having its roots in psychology, neuroscience, computer science, optometry, and aesthetics, among others (Palmer, 1999). Central is the idea that vision is the computation occuring in the eye and brain to build a representation of the world surrounding us. One of the goals of vision science is to uncover these mechanisms and reveal their implications. It covers the (neurological) make-up of the visual system, including that of the eye and the visual cortex. Insights from vision science help to understand what consumers are most likely to perceive centrally or consciously when, for instance, standing in their local supermarket in front of the soft drink shelf; what they perceive peripherally or subliminally, without conscious awareness; what aspects of the visual stimuli (packages, displays, shelves) affect this; and how they move the eyes to build up a representation of the shelf.

Vision science overlaps with cognitive psychology. Cognitive psychology has gained much knowledge about the influence of perceptual characteristics of rudimentary stimuli on attentional and cognitive processes. This research has laid the very foundation of the understanding of visual perception of marketing stimuli, and many studies in visual marketing build directly on it. For example, the extensive literature on eye tracking in psychology (see Rayner, 1998, for a review) has led to an important set of tools to evaluate visual marketing effort and to insights that help improve its effectiveness. It has impacted both the theory and practice of visual marketing, even early on (Russo, 1978). Initially this research emphasized fundamental attentional and perceptual processes, using abstracted stimuli under controlled conditions, with some notable exceptions including Broadbent's (1958) and Gibson's (1986) ecological approach to perception. As such, early research could not concentrate on the realistic, complex stimuli that consumers encounter daily, or on individual differences in processing due to consumers' momentary states and stable traits. This situation has rapidly changed, and fundamental research on scene perception and target search in cognitive psychology, for example, increasingly employs realistic scenes and complex stimulus configurations, under the typically cluttered exposure conditions that characaterize the marketing environment. Kingstone and his colleagues (Kingstone, Smilek, Ristic, Kelland-Friesen, & Eastwood, 2003) recently urged cognitive researchers to "get out of the laboratory and study how individuals actually behave in the real world" (p. 179), for example by observing and describing cognition and behavior as it happens in front of them. The spectacular findings of such work are immediately relevant to visual marketing.

Visual marketing is also at the intersection of vision science and social psychology, with the latter offering theories and methods to assess and understand the role of motivation and emotion in vision. Recent research in this area is fascinating, allowing insights into the influence of consumers' states and traits on attention and perception, and the other way around. This interface between motivation and attention may attract much interest in years to come. Research may build for instance on recent studies showing that people are more likely to perceive desirable than undesirable objects in ambigious figures (Balcetis & Dunning, 2006). Likewise, goal research in social psychology has found that priming a particular goal tends to activate the means to attain the goal, and to simultaneously inhibit conflicting goals (e.g., Kruglanski et al., 2002). This is in line with the research stream on activation and inhibition in vision science and cognitive psychology. Combining insights from social psychology and vision science will lead to better theories and models, and to better visual marketing practice.

It is important to establish that the focus on the "visual" aspect of marketing activity does not preclude a role for textual information, and other sense modalities. First, text is presented in a visual format, and logotype, word size, color, and other text features all may affect consumer experience and behavior (Doyle & Bottomley, 2006). Thus, both texts and pictorials are visual. Second, whereas a single picture may convey a thousand words, a single word may stimulate vivid images that may move consumers to attend, prefer, or buy (MacInnis & Price, 1987). These visual imagery effects of text can be part of the domain of visual marketing as well. Third, textual and pictorial processing may cooperate or conflict, and such cross-presentation effects are important to understand. For example, textual descriptions change the memory for pictures (Gentner & Loftus, 1979), and consumption vocabularies change and refine consumption experiences and memory, and allow them to influence future behavior (West, Brown, & Hoch, 1996). Fourth, the senses cooperate in task completion, and there is increasing insight into the role and influence of video, audio, tangible, smell, and other stimuli, and about the consumer operations on them (Meyer & Kieras, 1997). Such insights may be important for the development of, for example, visual radio (http://www.visualradio.com).

In sum, visual marketing covers the role and influence of visual (pictorial and textual) marketing stimuli in consumer behavior, as well as the visual processing mechanisms underlying consumer behavior. It is founded in vision science, cognitive psychology, and social psychology, and aims to understand and assess the influence of visual marketing activity, and to improve visual communication design.

Contributions

This book aims to further research and theory development in visual marketing. By bringing together leading researchers in the field, it strives to contribute to the establishment of visual marketing as a coherent discipline. The chapters represent a representative array of issues in visual marketing. They address three areas in visual marketing theory: attention and perception (chapters 2–5), visual cognition (chapters 6–9), and action and choice (chapters 10–12). The chapters go beyond what is known, and offer in many cases a more speculative and visionary account of the directions that visual marketing research could and should take.

In chapter 2, Rayner and Castelhano review foundational research on eye movements in reading, scene perception, and visual search. They discuss research in cognitive psychology on issues such as the size of the perceptual span and how decisions are made about when and where to move the eyes in each of the three tasks. Understanding eye movements in these three tasks is required to understand eye movements when viewers look at advertising. They show that the tasks differ considerably, and that eye movements also differ considerably as a function of the task. Research on eye movements while looking at ads is reviewed and discussed.

Pieters and Wedel, in chapter 3, propose six cornerstones to further eye tracking theory and research in visual marketing, and in this process remedy six common delusions about the role and utility of eye movements in assessing visual marketing effectiveness. The influences of consumers' processing goals on eye movements to print advertising are discussed as an important illustration of the new insights that can be gained from eye tracking research of visual marketing stimuli.

In chapter 4, Tavassoli shows how visual selection has affective consequences beyond and counter to mere exposure. This research promises a variety of new insights central to marketing. Instead of the old marketing dictum that *every exposure is a good exposure*, his research shows that marketers need to heed the fact that the mere act of observing an object changes it.

In chapter 5, McQuarrie develops a new rhetorical framework for differentiating the pictures that appear in magazine advertisements. This framework offers a system of distinctions among kinds of pictures. He shows that pictorial strategies in American magazine advertisements have changed significantly. Strategies that were common in the 1980s are relatively scarce today, and vice versa. Going beyond a mere statement of the phenomenon, he then discusses the changes in both the advertising environment and in consumer response to advertising that might be hypothesized to explain these changes.

Greenleaf and Raghubir revisit in chapter 6 a fundamental question in aesthetics: whether people prefer certain proportions for the sides of rectangles. This issue has attracted relatively little research in marketing, even though rectangles are perhaps the most common shape that consumers encounter in package design, product design, and print advertising. They show that people do prefer certain ratios of rectangular products and packages, and that people favor a range of proportions rather than any single proportion alone. They show that the ratios of rectangular products offered in the marketplace appear to reflect the effect of the marketing context.

Raghubir proposes a new *hard-wired* model of perceptual judgments in chapter 7. The model accounts for documented patterns of visual biases in spatial perception. It adds to information processing models that have been developed in the domain of semantic information processing.

Krishna, in chapter 8, brings together spatial perception research relevant to marketing in an integrated framework. She aims at making managers more aware of spatial perception biases. She focuses on factors that affect *spatial perceptions*, in particular, length, area, volume, and number perceptions, and their implications for consumer behavior.

Chapter 9 by Meyers-Levy and Zhu explores how structural aspects of shopping and consumption environments may affect consumers' cognition and responses. They consider a wide array of architectural, and free-standing, in-store elements that are often present in such environments. An application that they discuss pertains to ceiling height, showing that a high versus a low ceiling prompts individuals to activate concepts associated with *freedom* versus *confinement*, respectively. These then prompt more abstract and more specific associations.

In chapter 10, Chandon, Hutchinson, Bradlow, and Young show how commercially available eye-tracking data can be used to decompose a brand's consideration into its memory-based baseline and its visual lift, using a novel decision-path model of visual attention and brand consideration. They show the importance of visual-based factors in driving brand consideration. They also provide insight into the interplay between consideration decisions and visual attention to prices and packages during consumers' decision-making processes at the point of purchase.

In chapter 11, Cho, Schwarz, and Song describe the *feelings-as-information* perspective. They illustrate the misattribution of affective reactions to the visual context in which a product is presented as reactions to the product itself. They use the context of websites that provide consumers with an opportunity to virtually "try on" a product by displaying it on their own image. In a second application of the perspective, they show that the ease with which a print font can be read can have a profound impact on consumer judgment and choice.

In chapter 12, Janiszewski provides an epilogue to the book, with the goal to provide ideas that may spur additional research on visual communication. He reconsiders the role of key constructs in the information processing literature and reorients the focus of inquiry from information analysis to meaning and experience creation. In doing so, he uses construction and sculpturing metaphors.

The book is based on the presentations during the two-day IC1 Conference organized at the Ross School of Business at the University of Michigan, in June 2005, with the support of the Ross School and the Yaffe Center for Persuasive Communication. IC means "I see," and we did. Video streams of the presentations are available at http://www.bus.umich.edu/ic1/.

The collection of chapters in this book provides a representative sample of excellent research in the domain of visual marketing. The chapters are not meant to provide a definitive view on an issue or topic, but rather based on initial research, provide provocative and testable views that may stimulate future research in this area. We are truly grateful to the contributors for their time and their willingness to expose their ideas in this form, and for their important service to the emerging science of visual marketing.

References

Balcetis, E., & Dunning, D. (2006). See what you want to see: Motivational influences on visual perception. *Journal of Personality and Social Psychology, 91*, 612–625.

Broadbent, D. E. (1958). *Perception and communication*. London: Pergamon Press.

Doyle, J. R., & Bottomley, P. A. (2006). Dressed for the occasion: Font-product congruity in the perception of logotype. *Journal of Consumer Psychology, 16*(2), 112–123.

Gentner, D., & Loftus, E. F. (1979). Integration of verbal and visual information as evidenced by distortions in picture memory. *American Journal of Psychology, 92*(2), 363–375.

Gibson, J. J. (1986). *The ecological approach to visual perception*. Hillsdale, NJ: Lawrence Erlbaum Associates.

Kingstone, A., Smilek, D., Ristic, J., Kelland-Friesen, C., & Eastwood, J. D. (2003). Attention, researchers! It is time to take a look at the real world. *Current Directions in Psychological Science, 12*(5), 176–184.

Kruglanski, A. W., Shah, J. Y., Fishbach, A., Friedman, R., Chun, W. Y., & Sleeth-Keppler, D. (2002). A theory of goal systems. *Advances in Experimental Social Psychology, 34*, 331–378.

MacInnis, D. J., & Price, L. L. (1987). The role of imagery in information processing: Review and extensions. *Journal of Consumer Research, 13*(4), 473–491.

Meyer, D. E., & Kieras, D. E. (1997). A computational theory of executive cognitive processes and multiple-task performance: Part 1. Basic mechanisms. *Psychological Review, 112*(1), 3–65.

Palmer, S. E. (1999). *Vision science: Photons to phenomenology*. Cambridge, MA: The MIT Press.

Rayner, K. (1998). Eye movements in reading and information processing: 20 years of research. *Psychological Bulletin, 124*(3), 372–422.

Russo, J. E. (1978). Eye fixations can save the world: A critical evaluation and a comparison between eye fixations and other information processing methodologies. *Advances in Consumer Research, 2*, 561–570.

West, P. M., Brown, C. L., & Hoch, S. J. (1996). Consumption vocabulary and preference formation. *Journal of Consumer Research, 23*(2), 120–135.

2

Eye Movements during Reading, Scene Perception, Visual Search, and While Looking at Print Advertisements

Keith Rayner and Monica S. Castelhano

Eye Movements

Where do people look in print advertisements? This question has recently generated a fair amount of research activity to determine the factors that influence which aspects of an ad are salient in capturing a viewer's attention (Goldberg, 1999; Pieters, Rosbergen, & Wedel, 1999; Pieters & Warlop, 1999; Pieters & Wedel, 2007; Radach, Lemmer, Vorstius, Heller, & Radach, 2003; Rayner, Miller, & Rotello, 2007; Rayner, Rotello, Stewart, Keir, & Duffy, 2001; Wedel & Pieters, 2000). Given that eye movement research has been so successful in illuminating how cognitive processes are influenced online in various information processing tasks such as reading, scene perception, and visual search (Rayner, 1978, 1998), such interest is not at all surprising. More recently, there have also been attempts to provide models of eye movement control in scanning advertisements (Liechty, Pieters, & Wedel, 2003; Reichle & Nelson, 2003).

Research on eye movements during reading, scene perception, and visual search is obviously quite relevant for understanding how people look at advertisements. Let us be very clear at the outset that our overview of reading will be more complete than our overview of scene perception or visual search. The reason for this is quite obvious. We know more about the nature of eye movements in reading than in the other two tasks. And, the reason for this is also quite apparent.

In reading, there is a well-defined task for the viewer: people generally read to understand or comprehend the text. This involves a sequence of eye movements that typically moves from left to right across the page and then down the page. Of course, the task can be varied somewhat so that, for example, readers are asked to skim the text, and this will result in different eye movement characteristics. Yet, the vast bulk of the research on eye movements during reading has utilized comprehension as the goal of the reader. On the other hand, in scene perception, the nature of the task is inherently more vague. Viewers may be asked to look at a scene to remember it, but the sequence in which they examine the scene may be highly idiosyncratic and variable. In visual search, there are many different types of search tasks (search for a letter, search for a colored object, search for a person in a large group picture, search for Waldo in a *Where's Waldo* children's book, and so on), and viewers can use idiosyncratic strategies in dealing with the task. Despite these differences, some information on the nature of eye movements in each task is available. In this chapter, we will review some of the main findings concerning eye movements in these tasks. Then we will move to a brief review of eye movements when looking at print advertisements (see also the chapters by Pieters & Wedel, and by Chandon, Hutchinson, Bradlow, & Young in this volume).

Basic Characteristics of Eye Movements

When we read or look at a scene or search for a target in a visual array, we move our eyes every 250–350 ms. Eye movements serve the function of moving the fovea (the high resolution part of the retina encompassing 2 degrees in the center of vision) to that part of the visual array that we want to process in detail. Because of acuity limitations in the retina, eye movements are necessary for processing the details of the array. Our ability to discriminate fine detail drops off markedly outside of the fovea in the parafovea (extending out to about 5 degrees on either side of fixation) and in the periphery (everything beyond the parafovea). During the actual eye movement (or saccade), vision is suppressed,* and new information is acquired

* Although vision is suppressed, for most cognitive tasks, mental processing continues during the saccade (see Irwin, 2004 for a review of when cognition is also suppressed during saccades).

only during the fixation (the period of time when the eyes remain still for about 250–350 ms). Although we have the impression that we can process the entire visual array in a single fixation and while we can rapidly obtain the gist of the scene from a single fixation, in reality we would be unable to fully process the information outside of foveal vision if we were unable to move our eyes (Rayner, 1978, 1998).

It is often assumed that we can move our attention so as to attend to one object while the eyes are fixated on another object. While it is indeed the case that in very simple tasks (Posner, 1980) attention and eye location can be separated, in tasks such as reading, scene perception, and visual search, covert attention and overt attention (the exact eye location) are tightly linked. To be sure, when looking at a complicated scene, we can dissociate covert and overt attention. But it generally takes either a certain amount of almost conscious effort to do so (as when we hold fixation and move our attention elsewhere) or it is a natural consequence of programming eye movements. That is, there is considerable evidence that attention typically precedes an eye movement to the intended target of the saccade (Deubel & Schneider, 1996; Hoffman & Subramaniam, 1995; Kowler, Anderson, Dosher, & Blaser, 1995; Rayner, McConkie, & Ehrlich, 1978).

An important point about eye movements is that they are more or less ballistic movements. Once initiated, it is difficult (though not impossible) to change their trajectory. Furthermore, since they are motor movements, it takes time to plan and execute a saccade. In simple reaction time experiments, where there is no necessity of cognitive processing of the fixated material and participants merely need to monitor when a simple fixation target moves from one location to another (and their eyes accordingly), it takes on the order of 175 ms to move the eyes under the best of circumstances (Becker & Jürgens, 1979; McPeek, Skavenski, & Nakayama, 2000; Rayner, Slowiaczek, Clifton, & Bertera, 1983).

Table 2.1 shows some summary information regarding mean fixation durations and saccade lengths in reading, scene perception, and visual search. From this table, it is evident that the nature of the task influences the average amount of time spent on each fixation and the average distance the eyes move. Furthermore, it is very important to note that while the values presented in Table 2.1, are quite representative of the different tasks, they show a range of average fixation durations and for each of the tasks there is considerable

TABLE 2.1 Eye Movement Characteristics in Reading, Scene Perception, and Visual Search

Task	Mean Fixation Duration (ms)	Mean Saccade Size (degrees)
Silent reading	225–250	2 (8–9 letter spaces)
Oral reading	275–325	1.5 (6–7 letter spaces)
Scene perception	260–330	4
Visual search	180–275	3

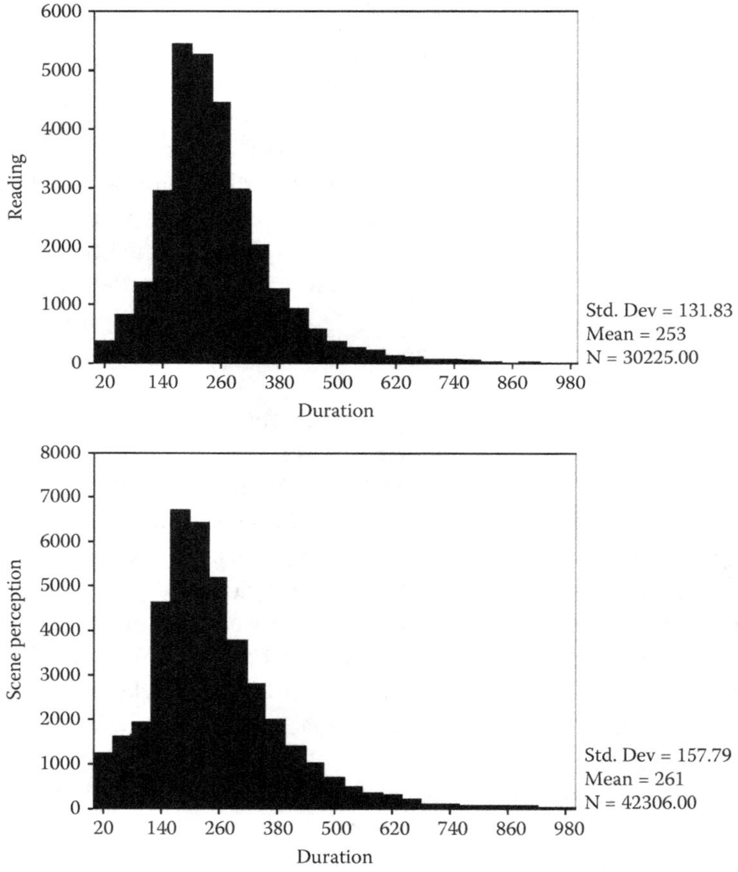

Figure 2.1 Fixation duration frequency distributions for reading, scene perception, and visual search. The data are from the same 24 observers engaged in the three different tasks. No lower cutoffs of fixation duration were used in these distributions while an upper cutoff of 1000 ms was used.

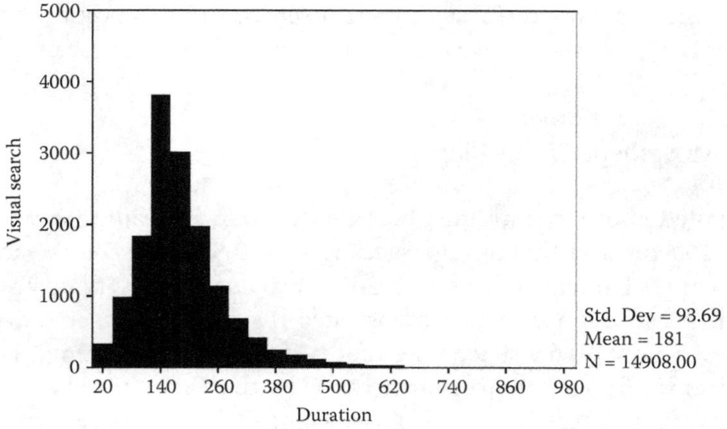

Figure 2.1 (continued)

variability both in terms of fixation durations and saccade lengths. To illustrate this, Figure 2.1 shows the frequency distributions of fixation durations in the three tasks. Here, it is very evident that there is a lot of variability in fixation time measures; although not illustrated here, the same point holds for saccade size measures.

At one time, the combination of the relatively long latency (or reaction time of the eyes) combined with the large variability in the fixation time measures led researchers to believe that the eyes and the mind were not tightly linked during information processing tasks such as reading, scene perception, and visual search. Basically, the argument was that if the eye movement latency was so long and if the fixation times were so variable, how could cognitive factors influence fixation times from fixation to fixation? Actually, an underlying assumption was that everything proceeded in a serial fashion and that cognitive processes could not influence anything very late in a fixation, if at all. However, a great deal of recent research has established a fairly tight link between the eye and the mind, and furthermore it is now clear that saccades can be programmed in parallel (Becker & Jürgens, 1979) and that information processing continues in parallel with saccade programming.

With this preamble (and basic information) out of the way, let's now turn to a brief overview of eye movements in each of the three tasks. We'll begin with reading (which will receive the most attention since there is more research on eye movements in this task than the other two), and then move to scene perception and visual search.

Eye Movements in Reading

As noted above, the average fixation duration in reading is about 225–250 ms and the average saccade size is 8–9 character spaces. Typically, character spaces in reading are used rather than visual angle because it has been demonstrated that character spaces drive the eyes more than visual angle. That is, if the size of the print is held constant and the viewing distance varied (so that there are either more or fewer characters per degree of visual angle), how far the eyes move is determined by character spaces and not visual angle (Morrison & Rayner, 1981). The other important characteristic of eye movements during reading is that about 10–15% of the time readers move their eyes back in the text to read previously read material. These regressions, as they are called, are somewhat variable depending on the difficulty of the text. Indeed, fixation duration and saccade size are both modulated by text difficulty: as the text becomes more difficult, fixation durations increase, saccade size decreases, and regressions increase. So, it is very clear that global properties of the text influence eye movements. The three main global measures mentioned here are also influenced by the type of reading material and the reader's goals in reading (Rayner & Pollatsek, 1989).

Likewise, there are also very clear local effects on fixation time on a word (see below). In these studies, rather than using global measures such as average fixation duration, more precise processing measures are examined for fixated target words. These measures include: first fixation duration (the duration of the first fixation on a word), single fixation duration (those cases where only a single fixation is made on a word), and gaze duration (the sum of all fixations on a word prior to moving to another word). If it were the case that readers fixated (a) each word and (b) only once on each word, then average fixation duration on a word would be a useful measure. But, the reality is that many words are skipped during reading (i.e., don't receive a direct eye fixation) and some words are fixated more than once. There is good reason to believe that the words that are skipped are processed on the fixation prior to the skip, and likewise there is good reason to think that words are refixated (before moving on in the text) in

Normal Line:

```
Where do people look in print advertisements and
```

Moving Window Paradigm (13 character window):

```
Where xx xeople look inxxxxxxxxxxxxxxxxxxxxxxxxx
                *
Where xx xxxxxxxxxxok in print axxxxxxxxxxxxxxxxx
                         *
```

Moving Mask Paradigm (7 character mask):

```
Where do people lxxxxxxxprint advertisements and
                    *
Where do people look in xxxxxxxdvertisements and
                           *
```

Boundary Paradigm:

```
Where do people look in house advertisements and
                  *
Where do people look in print advertisements and
                         *
```

Figure 2.2 Examples of a moving window (with a 13-character window), a moving mask (with a 7-character mask), and the boundary paradigm. When the reader's eye movement crosses an invisible boundary location (the letter *n*), the preview word *house* changes to the target word *print*. The asterisk represents the location of the eyes in each example.

order to fully process their meaning. The solution to this possible conundrum is to utilize the three measures just described, which provide a reasonable estimate of how long it takes to process each word (Rayner, 1998).

The Perceptual Span

A very important issue with respect to reading has to do with the size of the perceptual span (also called the region of effective vision or the functional field of view) during a fixation in reading. Each time the eyes pause (for 200–250 ms) how much information is the reader able to process and use during that fixation? We often have the impression that we can clearly see the entire line of text, even the entire page of text. But, this is an illusion as experiments utilizing a gaze-contingent moving window paradigm (see Figure 2.2) introduced by McConkie and Rayner (1975; Rayner & Bertera, 1979) have clearly demonstrated.

In these experiments, the rationale is to vary how much information is available to a reader and then determine how large the window of normal text has to be before readers read normally. Conversely, how small can the window be before there is disruption to reading? Thus, in the experiments, within the window area text is normally displayed, but outside of the window, the letters are replaced (with other letters or with Xs or a homogenous masking pattern). A great deal of research using this paradigm has demonstrated that readers of English obtain useful information from a region extending 3–4 character spaces to the left of fixation to about 14–15 character spaces to the right of fixation.* Indeed, if readers have the fixated word and the word to the right of fixation available on a fixation (and all other letters are replaced with visually similar letters), they are not aware that the words outside of the window are not normal, and their reading speed only decreases by about 10%. If two words to the right of fixation are available within the window, there is no slowdown in reading. Furthermore, readers do not utilize information from the words on the line below the currently fixated line (Rayner, 1998). Finally, in moving mask experiments (Rayner & Bertera, 1979; Rayner, Inhoff, Morrison, Slowiaczek, & Bertera, 1981) when a mask moves with the eyes on each fixation covering the letters in the center of vision (see Figure 2.2), it is very clear that reading is very difficult if not impossible when the central foveal region is masked (and only letters in parafoveal vision are available for reading).

A great deal of other research using another type of gaze-contingent display change paradigm (see Figure 2.2), called the boundary paradigm (Rayner, 1975), has also revealed that when readers have a valid preview of the word to the right of fixation, they spend less time fixating that word (following a saccade to it) than when they don't have a valid preview (i.e., another word or nonword or random string of letters initially occupied the target word location). The size of this preview benefit is typically on the order of 30–50 ms. Interestingly, research using this technique has revealed that readers don't combine a literal representation of the visual

* The nature of the writing system also very much influences the size of the perceptual span, but this is beyond the scope of the present chapter (see Rayner, 1998 for a review).

information across saccades, but rather abstract (and phonological) information is combined across eye fixations in reading (McConkie & Zola, 1979; Rayner, McConkie, & Zola, 1980).

Linguistic Influences on Fixation Time

Over the past few years, it has become very clear that the ease or difficulty associated with processing the fixated word strongly influences how long the eyes remain in place. How long the eyes remain in place is influenced by a host of linguistic variables such as the frequency of the fixated word (Inhoff & Rayner, 1986; Rayner & Duffy, 1986), how predictable the fixated word is (Ehrlich & Rayner, 1981; Rayner & Well, 1996), how many meanings the fixated word has (Duffy, Morris, & Rayner, 1988; Sereno, O'Donnell, & Rayner, 2006), when the meaning of the word was acquired (Juhasz & Rayner, 2003, 2006), semantic relations between the word and prior words (Carroll & Slowiaczek, 1986; Morris, 1994), how familiar the word is (Williams & Morris, 2004), and so on (see Rayner, 1998 for review).

Perhaps the most compelling evidence that cognitive processing of the fixated word is driving the eyes through the text comes from experiments in which the fixated word either disappears or is masked after 50–60 ms (Ishida & Ikeda, 1989; Liversedge et al., 2004; Rayner et al., 1981; Rayner, Liversedge, White, & Vergilino-Perez, 2003; Rayner, Liversedge, & White, 2006). Basically, these studies show that if readers are allowed to see the fixated word for 60 ms before it disappears, they read quite normally. Interestingly, if the word to the right of fixation also disappears or is masked, then reading is disrupted (Rayner et al., 2006); this quite strongly demonstrates that the word to the right of fixation is very important in reading. More critically for our present purposes, when the fixated word disappears after 60 ms, how long the eyes remain in place is determined by the frequency of the word that disappeared: if it is a low frequency word, the eyes remain in place longer (Rayner et al., 2003, 2006). Thus, even though the word is no longer there, how long the eyes remain in place is determined by that word's frequency. This is very compelling evidence that the cognitive processing associated with a fixated word is the engine driving the eyes through the text.

To summarize the foregoing overview, it is now clear that readers acquire information from a limited region during a fixation (extending to about 14–15 character spaces to the right of fixation). Information used for word identification is obtained from an even smaller region (extending to about 7–8 character spaces to the right of fixation). Furthermore, the word to the right of fixation is important and readers obtain preview benefit from that word. On some fixations, readers can process the meaning of the fixated word and the word to the right of fixation. In such cases, they will typically skip over the word to the right of fixation. Finally, the ease or difficulty associated with processing the fixated word strongly influences how long readers look at that word.

Models of Eye Movements in Reading

Given the vast amount of information that has been learned about eye movements during reading in the last 25–30 years, a number of models of eye movements in reading have recently appeared. The E-Z Reader model (Pollatsek, Reichle, & Rayner, 2006; Rayner, Ashby, Pollatsek, & Reichle, 2004; Rayner, Reichle, & Pollatsek, 1998; Reichle, Pollatsek, Fisher, & Rayner, 1998; Reichle, Pollatsek, & Rayner, 2006; Reichle, Rayner, & Pollatsek, 2003) is typically regarded as the most influential of these models. In the interests of space limitations, other models will not be discussed here.* Basically, the E-Z Reader model accounts for all of the data and results discussed above, and it also does a good job of predicting how long readers will look at words, which words they will skip, and which words will be refixated. It can account for global aspects of eye movements in reading, while also dealing with more local processing characteristics; the competitor models also can account for similar amounts of data. In many ways, the models share many similarities, though they differ on some precise details and how they go about explaining certain effects varies between them. As a computational model, E-Z Reader has the virtue of being highly transparent, so it makes very clear predictions and when it can't account for certain data, it is very clear why it can't (thus enabling one to change parameter values in the model). The model has also enabled us to account for data patterns that in the past may have been difficult to explain. The model isn't perfect and has many limitations. For example, higher order processes due to

* For a comprehensive overview of these models, see the 2006, vol. 7 special issue of *Cognitive Systems Research.*

sentence parsing and discourse variables do not currently have an influence within the model. It basically assumes that lexical processing is driving the eyes through the text, but we believe that this isn't an unreasonable assumption.*

The main, and concluding, point from the foregoing is that great advances have been made in understanding eye movements in reading (and inferring the mental processes associated with reading) via careful experimentation and via the implementation of computational models that nicely simulate eye movements during reading. In the next two sections, eye movements during scene perception and visual search will be discussed. Although there hasn't been as much research on these areas as on reading, it is still the case that some clear conclusions emerge from the work that has been done.

Eye Movements and Scene Perception

Figure 2.3 shows the eye movements of a viewer on a scene. As is very evident in this figure, viewers don't fixate on every part of the scene. This is largely because information can be obtained over a wider region in scene perception than reading. However, it is clear that the important aspects of the scene are typically fixated (and generally looked at for longer periods than less important parts of the scene). In Figure 2.3, the fixations are on the informative parts of the scene, and viewers do not fixate on the sky or the road in front of the houses. As we noted at the outset, the average fixation in scene perception tends to be longer than that in reading, and likewise the average saccade size tends to be longer. In this section, a brief summary of where people tend to look in scenes will be provided, as well as information regarding the perceptual span region for scenes and the nature of eye movement control when looking at scenes.

Getting the Gist of a Scene

One very important general finding with respect to scene perception is that viewers get the gist of a scene very early in the process of

* Our primary argument is that lexical processing drives the eyes through the text and higher order processes primarily serve to intervene when something doesn't compute (see Rayner, Warren, Juhasz, & Liversedge, 2004).

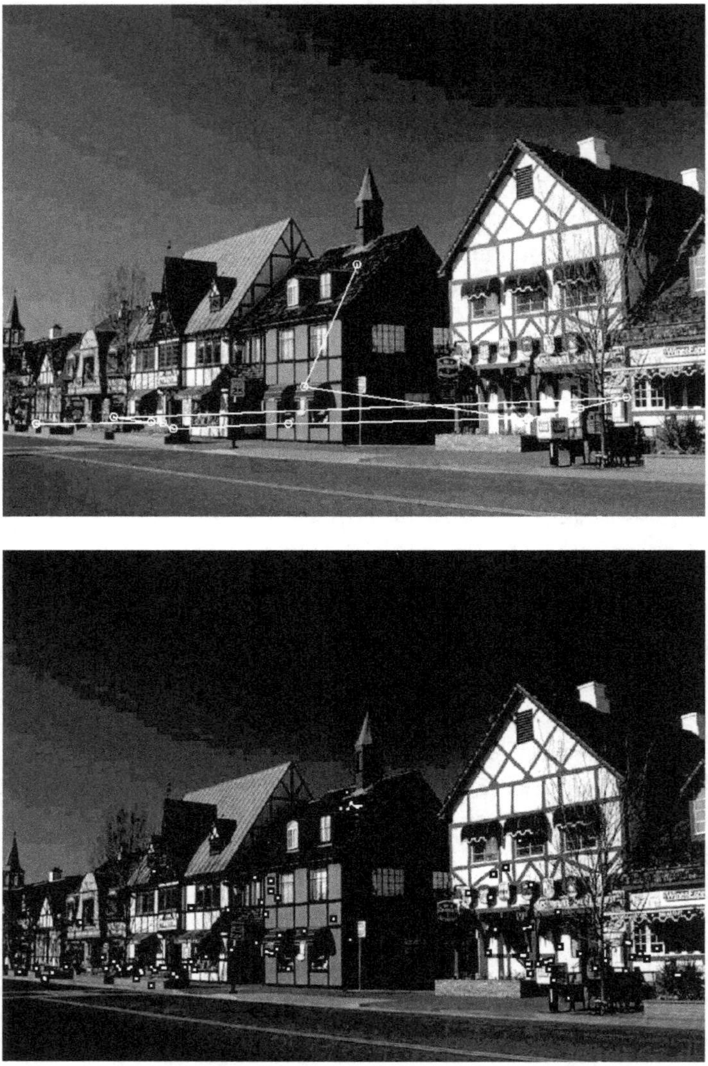

Figure 2.3 Examples of where viewers look in scenes. The top portion of the figure shows where one viewer fixates in the scene (the dots represent fixation points and the lines represent the sequence). The bottom portion shows where a number of different viewers fixate (with the dots representing fixation locations across a number of viewers).

looking, sometimes even from a single brief exposure that is so quick that it would be impossible to move the eyes (De Graef, 2005). In fact, in a recent study, Castelhano and Henderson (forthcoming b) showed that with exposures lasting as little as 40 ms, participants were able to extract enough information to get the gist of the scene. It has typically been argued that the gist of the scene is obtained in the first fixation, and that the remaining fixations on a scene are used to fill in the details.

Where Do Viewers Look in Scenes?

Since the pioneering work of Buswell (1935) and Yarbus (1967), it has been widely recognized that viewers' eyes are drawn to important aspects of the visual scene and that their goals in looking at the scene very much influence their eye movements. Quite a bit of early research demonstrated that the eyes are quickly drawn to informative areas in a scene (Antes, 1974; Mackworth & Morandi, 1967) and that the eyes quickly move to an object that is out of place in a scene (Friedman, 1979; Loftus & Mackworth, 1978). On the other hand, the out-of-place objects in these scenes tended to differ from the appropriate objects on a number of dimensions (Rayner & Pollatsek, 1992). For example, an octopus in a farm scene is not only semantically out of place, but it also tends to have more rounded features than the objects typically in a farm scene. So, these early studies confounded visual saliency and semantic saliency. More recent experiments in which appropriate featural information was well controlled raise questions about the earlier findings, and suggest that the eyes are not invariably and immediately drawn to out-of-place objects (De Graef, Christiaens, & D'Ydewalle, 1990; Henderson, Weeks, & Hollingworth, 1999).

But, it is certainly the case that the eyes do get quickly to the important parts of a scene. In a recent study, the influence that context has on the placement of eye movements in search of certain objects within pseudorealistic scenes was investigated (Neider & Zelinsky, 2006). Viewers were asked to look for target objects that are typically constrained to certain parts of the scene (i.e., jeep on the ground, blimp in the sky). When a target was present, fixations were largely limited to the area one would expect to find the target object (i.e., ground or sky); while, when the target was absent, the inclination to restrict search to these areas was less so. They also found that when the target was in the expected area, search times were on average 19% faster. From these results, they concluded that not only do viewers focus their fixations in areas of a scene that most likely contain the target to improve search times, but also that the visual system is flexible in the application of these restrictions and viewers very quickly adopt a "look everywhere" strategy when the first proves unfruitful. Thus, it seems that search strategies in scenes are guided by the scene context, but not with strict adherence.

It is also clear that the saliency of different parts of the scene influences what part of the scene is fixated (Parkhurst & Niebur, 2003; Mannan, Ruddock, & Wooding, 1995, 1996). Saliency is typically defined in terms of low-level components of the scene (such as contrast, color, intensity, brightness, spatial frequency, etc.). Indeed, there are now a fair number of computational models (Baddeley & Tatler, 2006; Itti & Koch, 2000, 2001; Parkhurst, Law, & Niebur, 2002) that use the concept of a saliency map to model eye fixation locations in scenes. In this approach, bottom-up properties in a scene (the saliency map) make explicit the locations of the most visually prominent regions of the scene. The models are basically used to derive predictions about the distribution of fixations on a given scene.

While these models can account for some of the variability in where viewers fixate in a scene, they are limited in that the assumption is that fixation locations are driven primarily by bottom-up factors and it is clear that higher level factors also come into play in determining where to look next in a scene (Castelhano & Henderson, forthcoming a; Henderson & Ferreira, 2004). A model that includes more in the way of top-down and cognitive strategies has recently been presented by Torralba, Oliva, Castelhano, and Henderson (2006). Indeed, while there has been a considerable amount of research to localize *where* viewers move their eyes while looking at scenes, there has been precious little in the way of attempting to determine what controls *when* the eyes move. This is in contrast with reading where the issues of *where* to move the eyes and *when* to move the eyes have both received considerable attention. One recent study attempting to correct this imbalance investigated the effect of repeated exposure to a scene and its effect on fixation durations (Hidalgo-Sotelo, Oliva, & Torralba, 2005). Observers were asked to search for a target and respond whether it was present in a scene while their eye movements were tracked. Unbeknownst to them, there were certain scene-target combinations that repeated throughout the experiment twenty times. As expected, these repeated searches showed a large decrease in response time. Interestingly though, the number of fixations did not decrease as much as the average fixation duration prior to fixating the target object. Furthermore, the results showed that the proportion of target objects that were fixated before a response was made did not change with increased repetitions (85%). And although the average gaze durations on the target fell from 450 ms during the first exposure to 310 ms in the twentieth, it seems that observers chose to verify the target object before making a response. These results showed that with repeated exposure, the reduced response time is primarily due to a decrease in the average duration of fixations during the search and in the time to verify the target object. Thus, it seems that in this study it became easier to identify the fixated regions as nontargets and targets, but not to cut down on the number of fixations made.

Another difference between scenes and reading is the question of what information is used from memory. We know that memory for the information read plays a large role in integrating information from the current fixation with what has already been read and directing subsequent fixations (such as deciding whether to regress and reread a certain section). In scenes, the role that memory plays in directing fixations is not as clear. Many of the models using saliency as the primary driving force of eye movements do not consider how information gathered initially may influence the placing of subsequent fixations. In a recent study, Castelhano and Henderson (forthcoming a) investigated whether this initial representation of a scene can be used to guide subsequent eye movements on a real-world scene. Observers were shown a very short preview of the search scene and then were asked to find the target object using a moving window, thus eliminating any immediately available visual information. A preview of the search scene elicited the most efficient searches when compared to a meaningless control (the preview yielded fewer fixations and the shortest saccade path to the target). When a preview of another scene within the same semantic category was shown (thereby providing general semantic information without the same visual details), results revealed no improvement in search. These results suggest that the initial representation used to improve search efficiency was not based on general semantics, but rather on something more specific. When a reduced scale of the search scene was shown as the preview, search efficiency measures were as high as when the full-scale preview was shown. Taken together, these results suggest that the initial scene representation is based on abstract, visual information that is useful across changes in spatial scales. Thus, the information used to guide eye movements in scenes is said to have two sources: the saliency of the scene and the information in memory about that scene and scene type.

The Perceptual Span

How much information do viewers obtain in a scene? As noted at the outset of this section, it is clear that information is acquired over a wider range of the visual field when looking at a scene than is the case for reading. Henderson, McClure, Pierce, and Schrock (1997) used a moving mask procedure (to cover the part of the scene around the fixation point) and found that although the presence of a foveal mask influenced looking time, it did not have nearly as serious effects for object identification as a foveal mask has for reading.

Nelson and Loftus (1980) examined how close to fixation an object had to be for it to be recognized as having been in the scene. They found that objects located within about 2.6 degrees from fixation were generally recognized, but recognition depended to some extent on the characteristics of the object. They also suggested that qualitatively different information is acquired from the region 1.5 degrees around fixation than from regions further away (see also Nodine, Carmody, & Herman, 1979). While a study by Parker (1978) is often taken to suggest (see Henderson & Ferreira, 2004 for discussion) that the functional field of view for specific objects in a scene is quite large (with a radius of at least 10 degrees around fixation resulting in a perceptual span of up to 20 degrees), other more recent studies using better controlled stimuli and more natural images (Henderson & Hollingworth, 1999; Henderson, Williams, Castelhano, & Falk, 2003) suggest that the functional field of view extends about 4 degrees away from fixation.

An early study using the moving window technique by Saida and Ikeda (1979) suggested that the functional field of view is quite large, and can consist of about half of the total scene regardless of the absolute size of the scene (at least for scenes that are up to 14.4 degrees by 18.8 degrees). In this study and other studies using the moving window paradigm (van Diepen & D'Ydewalle, 2003; van Diepen, Wampers, & D'Ydewalle, 1998) normal scene information within the window area around a fixation point is presented normally, but the information outside of the window is degraded in some systematic way. Saida and Ikeda (1979) found a serious deterioration in recognition of a scene when the window was limited to a small area (about 3.3 degrees × 3.3 degrees) on each fixation. Performance gradually improved as the window size became larger, as noted, up to about 50% of the entire scene. Saida and Ikeda noted that there was considerable overlap of information across fixations.

It should be clear from the studies we have reviewed that the answer to the question of how large the perceptual span in scene perception is hasn't been answered as conclusively as it has in reading. Nevertheless, it does appear that viewers typically gain useful information from a fairly wide region of the scene, which also probably varies as a function of the scene and the task of the viewer. For instance, the ease with which an object is identified has been linked to its orientation (Boutsen, Lamberts, & Verfaillie, 1998), frequency within a scene context (Henderson & Hollingworth, 1999), and how well camouflaged it is (De Graef et al., 1990). As has been shown in reading (Henderson & Ferreira, 1990), it is likely that the ease of identifying a fixated object has an effect on the extent of processing in the periphery.

Preview Benefit

Just as in reading, viewers obtain preview benefit from objects that they have not yet fixated (Henderson, 1992; Henderson, Pollatsek, & Rayner, 1987, 1989; Pollatsek, Rayner, & Collins, 1984; Pollatsek, Rayner, & Henderson, 1990) and the amount of the preview benefit is on the order of 100 ms (so it is larger than in reading). Interestingly, viewers are rather immune to changes in the scene. In a series of experiments by McConkie and Grimes (Grimes, 1996; Grimes & McConkie, 1995; McConkie, 1991) observers were asked to view scenes with the task of memorizing what they saw. They were also informed that changes could be made to the image while they were examining it, and they were instructed to press a button if they detected those changes. While observers viewed the scenes, changes were made during a saccade. As discussed earlier, during saccades vision is suppressed meaning that these changes would not have been visible as they were occurring. Remarkably, observers were unaware of most changes, which included the appearance and disappearance of large objects and the changing of colors, all of which were happening while the scene was being viewed. Although later studies found that any disruption served to induce an inability to detect changes, such as inserting a blank screen in between two changing images (Rensink, O'Regan, & Clark, 1997), movie cuts (Levin & Simons, 1997), or the simultaneous onset of patches covering portions of the scene (O'Regan, Rensink, & Clark, 1999), these experiments highlighted the relation between what is viewed during the initial exploration of a scene and then what is remembered about that scene. Further studies have shown that this lack of awareness does not mean that there is no recollection of any visual details, but rather that the likelihood of remembering visual information is highly dependent on the processing of that information (Henderson & Castelhano, 2005; Hollingworth, 2003; Hollingworth & Henderson, 2002). This means that knowing something about the processes that go on during a fixation on a scene is extremely important if one would want to predict how well visual information being viewed is stored.

When Do Viewers Move Their Eyes When Looking at Scenes?

With the assumption that attention precedes an eye movement to a new location within a scene (Henderson, 1992; van Diepen & D'Ydewalle, 2003), it follows that the eyes will move once information at the center of vision has been processed and a new fixation location has been chosen. In a recent study, van Diepen and D'Ydewalle (2003) investigated when this shift in attention (from the center of fixation to the periphery) took place in the course of a fixation. They had observers view scenes whose information at the center of fixation was masked during the initial part of fixations (from 20–90 ms). In another case, the periphery was masked at the beginning of each fixation (for 10–85 ms). As expected based on the assumptions made above, they found that when the center of fixation was masked initially, fixation durations increased with longer mask durations (61% increase). When the periphery was masked, they found a slight increase in fixation durations, but not as much as with a central mask (15% increase). Interestingly, they found that the average distance of saccades decreased and the number of fixations increased with longer mask durations in the periphery. They surmised that with the longer peripheral masking durations the visual system does not wait for the unmasking of peripheral information, but instead chooses information that is immediately available. These results suggest that the extracting of information at the fovea occurs very rapidly, and the attention is directed to the periphery almost immediately following the extraction of information (70–120 ms) to choose a viable saccade target. Although the general timing of the switch between central and peripheral information processing is now being investigated, the variability of information across scenes makes it more difficult to come up with a specific time frame as has been done in reading.

Eye Movements and Visual Search

Visual search is a research area that has received considerable effort over the past 40 years. Unfortunately, the vast majority of this research has been done in the absence of considering eye movements (Findlay & Gilchrist, 1998). That is, eye movements have typically not been monitored in this research area, and it has often been assumed that eye movements are not particularly important in understanding search. However, this attitude seems to be largely changing as there are now many experiments reported each year on visual search utilizing eye movements to understand the process. Many of these studies deal with very low-level aspects of search and often focus on using the search task to uncover properties of the saccadic eye movement system (see Findlay, 2004; Findlay & Gilchrist, 2003).

In this chapter, we'll focus primarily on research that has some implications for how viewers search through arrays to find specific targets (as is often the case when looking at ads). As we noted at the outset, fixation durations in search tend to be highly variable. Some studies report average fixation times as short as 180 ms while others report averages on the order of 275 ms. This wide variability is undoubtedly due to the fact that how difficult the search array is (or how dense or cluttered it is) and the exact nature of the search task strongly influence how long viewers pause on average. Typically, saccade size is a bit larger than in reading (though saccades can be quite short with very dense arrays) and a bit shorter than in scene perception.

The Search Array Matters

Perhaps the most obvious thing about visual search is that the search array makes a big difference in how easy it is to find a target. When the array is very dense (with many objects and distractors) or cluttered, search is more costly than when the array is simple or less dense and eye movements typically reflect this fact (Bertera & Rayner, 2000; Greene & Rayner, 2001a, 2001b). The number of fixations and fixation duration both increase as the array becomes more complicated, and the average saccade size decreases (Vlaskamp & Hooge, 2006). Additionally, the configuration of the search array has an effect on the pattern of eye movements. In an array of objects arranged in an arc, fixations tend to fall in between objects, progressively getting closer to the area where viewers think the target is located (Zelinsky, 2005; Zelinsky, Rao, Hayhoe, & Ballard, 1997). On the other hand, in randomly placed arrays, other factors such as color of the items and shape similarity to the target object influence the placement of fixations (Williams, Henderson, & Zacks, 2005).

Does Visual Search Have a Memory?

This question has provoked a considerable amount of research. Horowitz and Wolfe (1998) initially proposed that visual search doesn't have a good memory and that the same item will be resampled during the search process. However, they made this assertion based on reaction time functions, and eye movement data are ideal for addressing the issue (since one can examine how frequently the eyes return to a previously sampled part of the array). And, eye movement experiments (Beck, Peterson, Boot, Vomela, & Kramer, 2006; Beck, Peterson, & Vomela, 2006; Peterson, Kramer, Wang, Irwin, & McCarley, 2001) make it quite clear that viewers generally do not return to previously searched items.

The Perceptual Span

Rayner and Fisher (1987a, 1987b) used the moving window technique as viewers searched through horizontally arranged letter strings for a specified target letter. They found that the size of the perceptual span varied as a function of the difficulty of the distractor letter; when the distractor letters were visually similar to the target letter, the size of the perceptual span was smaller than when the distractor letters were distinctly different from the target letter. They suggested that there were two qualitatively different regions within the span: a decision region (where information about the presence or absence of a target is available, and a preview region where some letter information is available but where information on the absence of a target is not available.

Bertera and Rayner (2000) had viewers search through a randomly arranged array of letters and digits for the presence of a target letter. They used both the moving window and moving mask techniques. They varied the size of the array (so that it was 13 degrees by 10 degrees, 6 degrees by 6 degrees, or 5 degrees by 3.5 degrees), but the number of items was held constant (so in the smaller arrays, the information was more densely packed). The moving mask had a deleterious effect on search time and accuracy, and the larger the mask, the longer the search time. In the moving window condition, search performance reached asymptote when the window was 5 degrees (all letters/digits falling within 2.5 degrees from the fixation point where visible with such a window size while all other letters were masked).

Where and When to Move the Eyes

While there have been considerable efforts undertaken to determine the factors involved in deciding where and when to move the eyes (Greene, 2006; Greene & Rayner, 2001a, 2001b; Hooge & Erkelens, 1996, 1998; Jacobs, 1986; Vaughan, 1982), a clear answer to the issue has not emerged. Some have concluded that fixation durations in search are the result of both preprogrammed saccades and fixations that are influenced by the fixated information (Vaughan, 1982). Others have suggested that the completion of foveal analysis is not necessarily the trigger for an eye movement (Hooge & Erkelens, 1996, 1998) while others have suggested that it is (Greene & Rayner, 2001b). Rayner (1995) suggested that the trigger to move the eyes in a search task is something like: is the target present in the decision area of the perceptual span? If it is not, a new saccade is programmed to move the eyes to a location that has not been examined. As with reading (and presumably scene perception), attention would move to the region targeted for the next saccade.

Finally, the decision about where to fixate next and when to move the eyes is undoubtedly strongly influenced by the characteristics of the specific search task and the density of the visual array. In a recent study, van Zoest, Donk, and Theeuwes (2004) investigated what type of information had more influence over the placement of fixations: goal-driven information (i.e., target knowledge) or distractor saliency. They found that when fixations were made quickly subjects tended to fixate the target and distractor equally, however for longer fixation latencies, the target was fixated more often. They concluded that the longer observers took to choose a location before executing a saccade, the more likely it would be influenced by goal-driven control. Thus, it seems that the parallels between visual search arrays and scenes are greater than with reading, in that visual saliency plays a greater role in directing fixations. Also, searches for targets within visual search displays and scenes have different dimensions that are not as variable as in reading. For instance, with respect to search tasks, there are many different types of targets that people may be asked to search for. Searching for a certain product in a grocery store shelf or searching for a particular person in a large group picture or for a word in a dictionary may well yield very different strategies than skimming text for a word (and hence influence eye movements in different ways). Although the task is generally much better defined in visual search than in scene perception, it cannot be as well specified as in reading.

General Comments on Eye Movements

In the preceding sections, we have reviewed research on eye movements in three tasks that are very much related to what happens when viewers look at print advertisements. Although there are obviously many differences between reading, scene perception, and visual search, there are some general principles that we suspect hold across the three tasks (and are relevant for considering eye movements when looking at ads). First, how much information is processed on any fixation (the perceptual span or functional field of view) varies as a function of the task. The perceptual span is obviously smaller in reading than in scene perception and visual search. Thus, for example, fixations in scene perception tend to be longer and saccades are longer because more information is being processed during a fixation. Second, the difficulty of the stimulus influences eye movements: in reading, when the text becomes more difficult, eye fixations get longer and saccades get shorter; likewise in scene perception and visual search, when the array is more difficult (crowded, cluttered, dense), fixations get longer and saccades get shorter. Third, the difficulty of the specific task (reading for comprehension versus reading for gist, searching for a person in a scene versus looking at the scene for a memory test, and so on) clearly influences eye movements across the three tasks. Finally, in all three tasks there is some evidence (Najemnik & Geisler, 2005; Rayner, 1998) that viewers integrate information poorly across fixations and that what is most critical is that there is efficient processing of information on each fixation.

Eye Movements and Advertisements

In comparison to reading, scene perception, and visual search, there has been considerably less research on eye movements when looking at ads than there has been on these other topics. Obviously, however, what is known about eye movements in these other tasks has some relevance to looking at ads because there is often a reading component, a scene perception component, and a search component to the task of looking at an ad. While there was some research on eye movements while viewers examined print advertisements prior to the late 1990s (see Radach et al., 2003, for a summary), it tended to be rather descriptive and nondiagnostic. More recent research has focused on attempts to analytically determine how (a) aspects of the ad and (b) the goal of the viewer interact to influence looking behavior and the amount of attention devoted to different parts of the ad. For example, Rayner et al. (2001) asked American participants to imagine that they had just moved to the United Kingdom and that they needed to either buy a new car (the car condition) or skin care products (the skin care condition). Both groups of participants saw the same set of 24 ads; participants in the car group saw 8 critical car ads, but they also saw 8 critical skin care ads and 8 filler ads (consisting of a variety of ad types) while participants in the skin care group also saw the same 8 car ads, the same 8 skin care ads, and the same 8 filler ads. Obviously, the two different types of ads should have differing amounts of relevance to the viewers. Indeed, viewers in the car condition spent much more time looking at car ads than at skin care ads, while viewers in the skin care condition spent much more time looking at skin care ads than car ads.

In a follow-up experiment, Rayner et al. (2007) used the same set of ads, but this time participants were asked to rate the ads in terms

TABLE 2.2 Mean Viewing Time (in Seconds) and Number of Fixations for the Text and Picture Parts of Ads as a Function of Task*

	Viewing Time		Number of Fixations	
	Text	Picture	Text	Picture
Rayner et al. (2007)	3.64 (39%)	5.72 (61%)	14.7 (39%)	22.7 (61%)
Rayner et al. (2001)				
Intended	5.61 (73%)	2.12 (27%)	25.2 (72%)	9.8 (28%)
Non-intended	3.60 (71%)	1.50 (29%)	16.4 (70%)	6.9 (30%)

Note: In the Rayner et al. (2001) study, intended refers to ads that viewers were instructed to look at to purchase whereas non-intended refers to the other ads they viewed.

*Values in parentheses equal the percent of time looked at the text or picture (for the viewing time) and the percent of fixations in the text or picture (for the number of fixations).

of (a) how effective each ad was or (b) how much they liked the ad. Interestingly, the pattern of looking times was very different in this experiment in comparison to the earlier Rayner et al. (2001) study. Indeed, when asked to rate pictures for effectiveness or likeability, viewers tended to spend much more time looking at the picture part of the ad in comparison to the text. In contrast, viewers in the Rayner et al. (2001) study spent much more time reading the text portion of the ad, particularly if the ad was relevant for their goal. Thus, viewers in the car condition spent a lot of time reading the text in the car ads (but not in the skin care ads), while those in the skin care condition spent a lot of time reading the text in the skin care ads (but not in the car ads). As seen in Table 2.2, the amount of time that viewers devoted to the picture or text part of the ad varied rather dramatically as a function of their goals. When the goal was to think about actually buying a product they spent more time reading; when the goal was to rate the ad, they spent much more time looking at the picture (for further evidence of the importance of the viewer's goals, see Pieters & Wedel, 2007).

Clearly, advertisements differ in many ways, yet from our perspective there appear to be some underlying principles with respect to how viewers inspect them. First, when viewers look at an ad with the expectation that they might want to buy a product, they often quickly move their eyes to the text in the ad (Rayner et al., 2001), especially the large text (typically called the headline). Second, viewers spend more time on implicit ads in which the pictures and text are not directly related to the product than they spend on explicit ads (Radach et al., 2003). Third, although brand names tend to take up little space in an ad, they receive more eye fixations per unit of surface than text or pictures (Wedel & Pieters, 2000). Fourth, viewers tend to spend more time looking at the text portion than at the picture portion of the ad, especially when the amount of space taken up is taken into account (Rayner et al., 2001; Wedel & Pieters, 2000). Fifth, viewers typically do not alternate fixations between the text and the picture part of the ad (Rayner et al., 2001, 2007). That is, given that the eyes are in either the text or picture part of the ad, the probability that the next fixation is also in that part of the ad is fairly high (about .75, Rayner et al., 2007). Rayner et al. (2001) found that viewers tended to read the headline or large print, then the smaller print, and then they looked at the picture (although some viewers did an initial cursory scan of the picture). However, Radach et al. (2003) found that their viewers looked back and forth between different elements (often scanning back and forth between the headline, the text, and the picture). Radach et al. (2003) argued that the differences lie in the fact that the tasks they used were more demanding than those used by Rayner et al. (2001). This brings us to the sixth important point: it is very clear that the goal of the viewer very much influences the pattern of eye movements and how much time viewers spend on different parts of the ad (Pieters & Wedel, 2007; Rayner et al., 2006). As noted above (see Table 2.2), where people look (and how soon they look at the text or the picture part of the ad) varies rather dramatically as a function of the goals of the viewer (Rayner et al., 2006).

Summary

In this chapter, we have reviewed the basic findings concerning eye movements when (a) reading, (b) looking at a scene, (c) searching through a visual array, and (d) looking at ads. Although there is no question that the tasks differ considerably, and that eye movements also differ considerably as a function of the task, it is the case that eye movements can be very informative about what exactly viewers do in each type of task. Each of these points has been discussed in the preceding sections. We didn't discuss how people look at ads on web pages (or eye movements on web pages in general) because such research is in its infancy. But, we do suspect that many of the findings we have outlined above with more traditional tasks will carry over to that situation. It will also be interesting to see how well the findings we have described hold up when viewers look at dynamically changing scenes (as virtually all of the work that we described has dealt with static scenes). Finally, our expectation is that eye movements will continue to play a valuable role for those interested in how ads are processed and how effective they are for consumers.

Acknowledgments

Preparation of this chapter was supported by a grant from the Microsoft Corporation and by Grant HD26765 from the National Institute of Health. Correspondence should be addressed to Keith Rayner, Department of Psychology, University of Massachusetts, Amherst, MA 01003, USA.

References

Antes, J. R. (1974). The time course of picture viewing. *Journal of Experimental Psychology, 103,* 62–70.

Baddeley, R. J., & Tatler, B. W. (2006). High frequency edges (but not contrast) predict where we fixate: A Bayesian system identification analysis. *Vision Research, 46,* 2824–2833.

Beck, M. R., Peterson, M. S., Boot, W. R., Vomela, M., & Kramer, A. F. (2006). Explicit memory for rejected distractors during visual search. *Visual Cognition, 14,* 150–174.

Beck, M. R., Peterson, M. S., & Vomela, M. (2006). Memory for where, but not what, is used during visual search. *Journal of Experimental Psychology: Human Perception and Performance, 32,* 235–250.

Becker, W., & Jürgens, R. (1979). Analysis of the saccadic system by means of double step stimuli. *Vision Research, 19,* 967–983.

Bertera, J. H., & Rayner, K. (2000). Eye movements and the span of effective stimulus in visual search. *Perception & Psychophysics, 62,* 576–585.

Boutsen, L., Lamberts, K., & Verfaillie, K. (1998) Recognition times of different views of 56 depth-rotated objects: A note concerning Verfaillie and Boutsen (1995). *Perception & Psychophysics, 60,* 900–907.

Buswell, G. T. (1935). *How people look at pictures.* Chicago: University of Chicago Press.

Carroll, P. J., & Slowiaczek, M. L. (1986). Constraints on semantic priming in reading: A fixation time analysis. *Memory & Cognition, 14,* 509–522.

Castelhano, M. S., & Henderson, J. M. (forthcoming a). Initial scene representations facilitate eye movement guidance in visual search. *Journal of Experimental Psychology: Human Perception and Performance.*

Castelhano, M. S., & Henderson, J. M. (forthcoming b). The influence of color on perception of scene gist. *Journal of Experimental Psychology: Human Perception and Performance.*

de Graef, P. (2005). Semantic effects on object selection in real-world scene perception. In G. Underwood (Ed.), *Cognitive processes in eye guidance.* Oxford: Oxford University Press, 189–212.

de Graef, P., Christiaens, D., & d'Ydewalle, G. (1990). Perceptual effects of scene context on object identification. *Psychological Research, 52,* 317–329.

Deubel, H., & Schneider, W. X. (1996). Saccade target selection and object recognition: Evidence for a common attentional mechanism. *Vision Research, 36,* 1827–1837.

Diepen, E. M. J. van, Wampers, M., & Ydewalle, G. d' (1998). Functional division of the visual field: Moving masks and moving windows. In G. Underwood (Ed.), *Eye guidance in reading and scene perception* (pp. 337–356). Oxford, England: Elsevier.

Diepen, E. M. J. van, & Ydewalle, G. d' (2003). Early peripheral and foveal processing in fixations during scene perception. *Visual Cognition, 10,* 79–100.

Duffy, S. A., Morris, R. K., & Rayner, K. (1988). Lexical ambiguity and fixation times in reading. *Journal of Memory and Language, 27,* 429–446.

Ehrlich, S. E, & Rayner, K. (1981). Contextual effects on word perception and eye movements during reading. *Journal of Verbal Learning and Verbal Behavior, 20,* 641–655.

Findlay, J. M. (2004). Eye scanning and visual search. In J. M. Henderson, and F. Ferreira (Eds.), *The interface of language, vision, and action: Eye movements and the visual world* (pp. 135–160). New York: Psychology Press.

Findlay, J. M., & Gilchrist, I. D. (1998). Eye guidance and visual search. In G. Underwood (Ed.), *Eye guidance in reading and scene perception* (pp. 295–312). Oxford, England: Elsevier.

Findlay, J. M., & Gilchrist, I. D. (2003). *Active vision. The psychology of looking and seeing.* Oxford: Oxford University Press.

Friedman, A. (1979). Framing pictures: The role of knowledge in automatized encoding and memory for gist. *Journal of Experimental Psychology: General, 108,* 316–355.

Goldberg, J. H. (1999). Visual search of food nutrition labels. *Human Factors, 41,* 425–437.

Greene, H. (2006). The control of fixation duration in visual search. *Perception, 35*, 303–315.

Greene, H., & Rayner, K. (2001a). Eye movements and familiarity effects in visual search. *Vision Research, 41*, 3763–3773.

Greene, H., & Rayner, K. (2001b). Eye-movement control in direction-coded visual search. *Perception, 29*, 363–372.

Grimes, J. (1996). On the failure to detect changes in scenes across saccades. In K. Akins (Ed.), *Vancouver studies in cognitive science: Vol. 5. Perception* (pp. 89–110). New York: Oxford University Press.

Grimes, J., & McConkie, G. (1995). On the insensitivity of the human visual system to image changes made during saccades. In K. Akins (Ed.), *Problems in perception*. Oxford, UK: Oxford University Press.

Henderson, J. M. (1992). Identifying objects across saccades: Effects of extrafoveal preview and flanker object context. *Journal of Experimental Psychology: Learning, Memory, and Cognition, 18*, 521–530.

Henderson, J. M, & Castelhano, M. S. (2005). Eye movements and visual memory for scenes. In G. Underwood (Ed.), *Cognitive processes in eye guidance* (pp. 213–235). Oxford: Oxford University Press.

Henderson, J. M., & Ferreira, F. (1990). Effects of foveal processing difficulty on the perceptual span in reading: Implications for attention and eye movement control. *Journal of Experimental Psychology: Learning, Memory, and Cognition, 16(3)*, 417–429.

Henderson, J. M., & Ferreira, F. (2004). Scene perception for psycholinguists. In J. M. Henderson, and F. Ferreira (Eds.), *The interface of language, vision, and action: Eye movements and the visual world* (pp. 1–58). New York: Psychology Press.

Henderson, J. M., & Hollingworth, A. (1999). High-level scene perception. *Annual Review of Psychology, 50*, 243–271.

Henderson, J. M., McClure, K. K., Pierce, S., & Schrock, G. (1997). Object identification without foveal vision: Evidence from an artificial scotoma paradigm. *Perception & Psychophysics, 59*, 323–346.

Henderson, J. M., Pollatsek, A., & Rayner, K. (1987). The effects of foveal priming and extrafoveal preview on object identification. *Journal of Experimental Psychology: Human Perception and Performance, 13*, 449–463.

Henderson, J. M., Pollatsek, A., & Rayner, K. (1989). Covert visual attention and extrafoveal information use during object identification. *Perception & Psychophysics, 45*, 196–208.

Henderson, J. M., Weeks, P. A. Jr., & Hollingworth, A. (1999). Effects of semantic consistency on eye movements during scene viewing. *Journal of Experimental Psychology: Human Perception and Performance, 25*, 210–228.

Henderson, J. M., Williams, C. C., Castelhano, M. S., & Falk, R. J. (2003). Eye movements and picture processing during recognition. *Perception & Psychophysics, 65,* 725–734.

Hidalgo-Sotelo, B., Oliva, A., & Torralba, A. (2005). Human learning of contextual priors for object search: Where does the time go? In *Proceedings of 3rd Workshop on Attention and Performance at the International Conference in Computer Vision and Pattern Recognition* (CVPR), San Diego, CA.

Hoffman, J. E., & Subramaniam, B. (1995). The role of visual attention in saccadis eye movements. *Perception & Psychophysics, 57,* 787–795.

Hollingworth, A., & Henderson, J. M. (2002). Accurate visual memory for previously attended objects in natural scenes. *Journal of Experimental Psychology: Human Perception and Peformance, 28*(1), 113–136.

Hollingworth, A. (2003). Failures of retrieval and comparison constrain change detection in natural scenes. *Journal of Experimental Psychology: Human Perception and Performance,* 29, 388–403.

Hooge, I. T. C., & Erkelens, C. J. (1996). Control of fixation duration during a simple search task. *Perception & Psychophysics, 58,* 969–976.

Hooge, I. T. C., & Erkelens, C. J. (1998). Adjustment of fixation duration during visual search. *Vision Research, 38,* 1295–1302.

Horowitz, T. S., & Wolfe, J. M. (1998). Visual search has no memory. *Nature, 94,* 575–577.

Inhoff, A. W., & Rayner, K. (1986). Parafoveal word processing during eye fixations in reading: Effects of word frequency. *Perception & Psychophysics, 40,* 431–439.

Irwin, D. E. (2004). Fixation location and fixation duration as indices of cognitive processing. In J. M. Henderson & F. Ferreira (Eds.), *The interface of language, vision, and action: Eye movements and the visual world* (pp. 105–134). New York: Psychology Press.

Ishida, T., & Ikeda, M. (1989). Temporal properties of information extraction in reading studied by a text-mask replacement technique. *Journal of the Optical Society A: Optics and Image Science, 6,* 1624–1632.

Itti., L., & Koch, C. (2000). A saliency-based search mechanism for overt and covert shifts of visual attention. *Vision Research, 40,* 1489–1506.

Itti, L., & Koch, C. (2001). Computational modeling of visual attention. *Nature Reviews: Neuroscience, 2,* 194–203.

Jacobs, A. M. (1986). Eye movement control in visual search: How direct is visual span control? *Perception & Psychophysics, 39,* 47–58.

Juhasz, B. J., & Rayner, K. (2003). Investigating the effects of a set of intercorrelated variables on eye fixation durations in reading. *Journal of Experimental Psychology: Learning, Memory & Cognition, 29,* 1312–1318.

Juhasz, B. J., & Rayner, K. (2006). The role of age-of-acquisition and word frequency in reading: Evidence from eye fixation durations. *Visual Cognition, 13, 846–863.*

Kowler, E., Anderson, E., Dosher, B., & Blaser, E. (1995). The role of attention in programming saccades. *Vision Research, 35*, 1897–1916.

Levin, D. T., & Simons, D. J. (1997). Failure to detect changes to attended objects in motion pictures. *Psychonomic Bulletin & Review, 4(4)*, 501–506.

Liechty, J., Pieters F. G. M., & Wedel, M. (2003). Global and local covert visual attention: Evidence from a Bayesian hidden Markov model, *Psychometrika, 68*, 519–541.

Liversedge, S. P., Rayner, K., White, S. J., Vergilino-Perez, D., Findlay, J. M., & Kentridge, R. W. (2004). Eye movements while reading disappearing text: Is there a gap effect in reading? *Vision Research, 44*, 1013–1024.

Loftus, G. R., & Mackworth, N. H. (1978). Cognitive determinants of fixation location during picture viewing. *Journal of Experimental Psychology: Human Perception and Performance, 4*, 565–572.

Mackworth, N. H., & Morandi, A. J. (1967). The gaze selects informative details within pictures. *Perception & Psychophysics, 2*, 547–552.

Mannan, S. K., Ruddock, K. H., & Wooding, D. S. (1995). Automatic control of saccadic eye movements made in visual inspection of briefly presented 2-D images. *Spatial Vision, 9*, 363–386.

Mannan, S. K., Ruddock, K. H., & Wooding, D. S. (1996). The relationship between the locations of spatial features and those of fixation made during visual examination of briefly presented images. *Spatial Vision, 10*, 165–188.

McConkie, G. W. (1991). Perceiving a stable visual world. In *Proceedings of the Sixth European Conference on Eye Movements* (pp. 5–7). Leuven, Belgium: Laboratory of Experimental Psychology.

McConkie, G. W., & Rayner, K. (1975). The span of the effective stimulus during a fixation in reading. *Perception & Psychophysics, 17*, 578–586.

McConkie, G. W., & Zola, D. (1979). Is visual information integrated across successive fixations in reading? *Perception & Psychophysics, 25*, 221–224.

McPeek, R. M., Skavenski, A. A., & Nakayama, K. (2000). Concurrent processing of saccades in visual search. *Vision Research, 40*, 2499–2516.

Morris, R. K. (1994). Lexical and message-level sentence context effects on fixation times in reading. *Journal of Experimental Psychology: Learning, Memory, and Cognition, 20*, 92–103.

Morrison, R. E., & Rayner, K. (1981). Saccade size in reading depends upon character spaces and not visual angle. *Perception & Psychophysics, 30*, 395–396.

Najemnik, J., & Geisler, W. S. (2005). Optimal eye movement strategies in visual search. *Nature, 434*, 387–391.

Neider, M. B., & Zelinsky, G. J. (2006). Scene context guides eye movements during search.*Vision Research, 46(5),* 614–621.

Nelson, W. W., & Loftus, G. R. (1980). The functional visual field during picture viewing. *Journal of Experimental Psychology: Human Learning and Memory, 6,* 391–399.

Nodine, C. E., Carmody, D. P., & Herman, E. (1979). Eye movements during visual search for artistically embedded targets. *Bulletin of the Psychonomic Society, 13,* 371–374.

O'Regan, J. K., Rensink, R. A., & Clark, J. J. (1999). Change blindness as a result of 'mudsplashes'. *Nature, 398,* 34.

Parker, R. E. (1978). Picture processing during recognition. *Journal of Experimental Psychology: Human Perception and Performance, 4,* 284–293.

Parkhurst, D., Law, K., & Niebur, E. (2002). Modeling the role of salience in the allocation of overt visual attention. *Vision Research, 42,* 107–123.

Parkhurst, D. J., & Niebur, E. (2003). Scene content selected by active vision. *Spatial Vision, 16,* 125–154.

Peterson, M. S., Kramer, A. F., Wang, R. F., Irwin, D. E., & McCarley, J. S. (2001). Visual search has memory. *Psychological Science, 12,* 287–292.

Pieters, F. G. M., Rosbergen, E., & Wedel, M. (1999). Visual attention to repeated print advertising: A test of scanpath theory. *Journal of Marketing Research, 36,* 424–438.

Pieters, F. G. M., & Warlop, L. (1999). Visual attention during brand choice: The impact of time pressure and task motivation. *International Journal of Research in Marketing, 16,* 1–16.

Pieters, R., & Wedel, M. (2007). Goal control of attention to advertising: The Yarbus implication. *Journal of Consumer Research*, forthcoming.

Pollatsek, A., Rayner, K., & Collins, W. E. (1984). Integrating pictorial information across eye movements. *Journal of Experimental Psychology: General, 113,* 426–442.

Pollatsek, A., Rayner, K., & Henderson, J. M. (1990). Role of spatial location in integration of pictorial information across saccades. *Journal of Experimental Psychology: Human Perception and Performance, 16,* 199–210.

Pollatsek, A., Reichle, E. D., & Rayner, K. (2006). Tests of the E-Z Reader model: Exploring the interface between cognition and eye-movement control. *Cognitive Psychology, 52,* 1–52.

Posner, M. I. (1980). Orienting of attention. *Quarterly Journal of Experimental Psychology, 32,* 3–25.

Radach, R., Lemmer, S., Vorstius, C., Heller, D., & Radach, K. (2003). Eye movements in the processing of print advertisements. In J. Hyönä, R. Radach & H. Deubel, (Eds.), *The Mind's Eyes: Cognitive and Applied Aspects of Eye Movement Research*. Amsterdam: Elsevier Science Publishers.

Rayner, K. (1975). The perceptual span and peripheral cues in reading. *Cognitive Psychology, 7,* 65–81.

Rayner, K. (1978). Eye movements in reading and information processing. *Psychological Bulletin, 85,* 618–660.

Rayner, K. (1995). Eye movements and cognitive processes in reading, visual search, and scene perception. In J. M. Findlay, R. Walker, & R. W. Kentridge (Eds.), *Eye movement research: Mechanisms, processes and applications* (pp. 3–22). Amsterdam: North Holland.

Rayner, K. (1998). Eye movements in reading and information processing: 20 years of research. *Psychological Bulletin, 85,* 618–660.

Rayner, K., Ashby, J., Pollatsek, A., & Reichle, E. D. (2004). The effects of frequency and predictability on eye fixations in reading: Implications for the E-Z Reader model. *Journal of Experimental Psychology: Human Perception and Performance, 30,* 720–732.

Rayner, K., & Bertera, J. H. (1979). Reading without a fovea. *Science, 206,* 468–469.

Rayner, K., & Duffy, S. A. (1986). Lexical complexity and fixation times in reading: Effects of word frequency, verb complexity, and lexical ambiguity. *Memory & Cognition, 14,* 191–201.

Rayner, K., & Fisher, D. L. (1987a). Eye movements and the perceptual span during visual search. In J. K. O'Regan & A. Levy-Schoen (Eds.), *Eye movements: From physiology to cognition* (pp. 293–302). Amsterdam: North Holland.

Rayner, K., & Fisher, D. L. (1987b). Letter processing during eye fixations in visual search. *Perception & Psychophysics, 42,* 87–100.

Rayner, K., Inhoff, A. W., Morrison, R. E., Slowiaczek, M. L., & Bertera, J. H. (1981). Masking of foveal and parafoveal vision during eye fixations in reading. *Journal of Experimental Psychology: Human Perception and Performance, 7,* 167–179.

Rayner, K., Liversedge, S. P., & White, S. J. (2006). Eye movements when reading disappearing text: The importance of the word to the right of fixation. *Vision Research, 46,* 310–323.

Rayner, K., Liversedge, S. P., White, S. J., & Vergilino-Perez, D. (2003). Reading disappearing text: Cognitive control of eye movements. *Psychological Science, 14,* 385–389.

Rayner, K., McConkie, G. W., & Ehrlich, S. F. (1978). Eye movements and integrating information across saccades. *Journal of Experimental Psychology: Human Perception and Performance, 4,* 529–544.

Rayner, K., McConkie, G. W., & Zola, D. (1980). Integrating information across eye movements. *Cognitive Psychology, 12,* 206–226.

Rayner, K., Miller, B., & Rotello, C. M. (2007). Eye movements when looking at print advertisements: The goal of the viewer matters. *Applied Cognitive Psychology,* in press.

Rayner, K., & Pollatsek, A. (1989). The *psychology of reading.* Englewood Cliffs, NJ: Prentice Hall.

Rayner, K., & Pollatsek, A. (1992). Eye movements and scene perception. *Canadian Journal of Psychology, 46,* 342–376.

Rayner, K., Reichle, E. D., & Pollatsek, A. (1998). Eye movement control in reading: An overview and model. In G. Underwood (Ed.), *Eye guidance in reading and scene perception* (pp. 243–268). Oxford, England: Elsevier.

Rayner, K., Rotello, C., Stewart, A., Keir, J., & Duffy, S. (2001). Integrating text and pictorial information: Eye movements when looking at print advertisements. *Journal of Experimental Psychology: Applied, 7,* 219–226.

Rayner, K., Slowiaczek, M. L., Clifton, C., & Bertera, J. H. (1983). Latency of sequential eye movements: Implications for reading. *Journal of Experimental Psychology: Human Perception and Performance, 9,* 912–922.

Rayner, K., Warren, T., Juhasz, B. J., & Liversedge, S. P. (2004). The effect of plausibility on eye movements in reading. *Journal of Experimental Psychology: Learning, Memory, and Cognition, 30,* 1290–1301.

Rayner, K., & Well, A. D. (1996). Effects of contextual constraint on eye movements in reading: A further examination. *Psychonomic Bulletin & Review, 3,* 504–509.

Reichle, E. D., & Nelson, J. R. (2003). Local vs. global attention: Are two states necessary? Comment on Liechty et al., 2003. *Psychometrika, 68,* 543–549.

Reichle, E. D., Pollatsek, A., Fisher, D. L., & Rayner, K. (1998). Toward a model of eye movement control in reading. *Psychological Review, 105,* 125–157.

Reichle, E. D., Pollatsek, A., & Rayner, K. (2006). E-Z Reader: A cognitive-control, serial-attention model of eye-movement behavior during reading. *Cognitive Systems Research, 7,* 4–22.

Reichle, E. D., Rayner, K., & Pollatsek, A. (2003). The E-Z Reader model of eye movement control in reading: Comparison to other models. *Behavioral and Brain Sciences. 26,* 507–526.

Rensink, R. A., O'Regan, J. K., & Clark, J. J. (1997). To see or not to see: The need for attention to perceive changes in scenes. *Psychological Science, 8,* 368–373.

Saida, S., & Ikeda, M. (1979). Useful field size for pattern perception. *Perception & Psychophysics, 25,* 119–125.

Sereno, S. C., O'Donnell, P.J., & Rayner, K. (2006). Eye movements and lexical ambiguity resolution: Investigating the subordinate bias effect. *Journal of Experimental Psychology: Human Perception and Performance, 32,* 335–350.

Torralba, A., Oliva, A., Castelhano, M. S., & Henderson, J. M. (2006). Contextual guidance of eye movements and attention in real-world scenes: The role of global features in object search. *Psychological Review, 113,* 766–786.

Vaughan, J. (1982). Control of fixation duration in visual search and memory search: Another look. *Journal of Experimental Psychology: Human Perception and Performance, 8,* 709–723.

Vlaskamp, B. N. S., & Hooge, I. T. C. (2006). Crowding degrades saccadic search performance. *Vision Research, 46,* 417–425.

Wedel, M., & Pieters, F. G. M. (2000). Eye fixations on advertisements and memory for brands: A model and findings. *Marketing Science, 19,* 297–312.

Williams, C. C., Henderson, J. M., & Zacks, R. T. (2005). Incidental visual memory for targets and distractors in visual search. *Perception & Psychophysics, 67,* 816–827.

Williams, R. S., & Morris, R. K. (2004). Eye movements, word familiarity, and vocabulary acquisition. *European Journal of Cognitive Psychology, 16,* 312–339.

Yarbus, A. (1967). *Eye movements and vision.* New York: Plenum Press.

Zelinsky, G. (2005). Specifying the components of attention in a visual search task. In L. Itti, G. Rees, & J. Tsotsos (Eds.), *Neurobiology of attention* (pp. 395–400). Elsevier.

Zelinsky, G. J., Rao, R. P. N., Hayhoe, M. M., & Ballard, D. H. (1997). Eye movements reveal the spatiotemporal dynamics of visual search. *Psychological Science, 8*(6), 448–453.

Zoest, L. J. F. M. van, Donk, M., & Theeuwes, J. (2004). The role of bottom-up control in saccadic eye movements. *Journal of Experimental Psychology: Human Perception and Performance, 30,* 746–759.

3

Informativeness of Eye Movements for Visual Marketing

Six Cornerstones

Rik Pieters and Michel Wedel

Vision in Marketing

The human visual system is central in natural tasks that consumers daily engage in, such as viewing and reading advertising, and inspecting, searching and choosing brands and products in brick and mortar and virtual shopping environments. The visual system rapidly and largely automatically accomplishes a host of functions that are vital to consumers' goal-directed behavior. Moreover, the visual system is most likely centrally implicated in learning, higher-order, cognitive-affective processes, decision making and its behavioral implementation and coordination. Yet, relatively little attention in marketing and consumer science is devoted to the role of such visual processes, with several notable exceptions in this edited volume. Aristotle (trans. 1991), in his theory of rhetoric, already stressed the importance of "bringing before the eyes," to actualize and bring to life rather than to rely only on the force of logical, verbal arguments in order to persuade people. In a recent analysis of decision-making research, Loewenstein (2001, p. 503) argues that people often do not choose between alternative courses of behavior by explicitly weighting their costs and benefits. Instead, "people rely on cognitive capabilities that are relatively well developed, such as visual perception and object recognition, rather than operations that they are not very good at, like addition and multiplication." If this holds true, what happens when consumers are exposed to advertisements and similar visual marketing stimuli, with various forms of text and pictorials? How do consumers move their eyes across such complex scenes to extract information that is relevant to their current goals, what do they pay attention to, and how does this affect their decision making and choices? And more generally, how are eye movements related to higher-order cognitive and affective processes and to consumer behaviors of interest in marketing?

This chapter explores such questions, and aims to make several contributions. First, it documents how eye movements can and have shed new light on the processing and effectiveness of visual marketing stimuli, such as advertisements, that cannot be obtained otherwise. Second and importantly, it corrects six common delusions about the role of eye movements in the processing and effectiveness of visual marketing stimuli, which have hampered progress in the field, and it offers six cornerstones of eye-tracking theory and research in visual marketing based on the amendments. Third, it provides directions for future research in visual marketing, and demonstrates the potential contributions of eye-movement analysis. To these ends, we first introduce a scene perception perspective on advertising processing. Then, we explore how meaning is extracted from an ad scene, and the role of informativeness versus salience in guiding eye movements. With eye-movement data becoming increasingly available, we point to the answers to long-standing theoretical and managerial questions that eye movement analysis can offer. In this way, the chapter aims to demonstrate the value of studying eye movements across advertisements and similar visual marketing stimuli to test fundamental theories of visual perception, and thereby to contribute to improved visual marketing practice.

Advertising Processing as Scene Perception

Visual marketing stimuli, such as print advertisements and television commercials, are specific types of scenes. Consumers are continuously exposed to scenes, defined as "semantically coherent (and often nameable) views of a real-world environment comprising background elements and multiple discrete objects arranged in a spatially licensed manner" (Henderson & Hollingworth, 1999, p. 244). Spatial licensing involves adherence to physical constraints of the universe, such as the laws of gravity and sunlight coming from above, and the semantic constraints imposed by object identities and functions, such as that cars do not fly, or that dolls do not speak to people.

Real-world scenes differ from Ersatz scenes that are sometimes used in fundamental perception research, such as arrays of dots or basic shapes and colors in target search tasks. Henderson (2005) urges to reserve the term *scene* for real-world scenes, because these are likely to be perceived differently from Ersatz scenes. For instance, and we will return to this, real-world scenes are identified as coherent meaningful entities using global image properties, with implications for the informativeness of the objects contained therein.

Within real-world scenes, natural and man-made scenes can be distinguished, and the latter category comprises visual marketing stimuli, such as advertisements. Whereas natural scenes are predominantly or exclusively pictorial, advertising scenes comprise combinations of pictorial and textual information, as different information modes. Advertising scenes are mixed-mode, real-world, man-made scenes with their own lawfulness (or licensing), because in advertisements cars can fly, dolls may talk to people, and dreams come true. This makes understanding eye movements across ad scenes both interesting and challenging.

Eye movements are deployed across advertisements and other visual marketing scenes in the service of perception and action, and they hold the promise of providing insights into the rapid, largely automatic processes during ad perception unobtainable from other data. For this reason, eye movement analysis has attracted interest since early times. The history of academic research in visual marketing started in the early 1900s, when Nixon (1924), Poffenberger (1925) and others described eye-movement research to determine the attention-capture value of magazine and newspaper advertisements. Since then and particularly in recent years, eye-movement research in marketing has grown, and there is now a sizeable database of published studies to draw upon (Wedel & Pieters, forthcoming). We believe, however, that eye-tracking research is at the verge of a new era in the marketing discipline, with an even broader acceptance and an even wider use, due to the growing realization of the opportunities provided by it to address fundamental marketing questions, and the availability of low-cost, easy-to-use eye-tracking systems.

Six Cornerstones of Eye-Tracking Theory and Research in Visual Marketing

There are common misconceptions about the human visual system, and its role in visual marketing processing and effectiveness, and we believe that resolving these will enable eye-tracking theory and research to reach its full potential. Six such delusions are that people (a) move their eyes consciously, smoothly and orderly, (b) are aware of individual eye movements, (c) see well beyond their current point of fixation into the periphery of the perceptual field, (d) can routinely attend to objects they do not look at, and look at objects they do not attend to, (e) need to attend to objects only as a precondition for downstream cognitive processes that are more important, and beyond the scope of eye tracking, (f) use eye movements only to select objects for attention. It would be pointless to track eye movements if these beliefs would be accurate. Fortunately, the actual situation is different, which leads to the six cornerstones for eye-tracking theory and research of visual marketing that we propose next.

1. Eye Movements Reflect Information Sampling in Time and Space

The continuous and orderly flow of visual input over time and space that people experience during the perception of scenes, such as advertisements, is a major accomplishment of the visual system, and is based on an interrupted and incomplete visual input signal.

That is, rather than smoothly and continuously moving the eyes across visual scenes, people abruptly move their eyes about 3 to 6 times per second. During such saccades, the eyes reach a peak speed of 500 degrees per second. In between saccades, which normally last about 20–40 ms, the eyes are fairly still for about 100–400 ms, and it is only during these eye fixations that information intake from the scene can occur (Rayner, 1998; Wedel & Pieters, 2000; see also the chapter by Rayner & Castelhano in this volume). Thus, "Why and how people perceive the visual world as continuous and stable, despite the gross changes of its retinal projection that occur with each saccade, is certainly one of the classic problems in perception" (Deubel, Schneider, & Bridgeman, 2002, p. 165). People blink spontaneously about 10 to 15 times per minute to moisten and oxygenate the cornea, the front layer of the eyeball, and reflexively to prevent potential damage from strong light sources, dust, and so forth. Each blink lasts about 100–150 ms, during which stimulation of the retina by incoming light is attenuated 100-fold (Burr, 2005).

During and immediately before and after saccades and blinks, vision is actively suppressed to prevent blurring and smearing of the retinal image, in which presumably the magnocellular visual pathway in the brain plays a role, although the exact neural mechanisms are still unknown (Bristow, Frith, & Rees, 2005; Ridder & Tomlinson, 1997). Due to saccadic and blink suppression during scene perception, people are in fact up to 15% of the time *functionally blind.* One only needs to look at one's own eyes in a mirror to experience saccadic suppression: try to first fixate one eye and then fixate the other. Notice that no movement of the eyes is detectable, and the motionless stare of one's own eyes is an awkward experience at first. The visual brain not only accommodates image stabilization and saccadic and blink suppression, but also the maintenance of visual continuity through trans-saccadic memory (Deubel et al., 2002; Verfaillie & De Graef, 2000), by filling in the blanks, without which vision would be a smeared, shaky, and stuttering venture. Thus, to retain a stable view of the world, displacements of the image that take place during the course of eye saccades are actively suppressed. This phenomenon is related to *change blindness*, which reveals itself vividly in experiments when people are blind to actual and even gross changes in the position of objects in a scene when these occur during a saccade (Simons & Rensink, 2005), see later. Thus, in scene perception discrete sampling processes (eye) and continuous experiential processes (brain) are functionally coupled.

The spatio-temporal sampling pattern of eye fixations and saccades between them are the input for eye movement analysis. In fact, if the eyes would move continuously across the scene, eye movement analysis would be seriously challenged, due to the inferential demands of determining in continuous time and space what information in the scene consumers exactly process.

2. Awareness of Individual Eye Movements Is Limited

Despite the common thought that "one knows what one is looking at," awareness of the individual eye movements that are made during scene perception and action execution is typically low, and one may forget having fixated objects that were present (error of omission), and remember having fixated objects that were actually absent (error of commission), even very shortly after exposure. People are often not even aware that they make eye fixations during scene perception in the first place, because of their experiencing smooth, uninterrupted vision (see above). In addition, the feeling that the perceptual field during eye fixations is large (see below) hampers people accurately identifying their point-of-regard. This may hold even more for certain types of eye movements and entire scanpaths. As a case in point, Land and Hayhoe (2001) distinguish four different types of fixations during daily activities such as preparing breakfast: (a) locating (cup, teapot, spoon), (b) directing (hand to teapot), (c) guiding (teapot to cup), and (d) checking (cup is full enough). Here, locating and checking fixations are likely more important to be aware of and remember than directing and guiding fixations are, because it is crucial to know if the cup is present and when it is almost full, which may bring these fixations to consciousness, in particular when task failure is costly.

Because humans make over 100,000 saccades in the course of a waking day, with about the same number of eye fixations in between, it would be too taxing for any conscious system to be aware of each of these movements. Such "micro" awareness of individual eye movements would also be inefficient, as the vast majority of them are part of overlearned routines, which are governed by specific goals, but with little conscious control over and awareness of each specific eye movement (see for a more general discussion Bargh, 2002). There is abundant evidence that "the mind operates quite efficiently by relegating to the unconscious 'normal' processes of perception, attention, learning and judgment" (Wilson & Dunn, 2004, p. 499). Even in novel tasks, such as learning to play tennis, golf, or soccer, people often have limited conscious access to the specific eye movements that they make (see Duchowski, 2003). Forced conscious awareness of overlearned eye movements could even be dysfunctional by drawing on resources required elsewhere, or disrupting the efficiency of automated eye-movement processes (Wilson & Dunn, 2004).

Using think-aloud protocols to collect information about individual eye movements is not an obvious alternative in view of the large volume of rapid eye movements, the experience of smooth and uninterrupted vision, and the bias and task disruption that the verbalizations may engender. Memory measures of prior eye movements are likely to be prone to systematic reconstruction errors based on lay theories of how and where attention is and should be allocated and the salience of specific retrieval cues (e.g., D'Ydewalle & Tamsin, 1993; Schacter, 1999). Because of this, eye tracking is needed.

3. The Perceptual Field during Eye Fixations Is Narrow

"Both naïve individuals and many visual scientists consistently overestimate their abilities to use peripheral vision" (Findlay, 2004, p. 136). That is, the misconception that people can discern much detail in a fairly large area around the exact fixation location is pervasive. That illusion is created because the brain automatically and unconsciously moves the center of vision into any area of interest in the field of view, and therefore one sees much detail wherever one looks. Detailed perceptual analysis of a scene can only take place in the small area of about 2 degrees of visual angle around the exact fixation location which projects on the fovea centralis in the back of the eye, housing among others most of the 5 million cones in the retina that account for color vision. This small area of foveal vision is equivalent to about the size of one's thumbnail at arm's length. Outside the center of the fovea toward the parafovea and periphery, visual acuity rapidly tapers off, and colors, details, edges, and shapes are quickly lost to detailed analysis, up to the point that in the far periphery only large patches or blobs of luminance differences and movement are discernible (Anstis, 1974, 1998). Nelson and Loftus (1980) showed that performance in a memory task was related to the eye fixations closest to the target objects during a previous exposure task, and that memory performance dropped to chance levels when the eye fixations were over 2 degrees removed from them. Likewise, Henderson, Williams, Castelhano, and Falk (2003) found no evidence that objects in the visual periphery that were deleted or substituted between a previous and the current scene exposure could be recognized, which expresses the change blindness phenomenon. In other words, the perceptual field is small and objects outside it cannot reliably be identified or remembered. Consumers sample snapshots of detailed information in a small region around eye fixations, rather than continuously and orderly viewing big parts of the scene in full detail. Thus, if the interest is in information acquisition processes, eye fixations are the key measures of interest.

4. Eye Movements Are Tightly Coupled with Covert Attention

The belief that covert and overt attention can be easily and routinely dissociated in time and space during task performance is persistent. It is true that covert attention—the focus of the *internal eye*—and overt attention—the focus of the *external eye*—can be dissociated at specific points in time and space. Yet, during normal task completion, the coupling between covert and overt attention is like a firm rubber band (Henderson, 1992), with the eyes closely following attention, and attention closely following the eyes.

First, because objects in the periphery need to be progressively larger to become as discernible as when they would be fixated, and in view of the high speed of eye movements, it is much more efficient to move the eyes to the objects rather than to test hypotheses about their identity and specific features using peripheral vision only, which isn't designed for the task in the first place (Findlay & Gilchrist, 2003), see also later. Of course, covert spatial attention can be consciously allocated independent of eye movements. For instance, response times to the appearance of visual targets in displays are faster when cued with an arrow at the current fixation location that points to the likely position of the targets, although the benefits in such cueing tasks are usually no greater than 40 ms (Posner, 1980). Then, covert and overt attention are temporarily dissociated in anticipation of a soon-to-happen event outside the current perceptual field. But the important question is whether consumers persistently and routinely look "from the corner of their eyes," if it is more difficult to *not fixate* an object that is peripherally noted, than to fixate it (Findlay, 2004)? In general, many of the findings on the dissociation of covert attention and eye movements may arise because it is *possible* to consciously suppress the natural eye movement that normally follows a shift in covert attention directly, not that it is natural and common. Second, because it is effortful to buffer large sequences of fixated objects and locations in working memory before processing them, it is more efficient to process incoming information as quickly as possible. There is evidence for the *immediacy hypothesis* that "interpretations at all levels of processing are not deferred; they occur as soon as possible" (Just & Carpenter, 1980, p. 330). It was originally proposed based on reading research findings that fixation frequencies and durations depend on characteristics of the currently fixated word and on all levels of processing it, more so than on those of preceding and subsequent words. Countering the immediacy hypothesis, there is now evidence that linguistic processing of a word can be initiated before it is fixated (preview benefit), and that processing *can* continue afterward, but these dissociations between covert and overt attention are typically up to 60 ms only (Rayner, Reichle, & Pollatsek, 1998). Given the magnitude of the latencies, these findings do not contradict but support Henderson's rubber band metaphor of attention coupling.

It has been shown that covert attention derives from activation of the same neural circuits that determine eye-movement activity (reviewed by Craighero & Rizzolatti, 2005). That is, in the organization of action (i.e., an eye movement), there is a stage in which the required motor programs are set, prior to being executed, and this state is what is experienced as (covert) attention, hence the name *premotor theory of attention*. In other words, there may be no separate area in the visual brain for covert attention, which is independent of overt attention movements, but the two expressions of attention seem to follow from the same neural circuitry. Both covert (without saccadic eye movements) and overt (with saccadic eye movements) shifts of visuospatial attention are induced by activation of the Frontal Eye Fields (FEF; located in the prefrontal cortex) that operate in a network of areas involved in the control of eye movements, including the Superior Colliculus (SC) and the saccade generator in the brainstem. The SC guides eye movements to salient regions in the visual field through direct projections from the retina and contains a topographical representation of the visual field. The FEF have been implicated in voluntary eye movements and saccades to remembered targets (Schall, 2004). The recent discovery of *mirror neurons* in the ventral premotor area (F5) of the frontal lobes adds further support for the close connection between motor and sensory processes (Gallese, Fadiga, Fogassi, & Rizzolatti, 1996). It turns out that these mirror cells not only fire when an action is performed, but also when this same action is seen in others (Keysers et al., 2003). Thus, under normal task conditions, patterns of eye movements are closely aligned with covert attention, and there is evidence for a neurological basis of this connection.

5. Attention Is Central to Ad Processing

There is a generally held belief that attention is merely a selection mechanism that operates before the truly interesting downstream communication processes and effects occur. But in fact, attention is central to ad processing, both as a selection and an executive mechanism (Fuster, 2003, ch. 6).

Inspired by the popular AIDA (Attention, Interest, Desire, Action) model and its successors in marketing (Starch, 1923; Strong, 1920), attention is commonly considered to be an early gatekeeper that is qualitatively different and temporally separated from cognitive and affective processes. That is, such models assume that one can attend without interpreting, comprehending, and evaluating, and that there is a separate attention stage that selects only. The majority of alternatives to and successors of AIDA essentially retain this view, with attention, or its twin brother awareness, as a first step (see the review of Vakratsas & Ambler, 1999). For instance, Aaker, Myers, and Batra (1996) indicate: "attention can be viewed as an information filter—a screening mechanism that controls the quantity and nature of information any individual receives" (p. 221). Thus, they continue, "One might say that getting (and holding) a consumer's attention is a necessary but not sufficient condition in creating effective advertising. In the second step, a consumer who does pay attention to an ad must interpret and comprehend it in the way the advertiser intended it to be interpreted" (p. 220). Although there is little empirical support that consumers' ad processing follows such a strict hierarchy (in whatever form), managerial recommendations for communication nevertheless remain based on AIDA-like models (e.g., Belch & Belch, 2001, ch. 5).

We believe that the survival of AIDA is due, at least partly, to confusing the stages that advertising could go through in order to be effective, with the processes that consumers engage in when being exposed to advertisements. That is, AIDA-like frameworks may be useful as *communication planning models*, but they should not be taken as *consumer process models*. With respect to the former, Colley (1961, pp. 37–38) in his report to the Association of National Advertisers explained that prior to an advertising campaign aimed at increasing awareness, one needs to determine: "How many (of the target audience) have heard about or are aware of the existence of our product, company or the particular idea we wish to advance in our advertising." Pre–post comparison then establishes the percentage of the target audience converted. From a marketing or sales perspective, a sequential view of converting consumers may be useful, but there is no reason that these stages should map exactly on stages in consumers' ad processing (in content and timing), and in fact they don't, since even to be able to report awareness, consumers need to have memory of, and most likely need to have comprehended and evaluated the advertising message.

Rather than attention, comprehension, and evaluation being discrete, sequential processes well separated in time, there is growing evidence that comprehension processes occur (almost) simultaneously with attention (Grill-Spector & Kanwisher, 2005), and the same holds for evaluation (Bargh, 2002). For instance, both object detection (selection: does a scene contain an object or not) and object categorization (comprehension: what kind of object is it) in ambiguous scenes is already more than 80% after fewer than 100 ms (Grill-Spector & Kanwisher, 2005).

Attention serves to improve the speed, accuracy and maintenance of mental and behavioral processes over time, and it manifests itself in selection, preparation and maintenance (LaBerge, 1995). Attention operates by simultaneously enhancing the processing of some objects or locations (inclusion) while suppressing others (exclusion). In this way, it reduces uncertainty about the identity of objects or locations, and it enhances discriminations between them (Wolfe, 2000). Without maintaining attention, the speed and accuracy of ongoing mental and behavioral processes, such as message learning, is decreased, and even hedonic experience is reduced.

Accordingly, attention is an emergent property of the whole (visual) brain rather than a localized property of some area of it. That is, "Nowhere in the central nervous system is there evidence of a separate structure or group of structures dedicated to attention as a separate function" (Fuster, 2003, p. 148), but instead, Fuster continues, attention "is inherent in the processing of adaptive action at any level of the central nervous system" (p. 165). In other words, attention not only selects (ad) objects and locations for processing, but also reflects coordination of ad processing over time and space, and it is thus central in determining ad effectiveness.

6. Eye Movements Reflect Ad Processing

In a comparison of various methodologies for decision process tracing, Russo (1978, p. 561) argued that eye movements reflect information acquisition, and that "[a]ny strategy for performing a cognitive task, such as consumer decision making, will exhibit a characteristic pattern of information acquisition and internal computation. The task of the researcher is to identify the consumer's strategy from only what is observable." In an eye-tracking study demonstrating this, Pieters and Warlop (1999) inferred from eye movements that under time pressure, consumers who were engaged in a stimulus-based choice task progressively switched from a processing-by-brand strategy, as reflected in a higher proportion of saccades within brands, to a processing-by-attribute strategy, as reflected in a higher proportion of saccades between brands. Earlier, Russo and Leclerc (1994) inferred three different stages in stimulus-based choice process, based on eye-movements observations, between which consumers adaptively switched: orientation, evaluation, and verification, respectively. Orientation entailed getting an overview of the products. In the evaluation stage, direct comparisons between two or three alternative products were made—saccades between brands. The verification stage involved further examination of the already chosen brand—saccades within brands. Both of these studies demonstrated that brand choice could be predicted from eye movements (see for new evidence and directions the chapter by Chandon, Bradlow, Hutchinson, & Young in this volume).

There is initial support that the intensity of processing during scene perception is reflected in eye-movement measures as well. In an early study, Gould (1967), asked participants to report how many times a specific pattern of symbols occurred among a set of comparison patterns. He observed longer fixation durations (340 ms as opposed to 280 ms) for highly similar target and comparison patterns, which suggests that differences in fixation durations between stimuli reflect the complexity of processing them. This is consistent with Kahneman's (1973, p. 65) suggestion that "the rate of eye movements often corresponds to the rate of mental activity," as longer fixation durations lead to lower fixation frequencies per unit of time.

There is also evidence that emotional stimuli are likely to draw and hold attention, and to be more rapidly detected than neutral ones (Zeelenberg, Wagenmakers, & Rotteveel, 2006), and that this enhances long-term memory (Christianson, Loftus, Hoffman, & Loftus, 1991). For instance, Calvo and Lang (2004) asked participants to determine whether pairs of pictures were the same or different, while their eyes were being tracked. Consistently, the first eye fixation was more likely to be devoted to positively and negatively valenced pictures (scenes of affection versus threat) as compared to neutral pictures (matched on complexity, luminance, and size of faces). Also, the last eye fixation was more likely to be devoted to threatening rather than to neutral pictures. Related research further supports the initial enhancement and later active inhibition of visual attention to threatening stimuli (Hermans, Vansteenwegen, & Eelen, 1999). Thus, emotional valence of stimuli is reflected in eye movements, and a pioneering PhD thesis by Witt (cited in Kroeber-Riel, 1979) already demonstrated this phenomenon in advertising. Witt created two versions of ads by manipulating the pictorial to invoke mild versus intense arousal. The average number of fixations on the pictorial of the two ad types was 3.9 and 5.5, respectively, indicating more information intake under higher arousal. And there is even reason to believe that eye movements actively influence preferences, such that prolonging the gaze on objects raises preferences for them (Shimojo, Simion, Shimojo, & Scheier, 2003, experiment 2).

Tapping Informativeness in Eye Movements

When do consumers know they are looking at an ad, and what the ad is all about? How is the informativeness of objects and locations in the scene reflected in the eye, and how long, and where, do people actually look at in ads? These questions are at the heart of a better understanding of advertising processing as a special instance of scene perception. Whereas eye movement research has long emphasized perceptual and linguistic processes in text processing (Rayner, 1998), it has recently also begun to address scene perception issues (Henderson, 2003). Because of their importance to understanding visual attention to advertising, we elaborate on these in the remainder, as an illustration of the information value of eye movements to visual marketing.

The Advertising Exposure Task: The Brief Duration of Self-Controlled Exposure to the Ad and Its Context

Exposures to advertising and other visual marketing scenes under normal conditions are usually remarkably brief, compared to the much longer ad exposures under experimental conditions in (academic) advertising research, and differ in other important respects as well. Recently, Maret (2005) conducted a literature search of seven major marketing journals between 1972 and 2003, for all articles on memory for and persuasion by advertising. He located 38 relevant articles, which tested 239 specific relationships between memory and persuasion, finding that the average exposure duration to the advertisements in the studies was over 25 seconds, that ads most often were shown without facing editorial material, and that in 74% of the cases there were less than five ads, and usually only a single ad was the target ad. These exposure conditions may hamper valid generalizations about advertising effectiveness across ads, because (a) the forced exposure conditions are over five times as long as under natural exposure conditions, (b) the attention demands of exposure to multiple ads, as under natural conditions, are ignored, (c) the obtained effects may be idiosyncratic to the design and contents of the specific target ad, and (d) the influence of advertising context is lacking.

Pieters and Wedel (2004) conducted an analysis of over 1,363 full-page magazine print advertisements for various products and brands that were tested under natural exposure conditions, with exposure duration being self-controlled by consumers (age 18–55), and advertisements shown in their editorial context with multiple ads and editorials competing for attention in the same magazine. Consumers examine advertisements for 1.73 seconds on average, with a range from 0.37 to 5.30 seconds. Of course, differences exist between consumers high versus low in involvement. Rosbergen, Pieters, and Wedel (1997) identified from eye movement recordings three consumer segments with total ad viewing time increasing from the first to the third segment from .63–2.71 seconds. Despite significant differences between segments in involvement and other top-down factors, the notable result here is the brief ad durations when consumers control exposure, even under high involvement. In these studies, ads were faced by editorial material and consumers were exposed to multiple ads as normally in magazines.

What are the patterns of eye movements across ads and their editorial context, when exposure is so brief? If consumers look at the editorial context and the ad strictly sequentially, this could justify the use of exposure conditions where ads are shown in isolation. To explore this, we had a sample of 104 male consumers (age 18–55) examine a new ad in its editorial context, preceded and followed by other ads, while their eye movements where being tracked

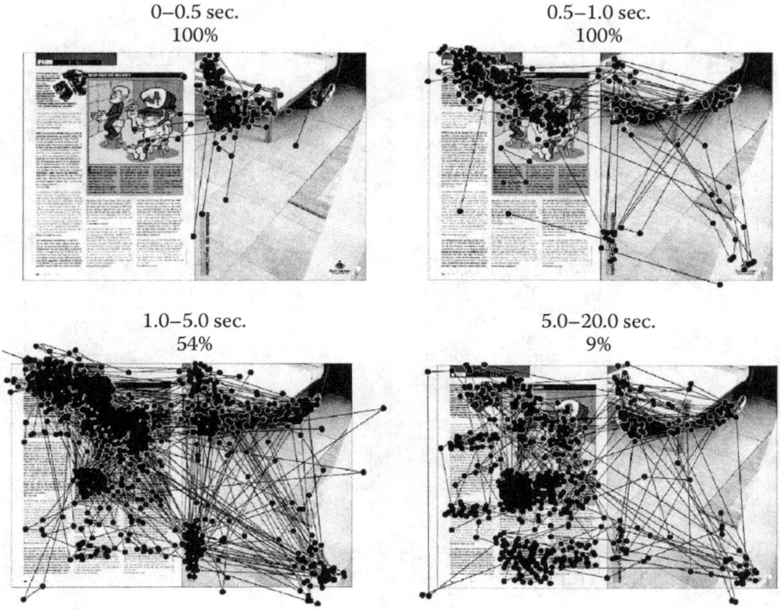

Figure 3.1 The trajectory of attention to an advertisement and editorial (ad for "Footlocker" on the right; $n = 104$).

with infrared corneal reflection methodology. Participants were instructed to "explore the pages as they would do at home or in a waiting room," and could continue to a next page at will. The ad was for the Foot Locker retail chain (right page). On average, consumers examined this double page for 6.45 seconds, with 27% of the time (1.74 seconds) being spent on the ad and the other 73% (4.71 seconds) on the editorial. During ad exposure only 31% of the participants fixated the Foot Locker brand logo (bottom right).

Figure 3.1 shows four episodes in the ad trajectory, with fixations as dots, and saccades as black lines. The first fixations (0–0.5 seconds) appear to be mostly on the ad pictorial, on the region that apparently is most informative or surprising (the feet under the bed). Then, from 0.5–1.0 seconds, when still all consumers are looking, the variance of fixation locations increases, and a large cluster of fixations on the editorial appears, in particular on the cartoon. In the next four seconds (1–4 seconds) only about half of the participants remain and they explore both the editorial and the ad in more detail, the clusters of fixations (the scanpath on regions of interest) remaining

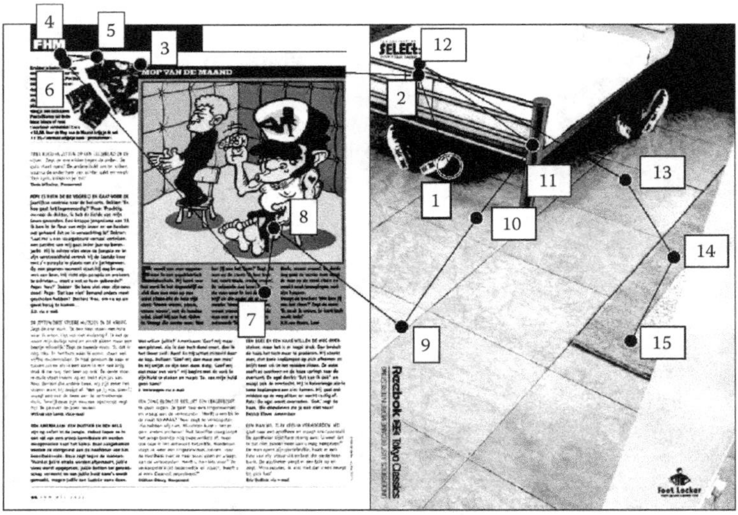

Figure 3.2 Scanpath of a single person across a double page: Footlocker advertisement on right page.

relatively similar. In addition, participants now also fixate secondary elements: the informative textual elements of the editorial and the ad, as well as the brand logo. In the final 15 seconds, the few (9%) remaining participants continue to explore the same regions of interest in the editorial and the ad, but now also sequences of fixations that indicate reading become apparent. The few participants reading the text may cause the long average exposure durations of this double page. The scanpath of a single consumer from the sample, Figure 3.2, adds further detail. This person fixated the double page 15 times (3.53 seconds of gaze duration). The fixations are numbered in Figure 3.2; the first two fixations are on the ad, the next seven on the editorial material, and the final seven again on the ad. The brand name and logo (bottom left) and the product information (bottom left in the ad) were never fixated. It is striking that the ad and editorial are explored intermittently, with saccades back and forth between them, rather than strictly sequentially.

This case study illustrates that: (a) self-controlled exposure durations to print ads are brief, (b) the spatial distribution of eye fixations is highly nonrandom, with specific regions receiving a disproportionate amount of eye fixations while other regions are almost skipped, (c) a few consumers typically start reading the body text only later during exposure, leading to much longer exposure durations, (d) consumers switch back and forth between the ad and the editorial material, rather than exploring them strictly sequentially, which highlights that information sampling takes place both within and between subscenes, and (e) eye movement patterns of consumers across the same ad are relatively similar, expressing a dominant scanpath (Noton & Stark, 1971). This scanpath is more likely due to low-level perceptual features in the scene strongly guiding attention bottom-up (see below, and the chapter by Greenleaf and Raghubir in this volume). It differs qualitatively from earlier observations (e.g., Yarbus, 1967) that people use additional time after a first scan to re-cycle through the key elements again. Instead, our case study indicates that consumers quit after a quick scan, or use the additional time to fixate the *secondary* elements, such as the body text, which is probably a consequence of self-controlled short exposure in our experiment, as in practice.

The case study indicates that eye fixations go to potentially informative regions of the advertisement and the editorial to sample detailed information. But given the short exposure and the eyes jumping back and forth between the *ed* and the ad, two questions come into sight: at what point is it clear to a consumer that he or she looks at an ad, and which regions of the ad does he or she consider informative?

The Gist of the Ad Is in the First Fixation

The gist is the basic meaning of a scene, such as its conceptual category (e.g., is the scene indoor or outdoor), spatial layout (are there aisles or islands), and level of clutter (how many aisles or islands). There is evidence that the gist of a scene is already known early during the first eye fixation, within less than 100 ms (Biederman, 1981; Friedman, 1979; Oliva, 2005). Introspection suggests this when paging through consumer magazines or flipping through television channels, when *knowing* to look at an advertisement, commercial or other scene, within a fraction of a second. This seems at odds with the perceptual field around a fixation being small, and with eye movements being needed for detailed ad processing, but is it? The explanation lies in the different functions of foveal versus peripheral vision.

Since the fovea has a much larger representation in the cortex than the peripheral parts of the retina, stimuli in the periphery would be as perceptible as in the fovea if they were enlarged by the reciprocal of this cortical magnification factor (the number of mm on the cortex to which one degree on the retina projects) (Anstis, 1998; Janiszewski, 1998). Anstis (1998) calculates that if the entire retina would have the fovea's acuity, the eyeball would need to be the size of one's current head. This might suggest that peripheral and foveal vision are essentially the same, but that peripheral vision is coarser, only because it would be physiologically impossible to sustain the acuity of the fovea across the whole retina. Instead, however, foveal and peripheral vision are qualitatively very different, as already indicated before, and even to some extent functionally separated in the brain, working in tandem for optimal perception. Foveal vision, in which the parvocellular pathway is involved, is detailed (sensitive to high spatial frequency and color) but slow, and peripheral vision, in which the magnocellular pathway is involved, is coarse (sensitive to low spatial frequency and motion) but fast.

Gist extraction most likely takes place preattentively and peripherally, in parallel across the whole retina. It has been shown that under short exposure duration (30 ms), low spatial frequency (luminance blobs, as in a blurred picture) rather than high spatial frequency (boundary edges, as in a line drawing) information determines gist extraction (Schyns & Oliva, 1994). There is evidence that gist extraction occurs before specific objects are identified, which supports the *global precedence hypothesis* that scene perception unfolds from the whole to the parts (Navon, 1977), but is at variance with dominant theories that perception proceeds from low-level perceptual features via mid-level objects to high-level scenes (e.g., Treisman & Gelade, 1980). The situation in reading tasks, which have generated most eye movement research, is quite different, because rapid gist extraction based on global structure is not possible, while text induces a constrained order of fixations. It seems that real-world scenes are initially processed holistically, and that there are global scene dimensions that distinguish them (in the same way as low-level perceptual features such as color and edges distinguish objects). The following eight dimensions, derived empirically using computer vision routines, have been proposed: naturalness, openness, perspective or expansion, size or roughness, ruggedness, mean depth, symmetry and complexity (see Oliva, 2005). Scenes with similar perceptual dimensions are in the same semantic category.

Once the gist is extracted, schematic knowledge about the possible objects in the scene is activated, which facilitates object identification (Friedman, 1979): which objects or regions are informative depends on the categorization of the scene. Foveal vision accurately but slowly identifies informative objects, and relates these to each other for conceptual analysis, and eye movements are executed to this aim. Objects that are consistent with the overall scene schema attract less attention, and objects inconsistent with the scene attract more attention, but to be discernible the deviations need to be large, the objects attention capturing, or close to the fixation point (Henderson et al., 2003). Figure 3.1 illustrates this. Apparently, participants quickly identified the scene on the right-hand side as an advertisement. Initially, inconsistent or surprising regions in the pictorial are fixated by close to all participants, and the ad-scheme consistent product information and brand logo are only fixated relatively late by a small fraction of participants. That limited detail about specific objects is captured in the gist through peripheral vision converges with findings that even gross changes in the location, size, and identity of objects in scenes often go unnoticed (Simons & Rensink, 2005), a phenomenon that has been called change blindness.

The coarse scene gist and the rapidly activated schematic knowledge generate hypotheses about the possible objects in the scene, their likely locations, informativeness, and meaning. These hypotheses are tested using foveal attention, deployed across the scene by visiting potential areas of interest, for detail. But how are eye movements deployed to sample informative regions in the ad, after gist extraction?

Informativeness Is in the Eye and Depends on the Processing Goal

Eye movements may be captured bottom-up by salient locations, and devoted top-down to informative objects in the advertisements. Whereas salient locations capture attention reflectively, informative objects receive attention voluntarily (see the discussion on the functions of respectively the SC and the FEF above). Salient locations contrast locally from their environment on basic perceptual features such as their color (red bottle among green ones), shape, and size, with *perceptual pop-out* as a possible result (Itti, 2005). Although salience is no less important and the relative weight of the two processes may vary across contexts, here we focus on the informativeness of ad objects.

We distinguish two types of informativeness, namely *semantic incongruency* and *goal relevancy*. Semantic congruency is the extent to which an object matches the overall schema of the scene, with incongruent objects having been called more "informative." The idea is that because incongruent objects have a lower likelihood of occurring in the scene, they are surprising, and important in comprehending and memorizing it (Findlay & Gilchrist, 2003, ch. 7; Henderson & Hollingworth, 1998). Thus, a monkey in a farm scene would be more informative than a tractor. Research has examined whether semantically incongruent objects in scenes disproportionately attract the first fixation, as a measure of attention capture or *conceptual pop-out*, and more fixations of longer durations, as measures of the depth of processing or attention engagement. Empirical support for semantic pop-out would imply that objects are identifiable and associated with the scene's schema during rapid gist extraction, which goes against the global precedence hypothesis (Oliva, 2005). In fact, support for conceptual pop-out is mixed at best, but semantically incongruent objects do receive more and longer eye fixations (Henderson & Hollingworth, 1998; Henderson et al., 2003).

Semantic incongruency is related to ad originality, because original ads deviate in an artful manner from what is normal, and as such are incongruous (see Figure 3.1). Pieters, Warlop, and Wedel (2002) found that original compared to regular ads not only received higher fixation frequencies, in particular to their brand and pictorial, but also that this carried over to better brand memory. However, research in this area has mostly compared eye movements of participants who were exposed to *different* scenes (with and without, more and less incongruent objects) under a *single* task instruction. Then it is challenging to isolate the effects of semantic incongruency from the effects of perceptual saliency—the monkey and tractor also differ perceptually—and this needs to be controlled for, which is difficult (Henderson & Hollingworth, 1998; Henderson et al., 2003; Underwood, Foulsham, van Loon, Humphreys, & Bloyce, forthcoming).

Goal relevancy is the extent to which an object in a scene is instrumental to reach the current processing goal or complete the current task. Alfred Yarbus (1967) was the first to systematically examine the influence of processing goals on scene perception. In his pathbreaking research, mentioned earlier, a single participant was exposed to the painting "The Unexpected Visitor" for 3 minutes, under different task instructions. The participant was asked to freely view the scene, but also to judge, for example, the age of the people in the painting, their material circumstances, how long the unexpected visitor had been away, and his relationship with the other people in the painting. Inspection of the raw scan-paths revealed marked differences between the various task instructions and showed that: "Eye movements reflect the human thought processes; so the observer's thought may be followed to some extent from records of eye movements (the thought accompanying the examination of the particular object)" (Yarbus, 1967, p. 190). The experiments of Yarbus were the first to demonstrate that the informativeness of objects in scenes is contingent on their relevance to the current processing goal, instead of an intrinsic property of the object, the latter premise having been the basis for much research in this area. The key implication of his experiments is that the *same* scene should be compared under *different* task instructions to understand the informativeness of the objects in it, rather than comparing multiple scenes with different objects under the same task instruction, as in work on semantic incongruency. By keeping the scene constant and varying the task instructions, the perceptual salience of the scene and specific locations in it are constant, and differences in eye-movement patterns can be attributed unequivocally to the goal conditions and the informativeness of ad objects to them. To date, the implication of the work of Yarbus has only rarely been taken to heart.

Therefore, we conducted an experiment to examine Yarbus's implication for advertising (Pieters & Wedel, forthcoming). We tested the influence of four different processing goals and a free-viewing condition on eye movements across a set of 17 print advertisements for various food products in a between-subjects design, with 220 participants. We distinguished two processing goal dimensions, respectively, brand-related versus ad-related goals, and learning versus evaluation goals. For instance, participants in the *ad evaluation* goal condition were asked to judge how attractive–unattractive each of the ads was to them. Participants in the *brand learning* goal were asked to learn something new about the brands from the ads. In free viewing, participants were asked to explore the ads "as they would do at home or in a waiting room." Participants were exposed to all 17 ads faced with editorial material and self-controlled exposure duration, to increase generalizability. In each ad, the brand, headline, pictorial, and body text were coded as specific ad objects. Gaze selection and duration were the key eye movement measures of pop-out and processing depth, and analyzed with a hierarchical Bayesian model that accommodates the censoring of the gaze duration measure due to attention selection, heterogeneity among participants and top-down control of attention by goals.

Differences between the five goal conditions were large in gaze duration, reflecting depth of ad processing, but no differences for selection (conceptual pop-out) appeared. Overall gaze duration was longest for an ad-learning goal (memorization), lowest for an ad-appreciation goal and for free viewing, and intermediate for the two brand goals. Gaze duration to the specific ad objects differed substantially between goals, in ways that deviated from the overall gaze duration. That is, the informativeness of the body text, as expressed in gaze durations, was highest for a brand-learning goal, although on average only 1.1 seconds, and lowest for an ad-appreciation goal. Yet, the informativeness of the pictorial was highest for an ad-learning goal and lowest for a brand-learning goal. According to consumers, body text does not contribute to an ad's attractiveness, but much to learning about the brand, which is revealed by their eye movement patterns. Consumers also consider pictorials less useful to evaluate brands and more useful to memorize and evaluate ads. We explored the average duration of fixations to the ad objects across goal conditions as measures of processing intensity (not reported in the original article). Indeed, the average duration of fixations to the brand (234 ms) and pictorial (217 ms) were significantly ($p<0.01$) longer for an ad-learning goal, where participants tried to memorize the ad, than for the other conditions. The absence of any differences between goal conditions in attention to the headline is revealing, because it is of the same text mode as the body text for which large differences were found, and consistent with practitioners' beliefs about the headline's uniform function to summarize the ad's claim, irrespective of consumers' goals.

Of course, perceived informativeness, as reflected in consumers' eye movement patterns, need not match the actual potential information value of advertisements and their objects. For instance, the pictorial, which was considered least informative under a brand-learning goal, might contain the most information, in particular in food advertising where a picture may tell a thousand words (see the contribution of McQuarrie in this volume). The present results, obtained under short exposure durations and natural conditions, demonstrate how a particular goal schema rapidly sets the parameters in the eye movement control network without explicit or conscious effort from the participant, resulting in distinct and identifiable patterns of eye movements on objects that are informative under that goal.

Conclusion

We have described six cornerstones for eye-tracking theory and research in visual marketing, namely:

1. Eye movements reflect information sampling in time and space.
2. Awareness of individual eye movements is limited.
3. The perceptual field during eye fixations is narrow.
4. Eye movements are tightly coupled with covert attention.
5. Attention is central to ad processing.
6. Eye movements reflect ad processing. Jointly they underline the informativeness of consumers' eye movements to understanding visual marketing processing and effectiveness.

Thus, eye movements are real-time measures that reflect the discrete information sampling activity of the visual system in time and space. Information sampling occurs during fixations with a narrow beam of acuity, the perceptual field, around the exact point-of-regard. Outside the perceptual field, detailed information cannot accurately be detected and remembered. People are usually unaware of the specific eye movements that they make during task performance. Eye movements are tightly coupled with covert attention, sharing the same neural circuitry. Covert attention plays a central role in ad processing and decision making, not only by acting as a selection device but also by executing and maintaining central processing activity to ensure that this occurs fast and accurately. As a consequence, eye movements do not only reflect the selection by attention, but also the intensity and nature of the central cognitive processes in ad perception, evaluation and memory, providing real-time information about these ongoing processes that cannot be obtained otherwise. The visual brain uses eye movements to test hypotheses about the identity and meaning of objects in the scene, the gist of which being rapidly but coarsely grasped peripherally and preattentively.

Eye movement research can play an important role in developing and testing formal theories and quantitative models of the processing and effectiveness of visual marketing based on these cornerstones. Ad processing also presents a unique context to develop and test fundamental scene perception theories, because ad scenes are mixed-mode (text and pictures), appear in contexts with which they may cooperate or compete (editorial material and other ads), have their own lawfulness (in ads people may fly and dolls may talk), and are relevant under a variety of consumer processing goals that can be systematically varied (learning or evaluation, ad or brand-directed).

Future research could be directed at, among others, the influence of the editorial content on ad processing, through the activation of schematic knowledge. Whereas it seems reasonable to expect that attention devoted to the ed often compete with attention to the ad, there may be situations of perceptual or semantic ad–ed congruency, where attention to the ed promotes attention to the ad and vice versa. In addition, research on the gist of ad scenes is required, and much more needs to be discovered about the role that global scene dimensions (such as openness, symmetry, and complexity) play in how consumers discriminate between an advertisement and the editorial, or in rapidly identifying specific ad-scenes. Further, the tardy attention of only a small fraction of participants to the body text as compared to the large print, pictorials and brand may have consequences for future research on the role of arguments—typically presented in textual mode—and cues in persuasion. Finally, the study of goal control of attention to ads is a wide open area that was merely unlocked in this chapter. Interesting research questions in particular focus on the extent to which ads can induce goals (i.e., an ad with a large picture may induce an ad evaluation goal, and an ad with a large body text may induce a brand learning goal), heterogeneity of these goals across individuals, and the extent to which they can be identified from the ensuing eye movement patterns.

In sum and returning to the aims of this chapter, vision mirrors a large, and largely automatic, rapid hypothesis-generating and -testing system, with the eyes providing a window to its workings, from which visual marketing theory and practice can learn much. With the proposed six cornerstones in mind, visual marketing theory and research can now start to look at what consumers see.

References

Aaker, D. A., Myers, J. G., & Batra, R. (1996). *Advertising management* (5th ed.). London, UK: Prentice Hall International.

Anstis, S. M. (1974). A chart demonstrating variations in acuity with retinal position. *Vision Research, 14*, 589–592.

Anstis, S. M. (1998). Picturing peripheral acuity. *Perception, 27*, 817–825.

Aristotle. (1991). *Aristotle on rhetoric: A theory of civic discourse* (G. A. Kennedy, Trans). New York: Oxford University Press.

Bargh, J. A. (2002). Automatic influences on consumer judgment, behavior, and motivation. *Journal of Consumer Research, 29*, 280–285.

Belch, G. E., & Belch, M. A. (2001). *Advertising and promotion: An integrated marketing communications perspective* (5th ed.). Boston: McGraw-Hill.

Biederman, I. (1981). On the semantics of a glance at a scene. In M. Kubovy & J. R. Pomerantz (Eds.), *Perceptual organization* (pp. 213–263). Hillsdale, NJ: Lawrence Erlbaum.

Bristow, D., Frith, C., & Rees, G. (2005). Two distinct neural effects of blinking on human visual processing. *NeuroImage, 27*, 136–145.

Burr, D. (2005). Vision: In the blink of an eye. *Current Biology, 15*(14), 554–556.

Calvo, M. G., & Lang, P. J. (2004). Gaze patterns when looking at emotional pictures: Motivationally biased attention. *Motivation and Emotion, 28*(3), 221–243.

Christianson, S. A., Loftus, E. F., Hoffman, H., & Loftus, G. R. (1991). Eye fixations and memory for emotional events. *Journal of Experimental Psychology: Learning, Memory, and Cognition, 17*(4), 693–701.

Colley, R. H. (1961). *Defining advertising goals for measured advertising results*. New York: Association of National Advertisers.

Craighero, L., & Rizzolatti, G. (2005). The premotor theory of attention. In L. Itti, G. Rees, & J. K. Tsotsos (Eds.), *Neurobiology of attention* (pp. 181–186). Amsterdam: Elsevier Academic.

Deubel, H., Schneider, W. X., & Bridgeman, B. (2002). Transsaccadic memory of position and form. In J. Hyöna, D. P. Munoz, W. Heide, & R. Radach (Eds.), *Progress in brain research*, (vol. 140, pp. 165–180). Amsterdam: Elsevier Science.

Duchowski, A. T. (2003). *Eye tracking methodology*. London: Springer Verlag.

Findlay, J. M. (2004). Eye scanning and visual search. In J. M. Henderson & F. Ferreira (Eds.), *The interface of language, vision, and action* (pp. 135–159). New York: Psychology Press.

Findlay, J. M., & Gilchrist, I. D. (2003). *Active vision: The psychology of looking and seeing*. Oxford: Oxford University Press.

Friedman, A. (1979). Framing pictures: The role of knowledge in automatized encoding and memory for gist. *Journal of Experimental Psychology: General, 108*(3), 316–355.

Fuster, J. M. (2003). *Cortex and mind: unifying cognition.* Oxford, UK: Oxford University Press.

Gallese, V., Fadiga, L., Fogassi, L., & Rizzolatti, G. (1996). Action recognition in the premotor cortex. *Brain, 119,* 593–609.

Gould, J. D. (1967). Pattern recognition and eye-movement parameters. *Perception and Psychophysics, 2,* 399–407.

Grill-Spector, K., & Kanwisher, N. (2005). Visual recognition: As soon as you know it is there, you know what it is. *Psychological Science, 16,* 152–160.

Henderson, J. M. (1992). Object identification in context: The visual processing of natural scenes. *Canadian Journal of Psychology, 46*(3), 319–341.

Henderson, J. M. (2003). Human gaze control during real-world scene perception. *Trends in Cognitive Sciences, 7*(11), 498–504.

Henderson, J. M. (2005). Introduction to real-world scene perception. *Visual Cognition, 12*(6), 849–851.

Henderson, J. M., & Hollingworth, A. (1998). Eye movements during scene viewing: An overview. In G. Underwoord (Ed.), *Eye guidance in reading and scene perception* (pp. 269–293). Amsterdam: Elsevier.

Henderson, J. M., & Hollingworth, A. (1999). High-level scene perception. *Annual Review of Psychology, 50,* 243–271.

Henderson, J. M., Williams, C. C., Castelhano, M. S., & Falk, R. J. (2003). Eye movements and picture processing during recognition. *Perception & Psychophysics, 65*(5), 725–734.

Hermans, D., Vansteenwegen, D., & Eelen, P. (1999). Eye movement registration as a continuous index of attention deployment: Data from a group of spider anxious students. *Cognition and Emotion, 13*(4), 419–434.

Itti, L. (2005). Models of bottom-up attention and saliency. In L. Itti, G. Rees, & J. K. Tsotsos (Eds.), *Neurobiology of attention* (pp. 576–582). Amsterdam: Elsevier Academic.

Janiszewski, C. (1998). The influence of display characteristics on visual exploratory search behavior. *Journal of Consumer Research, 25,* 290–301.

Just, M. A., & Carpenter, P. A. (1980). A theory of reading: From eye fixations to comprehension. *Psychological Review, 87*(4), 329–354.

Kahneman, D. (1973). *Attention and effort.* Englewood Cliffs, NJ: Prentice Hall.

Keysers, C., Kohler, E., Umiltà, M. A., Nanetti, L., Fogassi, L., & Gallese, V. (2003). Audiovisual mirror neurons and action recognition. *Experimental Brain research, 153,* 628–636.

Kroeber-Riel, W. (1979). Activation research: Psychobiological approaches in consumer research. *Journal of Consumer Research*, 5, 240–250.

LaBerge, D. (1995). *Attentional processing: The brain's art of mindfulness.* Cambridge, MA: Harvard University Press.

Land, M. F., & Hayhoe, M. (2001). In what ways do eye movements contribute to everyday activities? *Vision Research*, *41*, 3559–3565.

Loewenstein, G. (2001). The creative destruction of decision research. *Journal of Consumer Research*, *28*(3), 499–505.

Maret, V. (2005). *On the relation between memory and persuasion: A meta-analysis of advertising research.* Unpublished master thesis. Marketing Department, Tilburg University.

Navon, D. (1977). Forest before trees: The precedence of global features in visual perception. *Cognitive Psychology*, 9, 353–383.

Nelson, W. W., & Loftus, G. R. (1980). The functional visual field during picture viewing. *Journal of Experimental Psychology: Human Learning and Memory*, 6, 391–399.

Nixon, H. K. (1924). Attention and interest in advertising. *Archives of Psychology*, *72*, 5–67.

Noton, D., & Stark, L. (1971). Scanpaths in saccadic eye movements while viewing and recognizing patterns. *Vision Research*, *11*, 929–942.

Oliva, A. (2005). Gist of the scene. In L. Itti, G. Rees, & J. K. Tsotsos (Eds.), *Neurobiology of Attention* (pp. 251–256). Amsterdam: Elsevier Academic.

Pieters, R., & Warlop, L. (1999). Visual attention during brand choice: The impact of time pressure and task motivation. *International Journal of Research in Marketing*, *16*, 1–17.

Pieters, R., Warlop, L., & Wedel, M. (2002). Breaking through the clutter: Benefits of advertisement originality and familiarity on brand attention and memory. *Management Science*, *48*(6), 765–781.

Pieters, R., & Wedel, M. (2004). Attention capture and transfer in advertising: Brand, pictorial and text-size effects. *Journal of Marketing*, *68*, 36–50.

Pieters, R., & Wedel, M. (forthcoming). Goal control of attention to advertising: The Yarbus implication. *Journal of Consumer Research*, forthcoming.

Poffenberger, A. T. (1925). *Psychology in advertising.* Chicago, IL: A.W. Shaw Company.

Posner, M. (1980). Orienting of attention. *Quarterly Journal of Experimental* Psychology, *32A*, 3–25.

Rayner, K. (1998). Eye movements and information processing: 20 Years of research. *Psychological Bulletin*, *124*, 372–422.

Rayner, K., Reichle, E. D., & Pollatsek, A. (1998). Eye movement control in reading: An overview and model. In G. Underwood (Ed.), *Eye guidance in reading and scene perception* (pp. 243–268). Amsterdam: Elsevier.

Ridder, W. H., & Tomlinson, A. (1997). A comparison of saccadic suppression and blink suppression in normal observers. *Vision Research, 37*(22), 3171–3179.

Rosbergen, E., Pieters, R., & Wedel, M. (1997). Visual attention to advertising: A segment-level analysis. *Journal of Consumer Research, 24,* 305–314.

Russo, J. E. (1978). Eye fixations can save the world: A critical evaluation and a comparison between eye fixations and other information processing methodologies. *Advances in Consumer Research, 21,* 561–570.

Russo, J. E., & Leclerc, F. (1994). An eye-fixation analysis of choice processes for consumer nondurables. *Journal of Consumer Research, 21*(2), 274–290.

Schacter, D. L. (1999). The seven sins of memory: Insights from psychology and cognitive neuroscience. *American Psychologist, 54*(3), 182–203.

Schall, J. D. (2004). Selection of targets for saccadic eye movements. In L. M. Chalupa & J. S. Werner (Eds.), *The visual neurosciences* (pp. 1369–1390). Cambridge, MA: MIT Press.

Schyns, P. G., & Oliva, A. (1994). From blobs to boundary edges: Evidence for time- and spatial-scale-dependent scene recognition. *Psychological Science, 5,* 195–200.

Shimojo, S., Simion, C., Shimojo, E., & Scheier, C. (2003). Gaze bias both reflects and influences preference. *Nature Neuroscience, 10,* 1–6.

Simons, D. J., & Rensink, R. A. (2005). Change blindness: Past, present, and future. *Trends in Cognitive Sciences, 9*(1), 16–20.

Starch, D. (1923). *Principles of advertising.* Chicago: A.W. Shaw Company.

Strong, E. K. (1920). Theories of selling. *Journal of Applied Psychology, 9,* 75–86.

Treisman, A. M., & Gelade, G. (1980). A feature-integration theory of attention. *Cognitive Psychology, 12,* 97–136.

Underwood, G., Foulsham, T., Loon, E. van, Humphreys, L., & Bloyce, J. (forthcoming). Eye movements during scene inspection: A test of the saliency map hypothesis. *European Journal of Cognitive Psychology.*

Vakratsas, D., & Ambler, T. (1999). How advertising works: What do we really know? *Journal of Marketing, 63*(1), 26–43.

Verfaillie, K., & Graef, P. de (2000). Transsaccadic memory for position and orientation saccade source and target. *Journal of Experimental Pychology: Human Perception and Performance, 26*(4), 1243–1259.

Wedel, M., & Pieters, R. (2000). Eye fixations on advertisements and memory for brands: A model and findings. *Marketing Science, 19*(4), 297–312.

Wedel, M., & Pieters, R. (forthcoming). A review of eye-tracking research in marketing. *Review of Marketing Research.*

Wilson, T. D., & Dunn, E. W. (2004). Self-knowledge: Its limits, value, and potential for improvement. *Annual Review of Psychology, 55*, 493–518.

Wolfe, J. (2000). Visual attention. In K. K. De Valois (Ed.), *Seeing* (pp. 335–386). San Diego, CA: Academic Press.

Yarbus, A. L. (1967). *Eye movements and vision.* New York: Plenum.

Ydewalle, G. d', & Tamsin, F. (1993). On the visual processing and memory of incidental information: Advertising panels in soccer games. In D. Brogan, A. Gale, & K. Carr (Eds.), *Visual search 2* (pp. 401–408). London: Taylor and Francis.

Zeelenberg, R., Wagenmakers, E. J., & Rotteveel, M. (2006). The impact of emotion on perception. *Psychological Science, 17*(4), 287–291.

4

The Effect of Selecting and Ignoring on Liking

*Nader T. Tavassoli**

> Millions of items of the outward order are present to my senses which never properly enter into my experience. Why? Because they have no interest for me. My experience is what I agree to attend to. Only those items which I notice shape my mind—without selective interests, experience is an utter chaos. Interest alone gives accent and emphasis, light and shade, background and foreground—intelligible perspective, in a word.
>
> William James (1890, p. 381)

Introduction

From web pages to store shelves in supermarkets, consumers visually select specific objects as the targets of their actions, while avoiding and ignoring others. The purpose of this chapter is to highlight and speculate on the affective consequences for a stimulus that is selected for attention and response, as well as for those nontarget stimuli that are simultaneously ignored. What is labeled as "interesting" or "uninteresting"—in the James (1890) sense of the word—in one situation should affect how that information is processed and evaluated when reencountered at a future time. The simple act of visual selection should increase an object's subsequent valuation; the simple act of ignoring an object should devalue it.

* The ideas put forth in this chapter—especially on the effect of choice—owe much to the inputs of Chris Janiszewski and Andrew Kuo of the University of Florida.

Visual objects compete to be selected for representation in multiple, concurrently activated brain systems: sensory and motor, cortical and subcortical. The selective attention system allows us to focus on task-relevant information while ignoring irrelevant information by amplifying and attenuating sensory input (Kastner & Ungerleider, 2000). It is complemented through the coordinated activities of a second major brain system: the emotional system. This interprets information in terms of current and future goals by creating *emotional* control signals (Ortony, Clore, & Collins, 1988).

I will review how attentional amplification and inhibition, combined with emotional control signals, can result in affective enhancements and devaluations as a natural by-product of ordinary perceptual and cognitive operations applied in the routine processing of information. I conclude by speculating on how current findings might relate to marketing applications such as banner ads on the Internet, product choice off the store shelf, branded material on video games, and roadside billboards.

Affective Consequences

Mere Exposure

In order to understand the effects of selection and nonselection, it is useful to consider situations in which objects are perceived without any intent on the behalf of the perceiver, when the perceiver is merely exposed. The mere exposure effect (Zajonc, 1968) refers to the more positive evaluation of objects that have been exposed repeatedly, without any reinforcement or even intent on the behalf of the individual to process the information (e.g., Janiszewski, 1993). Mere exposure effects are typically obtained for unfamiliar stimuli that are repeated for brief and even subliminal presentation durations and/or under impoverished encoding conditions, and without any response required for the target stimuli or another competing task (for a review, see Bornstein, 1989). In other words, the mere exposure effect is obtained preattentively, without selection.

There are various accounts for this phenomenon. A cognitive explanation posits that reexperiencing a stimulus results in perceptual fluency that is being misattributed as liking (e.g., Bornstein & D'Agostino, 1994), a mechanism that relates to well-known implicit

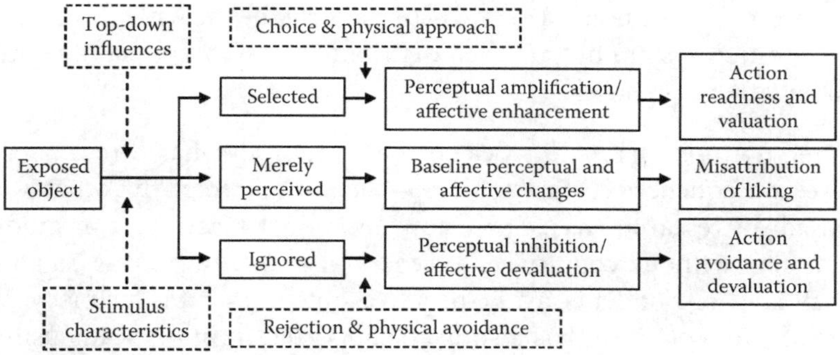

Figure 4.1 Summary of theoretical model.

memory effects found in repetition priming (for a review, see Schacter, 1987). In contrast, the primacy-of-affect account holds that the effect is independent of cognition and based on a distinct affective component (Zajonc, 1984), a conjecture that finds support in brain imaging studies (e.g., Elliott & Dolan, 1998). Other research has suggested the possibility that perceptual fluency is itself affectively positive rather than neutral (Reber, Winkielman, & Schwarz, 2000). I expect that the effect is probably codetermined by affective and perceptual mechanisms that operate in parallel.

To summarize, the mere exposure effect appears to be an automatic positive consequence of encountering a stimulus preattentively, without intent, and in the absence of any type of response. In that sense, it is useful to think of the mere exposure effect as a baseline condition for objects selected and ignored, in addition to the mere exposure's own baseline condition of items that have not been previously exposed. The next sections review how the affective and perceptual components of the mere exposure effect may be amplified or reduced (if not reversed) in the presence of active goals that serve to guide selective attention. The system of effects proposed in this chapter is illustrated in Figure 4.1.

Selecting

Perceptual Amplification Sensory input of items that are selected for attention is amplified (Kastner & Ungerleider, 2000). Single-neuron responses to a given input have been shown to be enhanced when this occurred at a specified (relevant) location (Bushnell, Goldberg, & Robinson, 1981) as well as toward a target object (Chelazzi, Miller,

Duncan, & Desimone, 1993). These patterns begin with the object recognition system but are then distributed to systems dealing with many other properties.

Affective Enhancement Selective attention also has direct affective consequences. Damasio's (1994) *somatic marker* hypothesis is based on research that shows how emotional reactions can guide actions—without cognitive awareness—by creating stress signals that help respondents avoid negative outcomes. This primacy of affect over cognition has also been supported in brain scans using marketing stimuli where the same brain regions in the prefrontal cortex implicated by Damasio have been found active in consumers' positive reactions to familiar brands in a visualized shopping environment (Ambler, Braeutigam, Stins, Rose, & Swithenby, 2004) and in a taste test preceded by a visual product cue (McClure, Li, Tomlin, Cypert, Montague, & Montague, 2004). Emotional control signals thus function both to signal approach and avoidance.

The emotional control signals instantiated in Damasio's (1994) studies are based on positive and negative feedback, a characteristic likely shared for familiar brands through repeated experience. It does not appear to be necessary, however, to receive overt feedback: objects selected for attention may be automatically emotionally enhanced in order to support future actions (Ortony et al., 1988). This is not a trivial hypothesis. Previous research had shown affect, as a stimulus characteristic, to operate preattentively to modulate attention: negative (threatening) information shifts attention away from the primary task resulting in behaviors such as conscious inhibition (Neely, 1977) and perceptual defense or vigilance (Erdelyi, 1974; Pratto & John, 1991); and emotional stimuli such as angry faces attract (Eastwood, Smilek, & Merikle, 2001) and maintain attention (Fox, Russo, Bowles, & Dutton, 2001). This chapter serves to highlight the reverse effect, that attention can modulate affect.

It should be pointed out that the emotional response considered here is not one the perceiver is necessarily aware of experiencing. Experienced emotions of the same valence tend to have specific and, at times, opposing influences on judgments and action tendencies, such as anger versus fear on risk perception (Lerner & Keltner, 2000), disgust versus sadness on sellers' prices and consumers' willingness to pay (Lerner, Small, & Loewenstein, 2004), or emotions such as fear, sadness, dislike, and guilt on action tendencies such as escape, doing nothing, rejecting, and undoing, respectively (Roseman, Wiest, & Swartz, 1994). Instead, the emotional control signals considered here are in the form of positive versus negative affect, and not in terms of differentiated emotions of the same valence. Moreover, unlike the research on the effects of diffuse affective states on general appraisal tendencies (Lerner & Keltner, 2000; Lerner et al., 2004) and action tendencies (Roseman et al., 1994), the emotional control signals considered here are object specific and the result of selective attention.

Top-Down Influences Both perceptual amplification and affective enhancement can be moderated by top-down influences. Selective attention can be moderated by the preactivation of certain attributes such as an object's color (e.g., Phaf, van der Heijden, & Hudson, 1990) or complex stimulus characteristics such as the distinction between digits and letters (Duncan, 1980; Schneider & Shiffrin, 1977). Searching for a Pepsi might, therefore, amplify sensory responses to blue objects but inhibit those to a red can of Coke. Goals can similarly increase the perceptual readiness of identifying goal-relevant information but inhibit that of goal-disabling information (Bruner, 1957). Goals may, therefore, serve to enhance perceptual fluency created by mere exposure and further enhance valuation (positive valuation).*

In terms of affective reactions, people also automatically and preattentively evaluate objects with respect to active goals (e.g., Ferguson & Bargh, 2004; Fiske, 1992; James, 1890) in order to orient attention (Roskos-Ewoldsen & Fazio, 1992) and guide behavior toward objects that satisfy a goal (Lewin, 1935). This research has empirically shown that goal-relevant objects are automatically evaluated more positively than goal-irrelevant objects; that automatic liking is ultimately in the service of actual "doing" (Ferguson & Bargh, 2004).

Choice Choosing an object should further amplify the valuation of selected outcomes. Consumers often show *brand choice inertia* (Jeuland, 1979) or a status quo bias (Samuelson & Zeckhauser, 1988) to the point at which their emotional attachment to their chosen brand outweighs objective preferences, an effect vividly demonstrated in the New Coke debacle (*Newsweek*, 1985). Merely owning an outcome

* Competition for representation may occur in limited visual short-term memory (Sperling, 1967) and/or for later stages of information processing such as semantic processing or the "selection for action" (Van der Heijden, 1991). For a marketing review of related other meta-cognitive assessments see Schwarz (2004).

changes the outcome, generally, by making it feel better (Beggan, 1992). Similarly, an initial choice, even if completely superfluous and unaccompanied by experience, can increase the likelihood that a consumer will persist with the same choice on future choice occasions (Muthukrishnan & Wathieu, 2007). Unlike the effects of mere exposure that appear to be eliminated by respondents' awareness of the source of perceptual fluency (Bornstein, 1989), selection and choice may persist as these behaviors can be seen as informative rather than resulting in a nondiagnostic misattribution. Furthermore, according to cognitive dissonance theory (Festinger, 1957), an option is judged as more desirable if it has been freely chosen rather than imposed.

Motor Responses In addition to thoughts, selection can be reinforced by motor responses through the integration between multiple brain systems, such as the functional link between visual and motor systems of eye movement and arm reaching (Posner, 1980). There are extensive cross-modal links in attention across the various modalities (audition, vision, touch, and proprioception), and attention typically shifts to a common location across the modalities, even preattentively (Driver & Spence, 1998). Previous research has also shown that motor action (arm movement) can directly bias attitude formation such that pulling one's arm toward oneself is a signal of approach and pushing it away from oneself is a signal of avoidance (Cacioppo, Priester, & Berntson, 1993). Motor responses toward an object should, therefore, compound the sensory-perceptual and affective enhancements of visual selection.

To summarize, selection is an event that occurs not only for visual attention and its associated sensory-perceptual and emotional responses, but one that relates to multiple levels of processing and, often, a response. This response can include volition and associated motor behaviors that enhance the future evaluation of a stimulus. These effects should combine to amplify the effects of mere exposure. Selective attention is a two-sided coin, however, and less well known are the affective consequences of being ignored or avoided while a competing object is selected for attention.

Ignoring

When items are not selected for attention, single-neuron responses to a given input have been shown to be suppressed at the irrelevant location (Bushnell et al., 1981; Moran & Desimone, 1985) as well as for nontarget objects (Chelazzi et al., 1993). Again, these patterns begin with the object recognition system but are then distributed to systems dealing with many other properties.

One of the most robust consequences of ignoring in a selective attention task has been demonstrated by the negative priming effect (Tipper, 1985). Negative priming describes the finding that, in selective attention tasks, responses to previously ignored stimuli are usually retarded (Tipper, 1985): if a stimulus serves as a distractor in one trial it is subsequently processed more slowly as a target on the next trial than when it had not been part of the previous choice set. The leading explanation of the effect is that it reflects the inhibitory mechanism of attention; that the activation level of the distractor's internal representation has been suppressed and that this inhibitatory state is not transient but reinstated at retrieval (for a review, see Tipper, 2001). This idea is supported by research showing repeated events to reactivate the same neural responses as during the initial experience (e.g., Nillson et al., 2000).

My coauthors and I asked the simple question: if perceptual fluency gives rise to a positive evaluative bias in the mere exposure effect, then should perceptual inhibition not create a negative bias? Any factors that inhibit an object's ease of processing can be inputs into affective devaluation as well as other judgments (Schwarz, 2004). This idea was further suggested by Zajonc's (1980) direct affective enhancement hypothesis that has its counterpart in negative control signals for ignored or avoided events (e.g., Damasio, 1994; Ortony et al., 1988). In other words, we expected that the reaction-time effects observed in negative priming were unlikely to be the only or even most important behavioral consequence of the visual attentional system.

Our inquiries resulted in the first article that demonstrated negative affective consequences of exposure (Raymond, Fenske, & Tavassoli, 2003). We presented participants with two images, one of which was a prespecified target respondents had to indicate the location of with the other simply being ignored. We found that the ignored image, that required no explicit action, was rated as less cheery (and more dreary) than the selected target item, as well as compared to a baseline rating for completely novel images to which respondents had not been preexposed (targets were rated similarly to the novel baseline condition). The ratings were completed immediately after the location task had been completed, after less than

1 second of the unmasked exposure to the stimuli. We replicated the effect and found that it also spills over to images of the same type (category) as that of the ignored image. It is known that even irrelevant inputs receive some semantic analysis (e.g., Eriksen & Eriksen, 1974) and our findings suggest that inhibition can be at the semantic level. This type of effect has its counterpart in the conceptual mere exposure literature where, for example, the mere exposure effect has been found to extend beyond an exposed product to members of the product category or subcategory (Lee & Labroo, 2004).

The finding that inhibited items are subsequently devalued has been replicated several times since. This idea is also supported by research on top-down influences on object evaluation. This has speculated that objects that impede goals will be automatically evaluated more negatively than goal-irrelevant objects (Ferguson & Bargh, 2004). Empirically, it has indeed been demonstrated that activating a focal need (e.g., to eat) devalues objects unrelated to that need (e.g., shampoo) without actually impeding the focal need (Brendl, Markman, & Messner, 2003).

The first replication of our finding was published by Fenske, Raymond, and Kunar (2004) who used the *preview task*—where a previewed distractor receives top-down inhibition (Watson & Humphreys, 1997)—in which the inhibited object was actually shown for a longer duration (1 additional second) than the target item. Targets were nevertheless evaluated more positively than distractors 1,300 ms after response/unmasked stimulus set (there was no novel-item baseline condition in this study).

The devaluation effect has also been shown for trustworthiness ratings of faces where inhibition had been created through withholding a response, a behavior that did not require, but inhibited a motor action (Fenske, Raymond, Kessler, Westoby, & Tipper, 2005). Two faces were shown on each trial and one of them either received a *go signal* that required a response, or a *no go signal* for which participants had to refrain from responding. This was indicated by a *no go signal* where attention was first drawn to a distractor and then withdrawn (e.g., Tipper, Grison, & Kessler, 2003). After a 9-second filler, both faces were again shown for 150 ms and participants had to select the face that they felt was more trustworthy (or untrustworthy) or for which they felt the background was darker (or lighter), the latter to measure a general response bias. While there were no significant effects for *go* trials, the items that were overlaid with the *no go signal* received a general negative response bias such that their backgrounds were judged both as *less* dark and as *less* light, depending on the question. Most significantly, inhibited faces were judged *less* often as "more trustworthy" but *more* often (i.e., in the opposite direction on the response scale) as "less trustworthy" than the faces that had appeared alongside of them (i.e., the devaluation was not the result of a response bias).

The effect of inhibition was also found to be moderated by factors that are known to moderate negative priming (Raymond, Fenske, & Westoby, 2005). Specifically, devaluation relative to the target (up to 2.5 seconds after exposure) was found to be stronger for distractors the closer they were to the target, and absent for peripherally presented distractors. In other words, inhibition was restricted to "inhibitory surrounds" (Mounts, 2000). Competion in V4—a cortical visual processing area that receives information already processed by other areas of the brain—may be spatially local such that an unattended stimulus is only suppressed if it falls within the receptive field (Moran & Desimone, 1985).

To summarize, it appears to be a robust effect that *not being selected for visual attention* in a competitive stimulus environment has negative consequences on the evaluation of a visual object. This effect appears to be moderated by similar factors as effects in paradigms on perceptual inhibition. These paradigms, therefore, appear to be a viable vantage point from which to extrapolate evaluative consequences of being ignored, as well as a promising starting point for further investigation into the phenomenon.

Marketing Implications

Kant's doctrine of idealism (1781) holds that experience is not solely the reflection of an object's intrinsic properties, but something that results from the interaction of the mind with the properties of the object. This chapter highlighted how visual observation is not a neutral endeavor but one during which an observer's goals create a subjective experience, where the coordinated activities of the brain systems for selective attention and emotional control converge to reinforce preference and choice. This appears to be a natural by-product of ordinary perceptual and cognitive operations applied in the routine visual processing of information.

There are several implications for marketing. The effects of mere exposure are well documented (Bornstein, 1989) and the effects of attentional or physical selection should amplify these. I will, therefore, primarily focus on the inhibitive and potentially devaluative effects of ignoring information. It should be noted from the onset that the delays between encountering a stimulus as a distractor and then as a target in negative priming studies or in studies on devaluative effects of inhibition have generally been in the mere seconds. However, long-term negative priming effects of over 10 minutes (Tipper et al., 2003) and even 1 month (DeSchepper & Treisman, 1996) have also been claimed. Inhibition and devaluation may, therefore, extend beyond the online encounter of information and exhibit carryover effects between repeated stimulus encounters more typical of marketing settings. Indeed, the retrieval account of the negative priming effect suggests that these effects may be lasting because inhibition should be reinstated when the stimulus is reencountered (Tipper, 2001) and devaluation may itself be integrated as an affective component of the object's mnemonic representation (Damasio, 1994). However, even if inhibition is transient and the effects are only momentary, this could significantly affect consumer search behavior and choice.

It should be noted that there are several scenarios in which I would expect effects not to differ from those of mere exposure. These include *divided attention* situations, for example, where a consumer is engaged in the primary task of driving while unattentively listening to a radio advertisement, or where a consumer is flipping through a magazine or chatting on the telephone during a commercial television break. Even though the advertisements are not the primary focus of attention, the consumer is not engaged in the process of selecting "this and not that" or preparing for a response. Similarly, roadside billboards or branded materials in, say, a race car video game might be peripherally distracting, but they are not selected against. Indeed, *divided attention* manipulations have not been found to eliminate the mere exposure effect (Seamon, Brody, & Kauff, 1983).

Instead, the mere exposure effect has been found to be impaired when participants had to select a response based on a property other than the one evaluated at a later point in time. When participants had to name the font color in which study words were presented, rather than name the words themselves, the advantages of exposure were eliminated (Stone, Ladd, & Gabrieli, 2000). As discussed, a selective attention task, where one object is selected for a response and the other is ignored, can actually devalue the subsequent rating of the ignored stimulus compared to stimuli that have not been pre-exposed (Raymond et al., 2003).

This might apply to settings such as video games in which players have to shoot branded "bad guys" while avoiding shooting branded "good guys." From a purely attentional perspective, this game should enhance the evaluation of the bad-guy brands but devalue the good-guy brands. The latter effect should also occur when the "good guys" appear by themselves and the player merely withholds the response of shooting them (Fenske et al., 2005).

Negative priming has been found to be stronger than the *activation* of the distracting stimulus, such as created via repetition or stimulus familiarity (Nagai & Yokosawa, 2003). For example, distractors that were previously targets show stronger negative priming (Strayer & Grison, 1999). This suggests that factors that increase salience and attract attention—physical properties such as motion, contrast and size (for reviews, see Broadbent, 1982; Pieters & Wedel, 2004; Rayner, 1998)—might also moderate devaluation such that large, bright, or flashing banner ads might be devalued more, and more often they are ignored. Unlike radio ads that do not detract from the activity of driving, one's cognitive mechanisms are often hard at work at inhibiting intrusive banner ads that interfere with processing the web content of interest. Physical proximity to the selected target object also increases negative priming and thus the intensity of devaluation (Raymond, Fenske, & Westoby, 2005). When selecting one's chosen brand from the store shelf, the physically closest competitor brands should, therefore, be automatically inhibited and devalued most strongly.

Studies using eye movements present an exciting method to explore the theoretical as well as the commercial implications of the model proposed. Eye-movement recording measurements have become highly accurate and are now easily obtained. Indeed, traditional recall measures are not a good indicator of what people look at. For example, consumers will report brands they normally buy instead of the products they actually saw just seconds after being asked what they looked at on a store shelf (Chandon, 2002).

Eye movements and fixations are sensitive to stimulus properties, their distinctiveness with a scene, as well as how interesting or important they are (for a review, see Rayner, 1998); within a marketing setting, the strength of different display or ad elements differs in terms of behaviors such as capturing attention (picture) or transferring attention to other elements (brand) (Pieters & Wedel, 2004). Knowing what consumers look at is important, because glancing at a product on the shelf has been found to be a good predictor of purchase consideration; visual attention to a detergent or juice brand, for example, on average, doubles the memory-based probability of consideration (Chandon, Hutchinson, & Young, 2001). Based on the ideas put forth in this paper, it would be interesting to observe the effect of brands that were not selected for attention, or attended and then ignored, especially in terms of their physical relation on the store shelf to those that held attention and were subsequently considered.

Finally, I had discussed that respondents' active goals create selection criteria and affect what inputs are amplified or inhibited, as well as automatically evaluated in a positive or negative light (Ferguson & Bargh, 2004). Distractor inhibition has similarly been shown to be a flexible process that adjusts to particular behavioral goals; that it is not an invariant process that occurs in the same way for each act of selection (Tipper, Bruce, & Houghton, 1994; Frings & Wentura, 2006). Specifically, those internal representations of the distractor that are most associated with the action to be directed toward the target are inhibited. Other properties of the ignored object can remain in an active state and can facilitate subsequent behavior. For example, features of a distractor, such as its shape and color, only become inhibited if they are the *defining features* in the search task (Simone, Carlisle, & McCormick, 1998). The color of the distractor (e.g., green), therefore, becomes inhibited only if the search task was based on color (e.g., "locate the red object") but not if the search was based on shape (e.g., "locate the square"). This suggests that a consumer's goals will affect the type of amplification or inhibition a stimulus receives. For example, an attention-grabbing banner ad for famine relief might receive perceptual inhibition when one has the goal of finding a plumber on the web, whereas it might receive *deeper* conceptual inhibition if one is searching for an all-you-can-eat restaurant.

Summary

This chapter has highlighted how visual selection and its flip-side, ignoring, have affective consequences beyond and counter to mere exposure. This research is nascent but promises a variety of new insights central to marketing. Instead of the old marketing dictum that *every exposure is a good exposure*, we need to pay heed to Heisenberg's (1927) discovery that the mere act of observing an object changes it … and not always for the better.

References

Ambler, T., Braeutigam, S., Stins, J., Rose, S., & Swithenby, S. (2004). Salience and choice: Neural correlates of shopping decisions. *Psychology & Marketing, 21*, 247–261.

Beggan, J. K. (1992). On the social nature of nonsocial perception: The mere ownership effect. *Journal of Personality and Social Psychology, 62*, 229–237.

Bornstein, R. F. (1989). Exposure and affect: Overview and meta-analysis of research, 1968–1987. *Psychological Bulletin, 106*, 265–289.

Bornstein, R. F., & D'Agostino, P. R. (1994). The attribution and discounting of perceptual fluency: Preliminary tests of a perceptual fluency/attributional model of the mere exposure effect. *Social Cognition, 9*, 103–128.

Brendl, C. M., Markman, A. B., & Messner, C. (2003). The devaluation effect: Activating a need devalues unrelated objects. *Journal of Consumer Research*, 29, 463–473.

Broadbent, D. E. (1982). Task combination and selective intake of information. *Acta Psychologica*, 50, 253–290.

Bruner, J. S. (1957). On perceptual readiness. *Psychological Review, 64*, 123–152.

Bushnell, M. C., Goldberg, M. E., & Robinson, D. L. (1981). Behavioral enhancement of visual responses in monkey cerebral cortex. I. modulation in posterior parietal cortex related to selective visual attention. *Journal of Neurophysiology, 46*, 755–772.

Cacioppo, J. T., Priester, J. R., & Berntson, G. G. (1993). Rudimentary determinants of attitudes. II: Arm flexion and extension have differential effects on attitudes. *Journal of Personality and Social Psychology, 65*, 5–17.

Chandon, P. (2002). Do we know what we look at? An eye-tracking study of visual attention and memory for brands at the point of purchase. Working paper. University of Pennsylvania.

Chandon, P., Hutchinson, J. W., & Young, S. H. (2001). Measuring the value of point-of-purchase marketing with commercial eye-tracking data. Working paper. INSEAD.

Chelazzi, L., Miller, E. K., Duncan, J., & Desimone, R. (1993). A neural basis for visual search in inferior temporal cortex. *Nature, 363*, 345–347.

Damasio, A. R. (1994). *Descartes' error: Emotion, reason and the human brain*. London: Papermac.

DeSchepper, B., & Treisman, A. (1996). Visual memory for novel shapes: Implicit coding without attention. *Journal of Experimental Psychology: Learning, Memory, and Cognition, 22*, 27–47.

Driver, J., & Spence, C. J. (1998). Crossmodal attention. *Current Opinion in Neurobiology, 8*, 245–253.

Duncan, J. (1980). The locus of interference in the perception of simultaneous stimuli. *Psychological Review, 87*, 272–300.

Eastwood, J. D., Smilek, D., & Merikle, F. P. M. (2001). Differential attentional guidance by unattended faces expressing positive and negative emotion. *Perception & Psychophysics, 63*, 1004–1013.

Elliott, R., & Dolan, R. J. (1998). Neural response during preference and memory judgments for subliminally presented stimuli: A functional neuroimaging study. *Journal of Neuroscience, 18*, 4697–4704.

Erdelyi, M. H. (1974). A new look at the new look: Perceptual defense and vigilance. *Psychological Review, 81*, 1–25.

Eriksen, B. A., & Eriksen, C. W. (1974). Effects of noise letters upon the identification of target letters in a non-search identification task. *Perception & Psychophysics, 16*, 143–149.

Fenske, M. J., Raymond, J. E., Kessler, K., Westoby, N., & Tipper, S. P. (2005). Attentional inhibition has social-emotional consequences for unfamiliar faces. *Psychological Science, 16*, 753–758.

Fenske, M. J., Raymond, J. E., & Kunar, M. A. (2004). The affective consequences of visual attention in preview search. *Psychonomic Bulletin and Review, 11*(6), 1055–1061.

Ferguson, M. J., & Bargh, J. A. (2004). Liking is for doing: The effects of goal pursuit on automatic evaluation. *Journal of Personality and Social Psychology, 87*, 557–572.

Festinger, L. (1957). *A theory of cognitive dissonance*. Stanford, CA: Stanford University Press.

Fiske, S. T. (1992). Thinking is for doing: Portraits of social cognition from daguerrotype to laserphoto. *Journal of Personality and Social Psychology, 63*, 877–889.

Fox, E., Russo, R., Bowles, R., & Dutton, K. K. (2001). Do threatening stimuli draw or hold visual attention in subclinical anxiety? *Journal of Experimental Psychology: General, 130*, 681–700.

Frings, C., & Wentura, D. (2006). Negative priming is stronger for task-relevant dimensions: Evidence of flexibility in the selective ignoring of distractor information. *Quarterly Journal of Experimental Psychology Sections A & B*, 59, 683–693.

Heijden, van der, A. H. C. (1991). *Selective attention in vision*. New York: Routledge.

Heisenberg, W. (1927). Über den anschaulichen inhalt der quantentheoretischen kinematik und mechanik. *Zeitschrift fur Physik*, 43, 172–198.

James, W. (1890). *The principles of psychology* (2nd ed.). New York: Holt.

Janiszewski, C. (1993). Preattentive mere exposure effects. *Journal of Consumer Research, 20,* 376–392.

Jeuland, A. P. (1979). Brand choice inertia as one aspect of the notion of brand loyalty. *Management Science, 25,* 671–682.

Kant, I. (1781). *Kritik der Reinen Vernunft [Critiques on just ratio].* Hamburg: Meiner.

Kastner, S., & Ungerleider, L. G. (2000). Mechanisms of visual attention in the human cortex. *Annual Review of Neuroscience, 23,* 315–341.

Lee, A. Y., & Labroo, A. (2004). The effect of conceptual and perceptual fluency on brand evaluation. *Journal of Marketing Research, 41,* 151–165.

Lerner, J. S., & Keltner, D. (2000). Beyond valence: Toward a model of emotion-specific influences on judgment and choice. *Cognition and Emotion, 14,* 473–493.

Lerner, J. S., Small, D. A., & Loewenstein, G. (2004). Heart strings and purse strings: Carryover effects of emotions on economic decisions. *Psychological Science, 15,* 337–341.

Lewin, K. (1935). *A dynamic theory of personality.* New York: McGraw-Hill.

McClure, S. M., Li, J., Tomlin, D., Cypert, K. S., Montague, L. M., & Montague, R. P. (2004). Neural correlates of behavioral preference for culturally familiar drinks. *Neuron, 44,* 379–387.

Moran, J., & Desimone, R. (1985). Selective attention gates visual processing in the extrastriate cortex. *Science, 229,* 782–784.

Mounts, J. R. W. (2000). Evidence for suppressive mechanisms in attentional selection: Feature singletons produce inhibitory surrounds. *Perception & Psychophysics, 62,* 969–983.

Muthukrishnan, A. V., & Wathieu, L. (2007). Superfluous choices and the persistence of preference. *Journal of Consumer Research, 33,* 454–460.

Nagai, J., & Yokosawa, K. (2003). Negative priming and stimulus familiarity: What causes opposite results? *Memory & Cognition, 31,* 369–379.

Neely, J. H. (1977). Semantic priming and retrieval from lexical memory: Roles of inhibitionless spreading activation and limited-capacity attention. *Journal of Experimental Psychology: General, 106,* 226–254.

Newsweek. (1985, June 24). Saying no to New Coke, pp. 32–33.

Nillson, L., Nyberg, L., Klingberg, T., Aberg, C., Persson, J., & Roland, P. E. (2000). Activity in motor areas while remembering action events. *Neuroport: For Rapid Communication of Neuroscience Research, 11*, 2199–2201.

Ortony, A., Clore, G. L., & Collins, A. (1988). *The Cognitive Structure of Emotions*. New York: Cambridge University Press.

Phaf, R. H., Heijden, van der, A. H., & Hudson, P. T. (1990). SLAM: A connectionist model for attention in visual selection tasks. *Cognitive Psychology, 22*, 273–341.

Pieters, R., & Wedel, M. (2004). Attention capture and transfer in advertising: Brand, pictorial, and text-size effects. *Journal of Marketing, 68*, 36–50.

Posner, M. I. (1980). Orienting of attention. *Quarterly Journal of Experimental Psychology, 32*, 3–25.

Pratto, F., & John, O.P. (1991). Automatic vigilance: The attention-grabbing power of negative social information. *Journal of Personality and Social Psychology, 61*, 380–191.

Raymond, J. E., Fenske, M. J., & Tavassoli, N. J. (2003). Selective attention determines emotional responses to novel visual stimuli. *Psychological Science, 14*, 537–542.

Raymond, J. E., Fenske, M. J., & Westoby, N. (2005). Emotional devaluation of distracting patterns and faces: A consequence of attentional inhibition during visual search? *Journal of Experimental Psychology: Human Perception and Performance, 31*, 1404–1415.

Rayner, K. (1998). Eye movements in reading and information processing: 20 Years of research. *Psychological Bulletin, 124*, 372–422.

Reber, R., Winkielman, P., & Schwarz, N. (2000). Effects of perceptual fluency on affective judgments. *Psychological Science, 9*, 45–48.

Roskos-Ewoldsen, D. R., & Fazio, R. H. (1992). On the orienting value of attitudes: Attitude accessibility as a determinant of an object's attraction of visual attention. *Journal of Personality and Social Psychology, 63*, 198–211.

Roseman, I. J., Wiest, C., & Swartz, T. S. (1994). Phenomenology, behaviors, and goals differentiate discrete emotions. *Journal of Personality and Social Psychology, 67*, 206–221.

Samuelson, W., & Zeckhauser, R. (1988). Status quo bias in decision making. *Journal of Risk and Uncertainty, 1*, 7–59.

Schacter, D. L. (1987). Implicit memory: History and current status. *Journal of Experimental Psychology: Learning, Memory, and Cognition, 13*, 501–518.

Schneider, W., & Shiffrin, R. M. (1977). Controlled and automatic human information processing: I. detection, search, and attention. *Psychological Review, 84*, 1–66.

Schwarz, N. (2004). Metacognitive experiences in consumer judgment and decision making. *Journal of Consumer Psychology, 14*(4), 332–348.

Seamon, J. G., Brody, N., & Kauff, D. M. (1983). Affective discrimination of stimuli that are not recognized: Effects of shadowing, masking, and cerebral laterality. *Journal of Experimental Psychology: Learning, Memory, and Cognition, 9*, 544–555.

Simone, P. M., Carlisle, E. A., & McCormick, E. B. (1998). Effect of defining features on inhibition in a spatial localization task. *Journal of Experimental Psychology: Human Perception and Performance, 24*, 993–1005.

Sperling, G. (1967). Successive approximations to a model of short-term memory. In A. F. Sanders (Ed.), *Attention and Performance I.* (pp. 285–292). Amsterdam: North-Holland.

Stone, M., Ladd, S. L., & Gabrieli, J. D. (2000). The role of selective attention in perceptual and affective priming. *American Journal of Psychology, 113*, 341–358.

Strayer, D. L., & Grison, S. (1999). Negative identity priming is contingent on stimulus repetition. *Journal of Experimental Psychology: Human Perception and Performance, 25*(1), 24–38.

Tipper, S. P. (1985). The negative priming effect: Inhibitory priming by ignored objects. *Quarterly Journal of Experimental Psychology A: Human Experimental Psychology, 37A*, 571–590.

Tipper, S. P. (2001). Does negative priming reflect inhibitory mechanisms? A review and integration of conflicting views. *The Quarterly Journal of Experimental Psychology, 54A*(2), 321–343.

Tipper, S. P., Bruce W., & Houghton, G. (1994). Behavioural goals determine inhibitory mechanisms of selective attention. *Quarterly Journal of Experimental Psychology A: Human Experimental Psychology, 47A*, 809–840.

Tipper, S. P., Grison, S., & Kessler, K. (2003). Long-term inhibition of return of attention. *Psychological Science, 14*, 19–25.

Watson, D. G., & Humphreys, G. W. (1997). Visual marking: Prioritizing selection for new objects by top-down attentional inhibition of old objects. *Psychological Review, 104*, 90–122.

Zajonc, R. B. (1968). Attitudinal effects of mere exposure. *Journal of Personality and Social Psychology, 9*, 1–27.

Zajonc, R. B. (1984). Feeling and thinking: Preferences need no inferences. *American Psychologist, 35*(2), 151–175.

5

Differentiating the Pictorial Element in Advertising

A Rhetorical Perspective

Edward F. McQuarrie

Introduction

It should not surprise readers of this volume that over the past 100 years, the picture has come to occupy a larger and larger portion of the typical American magazine advertisement. At the same time, the number of words, and the proportion of the ad devoted to text, has decreased. Pollay (1985), who was among the first to document this trend, also showed that the trend toward pictures and away from verbal text extends back throughout the 20th century. Pracejus, Olsen, and O'Guinn (2006), using a more fine-grained sampling strategy, confirm the trend and showed that it continued after the publication of Pollay (1985). McQuarrie and Phillips (2006) suggest that the trend toward picture-dominant ads may actually have accelerated after the mid-1990s. In summary, as of 2006, it is not uncommon to encounter a consumer magazine ad that contains a dozen or fewer words, while featuring a picture that fills the entire space of the ad, and it is now quite rare to find such an ad having more than a hundred words, and only a small picture.

Contemporary mass media print advertising is distinctive in its reliance on pictures to persuade. In most other domains, persuasion continues to be pursued via words, whether written or spoken, with pictures serving only as an adjunct or a supplement. Only in mass media print advertising do we see pictures supplanting words to carry the main burden of persuasion. Hence, no other scholarly discipline outside the marketing and consumer areas is as well-positioned to discover the scientific laws that govern persuasion via pictures. We have a wealth of material readily available, and we have the testimony of thousands of real marketing decision-makers, with billions of dollars at stake, whose freely chosen actions indicate their conviction that in print advertising today, persuasion is best pursued via pictures.

Differentiation of Pictures

Unfortunately, empirical scholarship in marketing has not caught up with the changes in magazine ad structure. One simple explanation for the relative rarity of experimental work on pictures in marketing would be that scholars lack a conceptual toolkit for differentiating pictures. By contrast, an abundance of distinctions is available if one wishes to focus on the underlying stuff of persuasion: one can design a study around central versus peripheral routes; systematic or heuristic processing; available cognitive resources; or motivation, opportunity, and ability to process, to name but a few. Similarly, a wealth of linguistic distinctions is available: claims can be easily manipulated with respect to either their syntactical form or their semantic content. This suggests that one of the best ways to stimulate scholarship on persuasion via pictures might be to develop what is now lacking: appropriate conceptual distinctions suitable for empirical investigation. That is the primary purpose of the present chapter.

The variety of pictures appearing in print advertisements is vast, and I make no attempt here to propose a comprehensive or encompassing framework (see Kenney & Scott, 2003 and Phillips, 2003, for useful introductions to the literature on visual rhetoric). Rather, I review a few examples of plausible differentiations, some of which have previously appeared in print and some of which are described here for the first time. The hope is that some of these distinctions will seem worth pursuing to other scholars, and also that the examples here may provide a model for how additional useful conceptual distinctions might be generated.

To begin, here are some desiderata that any candidate scheme for differentiating pictures must fulfill if it is to be attractive and worth pursuing. These include:

- The distinctions should be manifest in real advertisements.
- The distinctions should be native to the pictorial realm, rather than simply ported from some other, more extensively studied realm.
- The distinctions should be embedded in a larger framework, rather than being isolated, one-off categorizations, and the larger framework should be generative, i.e., should allow the derivation of multiple interlinked differences.
- There should be a plausible link between the elements of the differentiation, on the one hand, and variations in consumer response, on the other. In other words, interesting differences, in the picture, are those that also make a difference, to the consumer.
- The differences should be susceptible to experimental manipulation.

In summary, good pictorial differentiations are present in ads, specific to pictures, internally organized and structured, and causal in nature (McQuarrie, forthcoming).

The goal, then, is a set of useful differentiations that addresses the kinds of pictures that now dominate print advertising. However, we need a place to stand, a point of perspective, if we are to develop a theory of persuasion via pictures. For this purpose, in the next section I develop the idea of a rhetorical perspective on persuasion via pictures.

A Rhetorical Perspective on Advertising

The key difference between a rhetorical perspective and the social and cognitive psychological perspectives that have historically dominated scholarly work on advertising is as follows.

> Rhetoric assumes a few simple models of consumer response, and devotes effort at the margin to differentiating and structuring the stimuli capable of evoking one or another response.
>
> Cognitive and social psychology assume a few broad distinctions among stimuli, and devote effort at the margin to elaborating more detailed and nuanced models of consumer response to stimuli.

Elsewhere I have contrasted the two perspectives as focusing on the ad system on the one hand versus the human system on the other (McQuarrie & Mick, 2003b).

In the marketing area, the promise of rhetoric is that new insights into the structure of advertisements may be gained, and that the differences so identified will make a difference to consumer response. It is this commitment to causal understanding that permits one to call himself both a rhetorician and a marketing scientist. In general, the procedure of rhetoric is to identify the manifold (but limited) number of possibilities or options available in a given communication context, and then to determine the probability of achieving a desired audience response, given a choice to employ option A or option B, in context C.

A central distinction governing such a rhetorical procedure is the separation of content from style. In rhetoric, we distinguish what is said from how it is said. The idea is that almost any given content can be expressed using more than one style. In a marketing context, content might refer to the specific brand attribute being claimed. One can offer an explicit claim that a brand possesses that attribute, or make an implicit claim that requires an inference to be drawn; state it point blank, or give it an embellishment; express it pictorially instead of stating it verbally; and so forth. All of these are stylistic choices. Each instance shares the same underlying content, but each constitutes a different communication attempt that may fare well or poorly in a specific context. It is important to recognize that although style can be distinguished from content, style also communicates. Furthermore, the effectiveness of a communication attempt—the degree to which it fulfills the objective of the communicator—may be primarily a function of content, or primarily a function of the style selected for conveying that content.

In summary, when we take a rhetorical perspective on ad pictures, we expect to differentiate pictorial style. We also expect that the resulting differentiations will have a complex structure, and that this structure will have causal implications in terms of consumer response.

First-Level Differentiation of Visual and Pictorial Styles

To begin, let's define the visual element of an ad in broad terms, so that it includes the layout—the visual arrangement—of pictures, text, and brand components. We'll reserve the term *picture* for that component of the ad layout that is neither text nor brand identification.

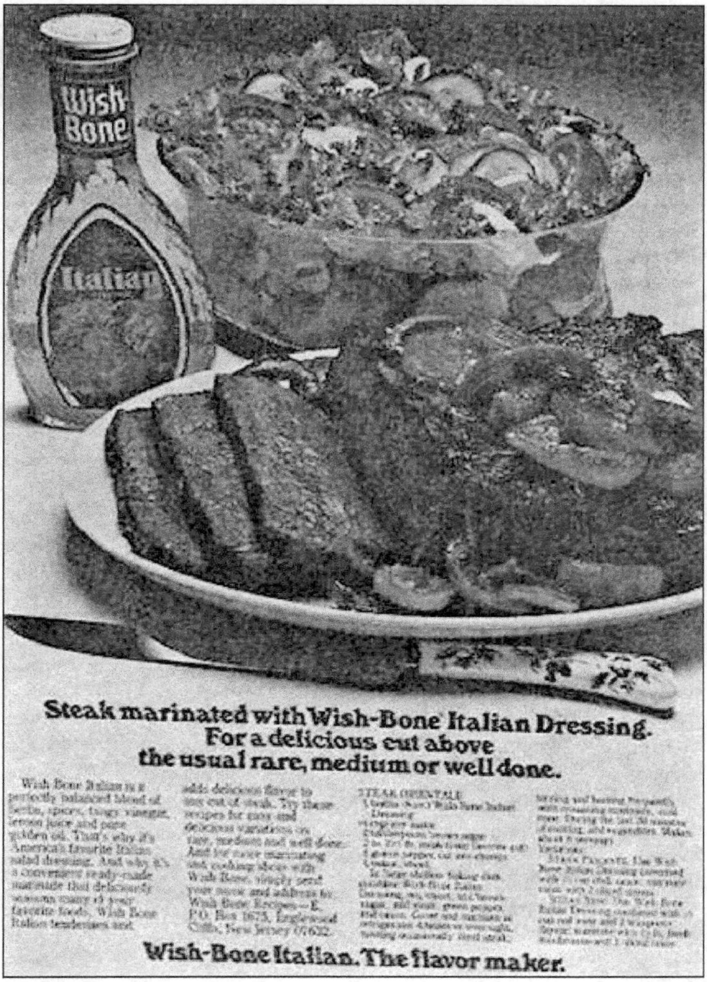

Figure 5.1 Conventional picture-window layout for a magazine ad.

The brand component of print ads tends to be a complex mélange of visual and verbal elements, which unfortunately I can't address here; see Henderson and Cote (1998) and Janiszewski and Meyvis (2001) for an introduction to some of the issues. Figure 5.1 shows a typical arrangement of pictorial, text, and brand components. This parsing of the elements that make up a print ad underlies work by Pieters and Wedel (2004) among others. This layout, which is clearly only one of several possible arrangements, actually has a name:

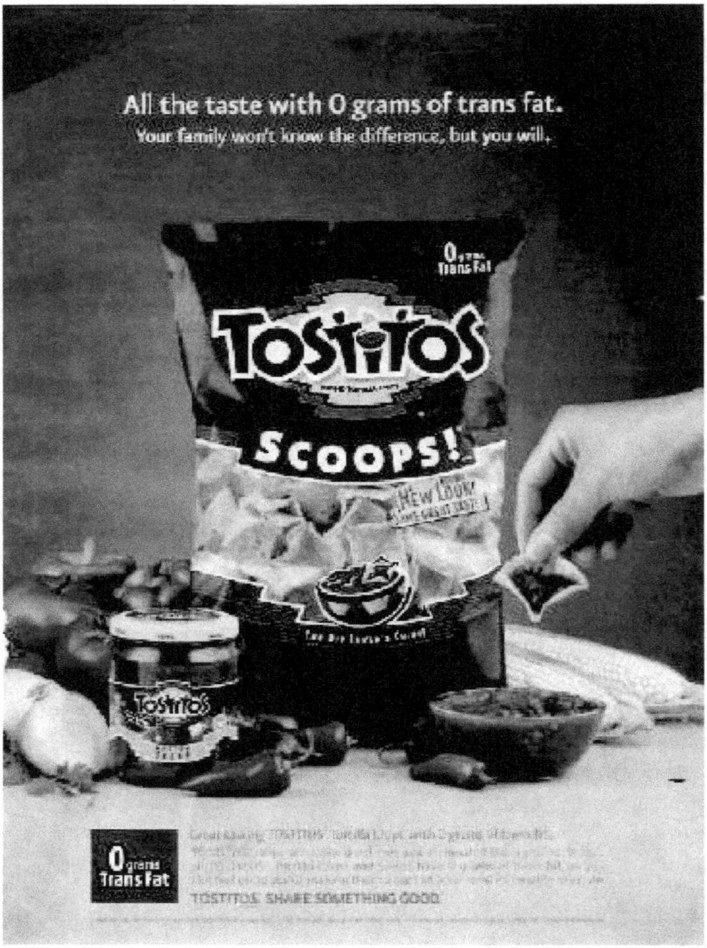

Figure 5.2 A newer ad that deviates from picture-window layout.

the *picture-window* layout, by analogy with typical mid-century American suburban residential architecture, where it was standard practice to place a single large window roughly centered on the upper two thirds of one wall of the living room.

One could interpret the trend data of Pollay (1985) and Pracejus et al. (2006) to conclude that the pictorial component of the sort of layout represented in Figure 5.1 got larger, and the real estate devoted to text got smaller, as time went on, without the arrangement itself changing. Although this may be the case, it turns out that something else was also going on, especially in more recent years. Figure 5.2 shows a recent ad for Tostitos that does not conform to the picture window layout. What has changed, exactly? Here is where rhetoric, with its sensitivity to stylistic elements, may be of assistance.

In the new ad, the picture has broken out of its window; in fact, the picture has taken over the ad, and occupies its entirety. There are still textual elements, but these occur in and on the picture. The words and the picture no longer hold separate territories—they no longer appear beside one another. The Tostitos ad is thus *picture dominant* in a double sense. On the one hand, there are not very many words; on the other, the entire ad is now a picture, so that the picture is primary as well as large.

Our first high level stylistic distinction can be captured by the terms documentary versus pictorial layout (see Table 5.1). In documentary layout, the ad is a document to be read. Words are primary, and the picture plays a secondary role—it illustrates the text. Ads produced in documentary style, like that shown in Figure 5.1, presume that the consumer is a reader who examines. That is how one treats documents—one examines them in order to render a judgment. Ads produced in pictorial style presume that the consumer is a viewer who glances. That is how one treats colorful pictures that may or may not be relevant to one's life project of the moment.

Elsewhere I have argued that the new pictorial style arose as an adaptation to changes in the consumer audience for advertising (McQuarrie & Phillips forthcoming; Phillips & McQuarrie, 2002). For purposes of this chapter, it is enough to point out that an ad designed as a document may fail if directed at a consumer who is merely a viewer; likewise, a pictorial ad may not produce the desired judgment if directed at a consumer prepared to examine ads. This is because the two styles assume very different consumer processing. Hence, this stylistic difference can be expected to have causal impact.

Second-Level Differentiation: Look Through versus Look At

We turn now to a differentiation that is conceptually independent of the documentary versus pictorial layout distinction (although in practice, this next distinction is particularly relevant to pictorial layouts, and correlated with it). Compare the Pampers ad in

TABLE 5.1 A Scheme for Conceptually Differentiating the Pictorial Element of Advertising

Level	Contrast	Distinguishing Characteristic	Expected Consumer Response
1	Documentary layout	Text dominant Picture confined to a window	Read and examine
	Pictorial layout	Text minimal Picture takes over the ad	View and glance
2	Look-through pictures	Picture is a copy of objects	Infer meanings from depicted objects
	Look-at pictures	Picture presents itself rather than representing objects	Enjoy artfulness of picture Infer meanings from pictographs and visual arrangements
3	Genres		
	Tableaux	Staged scene with pre-packaged elements	Time on ad
	Frozen narrative	Still shot from a movie	Time in story
	Rhetorical figure	Artful deviation from expectation	Elaboration Automaticity of inference generation
4	Types of figurative visual structure		
	Juxtaposition	A beside B	
	Inclusion	A inside B	
	Combination	A combined with B to form C	
	Fusion	A fused with B to form AB	
	Replacement	A in place of B	
	Removal	A and not-B	

Note: See text for additional discussion of levels 1 to 3, and Phillips and McQuarrie (2004) for further discussion of level 4. The list of genres is not exhaustive. For level 4, the visual structures are listed from simplest to most complex.

Figure 5.3, which, like the Tostitos ad, is in the newer pictorial style, with the Wrigleys ad in Figure 5.4, which is also in pictorial style, but which nonetheless differs from the Tostitos and Pampers ads in an important respect. The Pampers ad is a picture (of something), while the Wrigley's ad may be termed (some kind of) picture. The Pampers

Figure 5.3 An ad with a look-through picture.

picture is to look through, the Wrigley's picture is to look at. In the Pampers ad, one is intended to see the baby, see his red, raw skin and crumpled face, and feel his misery with a mother's concern (note the cast of her lips in the upper left). This is a picture of an unhappy baby in the arms of a devoted mother. By contrast, the Wrigley's ad is not a picture of two girls bicycling on a downtown street. It is a splash of fresh green amidst a grim gray urban scene. It is a staged tableau full of pictographs—the rows of treadmills, the stiff-legged, stressed-out strider yelling into his cell phone, etc. The Wrigley's ad is not a picture of anything except itself.

Figure 5.4 An ad from the tableaux genre containing a look-at picture.

Ad pictures designed for look-through function as transparent windows onto the objects and scenes they depict. The meaning of look-through pictures derives from these objects and scenes. Ad pictures designed to look at assemble pictographs rather than represent objects; they are not representations of objects, but representations of ideas, and their meaning lies in these ideas. Look-through pictures are instrumental; they are a means to the end of getting the consumer to think about certain objects or situations. As such, a strict photorealism is the dominant visual style (Schroeder, 2002). Look-at pictures are ends in themselves; they attempt to convey ideas directly, by means of their visual structure and the pictographs they construct. The goal of a look-through picture is to point to the objects whose meaning the consumer is to process; the goal of a look-at picture is to be looked at, so that the consumer can process the ideas represented therein.

I think it is fair to say that when many marketing and consumer scholars conceptualize *pictures in ads*, often the tacit assumption is that these are look-through pictures (Scott, 1994). Although I spend the remainder of this chapter attempting to further differentiate the category of look-at pictures, I don't mean to imply that the category of look-through pictures is either unimportant or undifferentiated within itself. Studies of how scenes such as that depicted in the Pampers ad are processed are a staple of contemporary perceptual and cognitive psychology (see Raymond, 2003, for an introduction). Quite a complex inference process is required to interpret the Pampers scene as I did above. Moreover, anthropological research has shown that diverse cultural competencies are required to effectively process such two-dimensional photographs (Scott, 1994). For examples of research strategies appropriate to the look-through domain, see Larsen, Luna, and Peracchio (2005), Meyers-Levy and Peracchio (1992), and Peracchio and Meyers-Levy (1994).

Tertiary Differentiation of the Pictorial Element: Genres

My goal now is to suggest avenues along which the category of look-at pictures can be further differentiated. The two central ideas in the account that follows are genre and rhetorical figure. A genre may be thought of as a set of settled expectations that a competent audience brings to an encounter with some category of cultural object; these expectations are genre rules. Detective novels are an example of a genre within the category of fiction. A reader pretty much knows what to expect from any novel that can be so tagged (i.e., the detective never dies; the crime will be solved). Implicit in the idea of a genre is that individual instances can be recognized as belonging to such and such a genre; there are tags that instruct a competent audience to apply the appropriate set of expectations. In what follows, I want to distinguish a number of genres within the category of look-at pictures, one of which will be the rhetorical figure genre; the idea of a visual rhetorical figure will be further developed in the next section.

The Wrigley's ad belongs to what might be called the tableaux genre (Figure 5.4). There are a plethora of elements, some of which cue culturally established knowledge (e.g., hectic city life). Other elements are pictographs, canned visual representations that the advertiser can rely on most consumers to interpret consistently (stressed-out cell phone user). Still other elements are bits of artistic license or cleverness (whimsical store signs such as "caffeine heaven"). The overall effect is not unlike such childhood puzzles as *Where's Waldo?*.

From a causal standpoint, what consumer response might an advertiser hope to achieve via use of the tableaux style? After all, Wrigley's could instead have surrounded a package shot with objects suggestive of fresh flavors, as did Tostitos in Figure 5.2. One possibility is that here the goal of the advertiser is to maximize *time on ad*. The tableaux style encourages the viewer to spend time on processing the picture. The goal would be to convert a glance into a lingering gaze. The expected result would be an increase in the salience of the brand, and/or a strengthened association between the brand and a desired attribute-benefit positioning (Wrigley's equals refreshment). Such salience, along with positioning reinforcement, may be all that an advertisement can accomplish for a familiar brand in a parity product category. In short, we are dealing here with what Kardes (1993) labeled as indirect persuasion.

The ad in Figure 5.5 introduces another genre, which might be termed *frozen narrative*. This is ad-picture-as-movie-still. Here we have not a picture of a handyman removing a hornet's nest, but a movie about inept foolishness, a little morality play, arrested just before its climax. In frozen narrative, we have not a picture of, but a story about. The goal of this kind of advertising is to engage the consumer, to get them to elaborate the story forward (and backward) in time. Rather than time-on-ad in association with the brand, we have time-in-story with a moral regarding the product category—the importance, perhaps, of a good worker's compensation policy. To get the ad viewer to "tell the story" may be an extremely potent gambit for motivating involvement with the ad message.

Doubtless there are other genres of ad pictures that can be identified (fashion ads would be on many scholars' short list of magazine ad genres). My goal here was not to construct an exhaustive categorization of ad picture genres, but simply to demonstrate how a rhetorician would proceed to differentiate ad pictures, while introducing the idea of genre as a means to organize the available possibilities for

Figure 5.5 An ad from the frozen narrative genre.

persuasion. It should also be clear that the genres discussed assume a very different consumer than the *reader of documents*. These ads are aimed at consumers who have developed antibodies to straightforward claims by brands. These ads assume that the consumer will give the ad no more than a passing glance unless given some kind of incentive to linger. In turn, the importance of this kind of advertising, or how it works, or even that it should exist, can never be revealed by an experimental tradition that works exclusively within a forced exposure paradigm (McQuarrie, 2004). These genres are conditioned on the idea that ad exposure cannot be forced, and is unlikely to be achieved, no matter how much money is spent on ad insertions, unless the ad is designed to break through the clutter.

A problem with genre as a tool for rhetorical differentiation is that conceptually speaking, it is list-like. As a simple list of possibilities, a set of genres has no internal structure, and hence it lacks generative power. Each genre discussed may seem reasonable, and distinct from the others; but there is no way to specify that there are *n* such genres, and only *n*. Similarly, there is no clear route for articulating what the $n + 1$ genre, or next genre, might be, after identifying the first two or three, and no way to know whether an exhaustive categorization has been achieved. If the list of genres is short, and can plausibly be claimed to be exhaustive, then these difficulties are ameliorated somewhat. Nonetheless, because we are dealing with an unstructured list, there is no clear route to predicting how different genres will evoke systematically different kinds of consumer response. For this reason, as a rhetorician, I prefer internally structured sets when building a scheme of differentiation, as discussed next.

Differentiating the Genre of Visual Rhetorical Figures

To conclude the discussion of pictorial differentiation, I turn now to a mode of differentiating pictures that addresses some of the shortcomings of the idea of genre. This is the idea that some ad pictures are structured as rhetorical figures. A rhetorical figure can be defined as an artful deviation from expectation, corresponding to a template; furthermore, these templates are limited in number, and internally organized. Deviations that do not correspond to a template are simply stylistic devices; like genres, multiple stylistic devices can be easily identified, but resist systematization (McQuarrie & Mick, 1996).

Metaphor, pun, rhyme, antithesis, hyperbole, and many more obscure terms (e.g., antimetabole) are all examples of specific verbal rhetorical figures. In each case of pun or any other rhetorical figure, there is a system of relations that is common to all puns; and—this is crucial for our present purposes—the system of relationships that defines a pun, and the system that defines a rhyme, are in turn integrated within a larger system. Such a system of systems, applicable to the language of advertising, is developed in McQuarrie and Mick (1996, 2003b). For our purposes, the important thing is the contrast between an unstructured list and a system of systems. From a scientific standpoint, it seems to me that a system of systems is much more appealing, particularly when that system can be linked to differences in consumer response.

The reader will be quick to note that *rhetorical figure* is not an idea that is native to pictures or the visual realm; it originated as a distinction among kinds of speech. Is it then an illegitimate extrapolation of linguistic ideas to speak of visual rhetorical figures? I think not; what is illegitimate is to extrapolate the specific systems used to subdifferentiate verbal rhetorical figures over onto visual rhetorical figures (compare McQuarrie & Mick, 1999, to Phillips & McQuarrie, 2004). The idea of a rhetorical figure is not a linguistic or literary concept per se but a more general semiotic idea, a type or mode of human communication. Evidence for this generality can be seen in the long history of its usage in art criticism as well as poetics (Scott, 1994). By contrast, the scheme-trope distinction, which is constitutive of the subsystems described in McQuarrie and Mick (1996), is a distinction specific to verbal material, and not useful in the pictorial realm. As I see it now, a rhetorical figure—an artful deviation from expectation—is an exceedingly general idea that can be used to distinguish a certain kind of word arrangement, a certain kind of pictorial arrangement, and much else besides. It is at the subsystem level—the typology within the category of visual rhetorical figures—that we must seek ideas native to, and appropriate for, the pictorial realm.

What follows builds on the typology introduced in Phillips and McQuarrie (2004). I will not go into as much detail here, and readers who wish to examine its foundations or conduct follow-up research should consult that paper. Here I want only to demonstrate how a structural differentiation of pictures can be developed, using visual rhetorical figures as an illustrative example. Phillips and McQuarrie (2004) differentiate visual figures along two dimensions: (a) the visual structure deployed on the page (juxtaposition, fusion, replacement); and (b) the meaning operation invoked (connection, similarity, opposition). Crossing three types of visual structure with three types of meaning operation produces nine distinct types of visual rhetorical figure—a great advance, they argue, over omnibus references to *visual metaphor* and the like. The dimension of meaning operation is not unique to pictures, so I won't consider it further here; the focus is on visual structure as an exemplary approach to differentiating ad pictures.

Recall that our goal is a generative structure of differentiations, having the potential to be exhaustive, with a clear association between its different categories and corresponding differences in consumer response. Let's see how visual structure fits the bill. The simplest kind of figurative visual structure is juxtaposition. Thus, one can show a shoe next to a made-up bed (to assert similar degrees of comfort), or a pair of cacti next to a pair of sock-covered feet (to cue the opposition between prickly and comfortable cloth). Stepping back to the conceptual level, we may say that juxtaposition is one of *k* possible relations between two pictorial elements. We may further say that there are only *k* possible visual arrangements of two objects, with *k* being a relatively small number on the order of a dozen or less. If so, then visual structure fits the desiderata for a conceptual differentiation. It has a rule for generating possibilities: simply find all possible ways of arranging two pictorial elements. Moreover, this rule seems likely to have a clear stopping point (there aren't many distinct ways of arranging two pictorial elements on a two-dimensional page). By analogy, there are only four ways to alter the disposition of an object in three-dimensional space: one can invert it (top to bottom), reverse it (left to right), obvert it (front to back), or transpose it (making top and bottom into sides, and vice versa).

Note that if the various arrangements can be arrayed onto a dimension (simple versus complex, in the case of visual structure), then a connection can probably be made to variations in consumer response. The underlying dimension then becomes the causal factor, and specific visual structures become a means to the end of occupying a particular position on that causal dimension, with juxtaposition being the simplest kind of visual structure. Such causal hypotheses are developed at more length in Phillips and McQuarrie (2004).

We now proceed to examine briefly other kinds of progressively more complex visual structures. Put another way, if juxtaposition is but one way in which two objects can be visually related, what are the other possibilities? We might next distinguish inclusion, in which one pictorial element includes another. An example would be a fire alarm box containing a heartburn medicine, or a colander containing a jar of salad dressing. Note that although juxtaposition and inclusion are relatively simple visual structures, the examples are nonetheless figurative, because they are deviant and unexpected. Next in the set of progressively more complex visual structures is combination, in which one element combines with another to create a third. An example would be a mistletoe hanging that combines gold-wrapped chocolate balls with sprigs of the plant. Just slightly more complex is fusion, in which two elements merge into one another.

An example would be a slice of bread with the texture of a cracker, or a blue towel whose folds become blue ocean waves. Finally, we come to replacement, in which one element substitutes for another, and removal, which is one element without its expected complement. An example of replacement would be a cracked package of Egg Beaters®, held just as the cracked halves of an egg would be held; an example of removal, for fruit-flavored water, would be a strawberry complete as to shape and texture, but drained of color. These possible structures for visually relating two elements on a two-dimensional surface are summarized in Table 5.1. Have we derived here a complete list of the possibilities for relating two pictorial elements? Probably not (it is a lengthier list than in Phillips & McQuarrie, 2004), but only time and human ingenuity will tell. The important point is that the generative rule is clear, and there is a definite stopping point. Hence, an exhaustive list of rule-generated visual structures is possible in principle.

A question not yet addressed is why a marketer would make use of any kind of figurative visual structure. This question is really two questions: Why use a rhetorical figure in an advertisement? And, why use a visual rhetorical figure? The answer to the first question is laid out in McQuarrie and Mick (1996, 2003b), with empirical tests in McQuarrie and Mick (1992, 1999, 2003a), McQuarrie and Phillips (2005) and Mothersbaugh, Huhmann, and Franke (2002). Simply put, rhetorical figures may be advantageous in processing contexts where exposure is not forced and/or processing effort will be minimal. They invite attention via their artful deviation, known more conventionally as incongruity, and then reward it with a pleasure-of-the-text, known more conventionally as cognitive elaboration. This incremental cognitive elaboration produces better recall and a more favorable attitude toward the ad. To answer the second question, we need to step back and answer a larger question that has probably been in the back of the reader's mind since the chapter began: why emphasize pictures in ads?

Why Have Pictures Come to Dominate Modern Magazine Advertisements?

What has to be explained are three interwoven trends: (a) the decrease in the portion of ads devoted to words and increase in the proportion devoted to pictures; (b) the transmutation of these pictures such that look-at styles become more common and look-through styles less common; and (c) the steady increase in the number of pictures that offer a visual rhetorical figure to look at. The last named trend is more recent, but unmistakable when I flip through magazines appearing after 2000.

We may also distinguish between dismissive and substantive explanations for these trends. A dismissive explanation treats the change in advertising as an epiphenomenon of some other change in the larger culture or society. A substantive explanation treats the change as a necessary and appropriate response by advertisers to some change in the consumer, competitive, or media viewing environment, which, absent such an advertiser response, would have rendered advertising increasingly ineffective. An example of a dismissive explanation would be the claim that the advent of first television and then the Web greatly increased the amount of visual stimulation to which consumers became accustomed. Hence, advertisements became more visual simply as a matter of fitting in with the Zeitgeist.

Any such dismissive explanation is really a matter of explaining away the change. If the change in advertising is simply a surface adaptation to its surround, then no change in substantive marketing theory is required. The problem with a dismissive explanation is that it has trouble accounting for all three trends. This is why the middle of this chapter was devoted to differentiating pictures. What has to be explained is the increase in pictures, plus the increase in a certain kind of picture, plus the increase in the use of a specific pictorial device. The explanation offered below rests on the following postulates:

- Advertisers and consumers are mutually adaptive. The goal of the advertiser is to capture consumer attention and processing, and the goal of the consumer is to elude this capture so as to preserve attentional resources for purposes other than processing advertising.
- Reading of text is voluntary and effortful, hence easy to abort and also likely to be stillborn even if initiated.
- Glancing at pictures is involuntary and comparatively effortless, hence spontaneous and difficult to derail once begun.
- Pictures are inferior to words with respect to the kind of communication endeavor wherein words excel, such as the ascription of properties to objects and the articulation of arguments in support of such ascriptions.

- In tightly scripted communication environments (such as advertising), where the message recipient knows pretty much what kind of message to expect ("this is a good brand for you to buy because…"), the aforementioned inferiority of pictures constitutes an advantageous incapacity.

In its essence, the argument is a combination of an ecological argument with a mode of processing argument. Specifically, I contend that by the 1990s, after decades of post-WWII affluence, the American consumer had adapted to incessant advertising by developing an immunity to straightforward verbal claims of the sort, "Tide gets clothes really clean." At the present juncture, pictures in ads do not suffer this fate; this is the first reason behind the switch to pictures in recent times. Second, the involuntary and (comparatively) effortless nature of picture processing makes it desirable to attempt to embed the advertiser's brand message into the picture—since fewer words are available for this purpose, and words don't work well anymore anyway. This drives the spread of look-at pictorial genres. Third, because pictures are such a poor tool for communicating detailed property ascriptions and supporting argumentation—in other words, because pictures are not a language—advertisers seek out the kind of pictures most suitable for this unpictorial activity. This turns out to be visual rhetorical figures, for the reasons explained below.

The ecological argument is developed in Phillips and McQuarrie (2002) and McQuarrie and Phillips (forthcoming). The mode of processing piece is developed and given empirical support in McQuarrie and Phillips (2005). This latter portion of the argument has two components: (a) that pictures have one inherent advantage over words; and (b) that pictures have another, inherent disadvantage over words. On the one hand, pictures in ads will be processed, whereas words may not; on the other, it's hard to design a picture from which the recipient will draw specific inferences, of the sort that are so easily encoded in words. Solution: a visual rhetorical figure, which guides the recipient's inference process. That is, the launch of inference processes is relatively automatic in the case of pictures, which is good, but may lead to unexpected, aberrant, or just uncontrolled outcomes, absent a channel to guide it. The visual rhetorical figure provides that channel. McQuarrie and Phillips (2005) show that visual metaphors unanchored by text do indeed appear to compel an involuntary inference process that is responsive to the advertiser's objective. The underdetermination of meaning in pictures thus becomes an advantageous incapacity, given the availability of a channeling device such as a rhetorical figure.

Conclusion

An underlying presupposition of this chapter has been that print advertising has changed over the past few decades, and that theories of consumer response to advertising—at least, midrange theories—have to change as well. Contemporary ads may be characterized as increasingly pictorial rather than verbal, as objects of visual consumption in their own right apart from any messaging function, and as figurative by design. If we wish to contribute to the scientific understanding of mass media advertising, we need to model these distinctive characteristics in our empirical work (McQuarrie, 2004). In this regard, rhetorical perspectives can guide empirical inquiry by differentiating causal factors within the pictorial element of advertisements.

References

Henderson, P., & Cote, J. A. (1998). Guidelines for selecting or modifying logos. *Journal of Marketing, 62*, 14–30.

Janiszewski, C., & Meyvis, T. (2001). Effects of brand logo complexity, repetition, and spacing on processing fluency and judgment. *Journal of Consumer Research, 28*(June), 18–32.

Kardes, F. (1993). Consumer inference: Determinants, consequences, and implications for advertising. In A. A. Mitchell (Ed.), *Advertising exposure, memory, and choice* (pp. 163–191). Hillsdale, NJ: Lawrence Erlbaum.

Kenney, K., & Scott, L. M. (2003). A review of the visual rhetoric literature. In L. M. Scott & R. B. Mahwah (Eds.), *Persuasive imagery: A consumer response perspective*, Mahwah, NJ: Lawrence Erlbaum, 17–56.

Larsen, V., Luna, D., & Peracchio, L. (2005). Points of view and pieces of time: A taxonomy of image attributes. *Journal of Consumer Research, 31*, 102–111.

McQuarrie, E. F. (2004). Integration of construct and external validity by means of proximal similarity: Implications for laboratory experiments in marketing. *Journal of Business Research, 57*, 142–153.

McQuarrie. E. F. (forthcoming). A visit to the rhetorician's workbench: Developing a toolkit for differentiating advertising style. In E. F. McQuarrie and B. J. Phillips (Eds.), *Go figure! New directions in advertising rhetoric*. Armonk, NY: M. E. Sharpe.

McQuarrie, E. F., & Mick, D. (1992). On resonance: A critical pluralistic inquiry into advertising rhetoric. *Journal of Consumer Research, 19*, 180–197.

McQuarrie, E. F., & Mick, D. (1996). Figures of rhetoric in advertising language. *Journal of Consumer Research, 22*, 424–438.

McQuarrie, E. F., & Mick, D. (1999). Visual rhetoric in advertising: Text-interpretive, experimental, and reader-response analyses. *Journal of Consumer Research, 26*, 37–54.

McQuarrie, E. F., & Mick, D. (2003a). Visual and verbal rhetorical figures under directed processing versus incidental exposure to advertising. *Journal of Consumer Research, 29*, 579–587.

McQuarrie, E. F., & Mick, D. (2003b). The contribution of semiotic and rhetorical perspectives to the explanation of visual persuasion in advertising. In L. Scott & R. Batra (Eds.), *Persuasive imagery: A consumer response perspective*. Mahwah, NJ: Lawrence Erlbaum, 191–122.

McQuarrie, E. F., & Phillips, B. J. (2005). Indirect persuasion in advertising: How consumers process metaphors presented in pictures and words. *Journal of Advertising, 34*, 7–20.

McQuarrie, E. F., & Phillips, B. J. (forthcoming). Not your father's magazine ad: Magnitude and direction of recent changes in ad style. *Journal of Advertising.*

Meyers-Levy, J., & Peracchio, L. A. (1992). Getting an angle in advertising: The effect of camera angle on product evaluations. *Journal of Marketing Research, 29*, 454–461.

Mothersbaugh, D. L., Huhmann, B. A., & Franke, G. R. (2002). Combinatory and separative effects of rhetorical figures on consumers' efforts and focus in ad processing. *Journal of Consumer Research, 28*, 589–602.

Peracchio, L., & Meyers-Levy, J. (1994). How ambiguous cropped objects in ad photos affect product evaluations. *Journal of Consumer Research, 21*, 190–204.

Phillips, B. J. (2003). Understanding visual metaphor in advertising. In L. M. Scott & R. Batra (Eds.), *Persuasive imagery: A consumer response perspective* (pp. 297–310). Mahweh, NJ: Lawrence Erlbaum.

Phillips, B. J., & McQuarrie, E. F. (2002). The development, change, and transformation of rhetorical style in magazine advertisements. *Journal of Advertising, 31*(4), 1–13.

Phillips, B. J., & McQuarrie, E. F. (2004). Beyond visual metaphor: A new typology of visual rhetoric in advertising. *Marketing Theory, 4*(1/2), 113–136.

Pieters, R., & Wedel, M. (2004). Attention capture and transfer in advertising: Brand, pictorial, and text-size effects. *Journal of Marketing, 68*, 36–50.

Pollay, R. W. (1985). The subsidizing sizzle: A descriptive history of print advertising, 1900–1980. *Journal of Marketing, 48*, 24–37.

Pracejus, J., Olsen, G. D., & O'Guinn, T. C. (2006). How nothing became something: White space, rhetoric, history, and meaning. *Journal of Consumer Research, 33*, 82–90.

Raymond, J. (2003). When the mind blinks: Attentional limitations to the perception of sequential images. In L. M. Scott & R. Batra (Eds.), *Persuasive imagery: A consumer response perspective* (pp. 59–74). Mahwah, NJ: Lawrence Erlbaum.

Schroeder, J. (2002). *Visual consumption.* London, UK: Routledge.

Scott, L. M. (1994). Images in advertising: The need for a theory of visual rhetoric. *Journal of Consumer Research, 21*, 252–273.

6

Geometry in the Marketplace

Eric Greenleaf and Priya Raghubir

Introduction

Consumer reaction to products can depend on aesthetic product features and product and package design (Bloch, 1995; Holbrook & Anand, 1992: Raghubir & Greenleaf, 2006). Product designers vary aesthetic features to appeal to consumer preferences for these features and to differentiate their products from competing products. While product design incorporates many kinds of attributes, such as the taste of a cereal, the resolution of a digital camera, or the gas mileage of an automobile, one design element that must be addressed for many products is geometric shape. A product's shape and geometry can be considered one of its most basic design features, especially from the perspective of a consumer who is viewing the product but has yet to use it. However, while research in psychology and aesthetics has paid considerable attention to perceptions of, and preferences for, different basic shapes, less attention has been given to this question in the realms of consumer behavior and marketing management.

We examine the issue of geometry in the marketplace from three perspectives. First, from an empirical perspective, we examine whether the relative seriousness versus frivolousness of a product category, which is a context effect that has been found to be related to the variation of consumer purchase intentions and preferences (Raghubir & Greenleaf, 2006), is also related to the variation of this ratio in marketplace offerings in different categories and subcategories.

Second, we propose an agenda for consumer behavior research on geometry, which focuses on marketplace concepts that are important in consumer behavior and marketing, such as competition and post-purchase satisfaction, but have been much less studied in research on geometry. Third, we propose a broader, integrative conceptual model to serve both as a set of testable hypotheses and as a research agenda for examining geometry in design from a consumer perspective. This model unites concepts from aesthetics, psychology, and consumer behavior into a single conceptual framework. This model delineates four primary geometric properties that we feel should relate to products and packages, proposes routes through which these properties affect consumer judgments, then proposes factors moderating their effect, and then links these factors to marketing implications, for marketing decisions in the realm of the "four Ps" of the marketing mix, such as product design, placement, promotion, and pricing. As examples of how this model incorporates geometric design features, we discuss in detail *planned distortion* and *incomplete patterns*, two design features found in the marketplace.

An Empirical Test of Variation in Rectangular Ratios in the Marketplace

We begin our examination of geometry in the marketplace by giving an example of how empirical research, in this case using the positivist method, can be applied to study geometry. This section presents the results of four studies of the variation of ratios in a variety of product categories. Rectangular ratios are one of the most frequently used shapes in product and package design (e.g., TVs, cereal boxes, greeting cards, books, print advertising), and the ratio of a rectangle's sides is one of its most salient attributes. Further, their quantifiable nature makes rectangular ratios a good starting point for examining marketplace variation in product features, especially as the results can inform one of the oldest controversies in psychology and aesthetics.

Research on Preferences for Rectangles

Aestheticians and psychologists have long been interested in preferences for rectangular ratios. Indeed, some of the earliest experimental work in psychology was Fechner's (Fechner, 1871, 1876, trans. 1997) investigation of whether people preferred the "golden ratio" rectangle (ratio of sides of Φ ≈ 1.618). Ancient Greek and Renaissance writers, as well as more recent aestheticians, have noted the special mathematical and aesthetic qualities of this number (Borissavliévitch, 1958; Ghyka, 1977; Herz-Fischler, 1987; Huntley, 1970; Livio, 2002; Pennick, 1980), and claim that it is used in the design of many admired buildings, such as the Parthenon, and recurs in natural formations such as shells and sunflowers. However, Fechner's conclusions remain controversial (Höge, 1997; Green, 1995, reviews this research). Other researchers have concluded that people prefer a range of rectangles, extending roughly from √2 (1.414) to √3 (1.732) and including Φ, rather than a single ratio (Benjafield, 1976; McManus, 1980; Piehl, 1978; Plug, 1976; Svensson, 1977). In recent work, Raghubir and Greenleaf (2006) showed that the preference for rectangles over squares is contextual—it is not found for contexts that are relatively frivolous in nature. The specific underlying reason for such a preference remains a matter of conjecture, with some possible routes through which it could manifest being discussed in our conceptual model.

Context Effects in Rectangular Preferences

Much of the research just discussed examines preferences for abstract rectangles (though a few have examined actual objects, such as Shortess, Clarke, and Shannon [1997], who examine the ratios of paintings and discuss Fechner's work [1871, 1876] examining ratios of actual objects). However, recent research in marketing has argued that since products and packages are typically used in particular contexts, consumer researchers need to study preferences for rectangular products and packages rather than abstract rectangles, and also need to examine how consumer preferences and purchase intentions vary with the context in which a rectangular product or package is used (Raghubir & Greenleaf, 2006). This research has found that consumers' preferences for rectangular products with different ratios depend on whether the product is intended to be used in a relatively serious or frivolous context. In particular, they found that consumers preferred a tighter range of rectangles in relatively serious contexts, but that the preference range was much wider for relatively frivolous ones. The context of relative seriousness versus frivolity was chosen because many of the reasons that have been offered in research on rectangular preferences to explain why people will prefer certain rectangles relate to properties—such as rationality, balance, harmony, proportion, and mathematical beauty (Ghyka, 1977; Huntley, 1970; Lawlor, 1982; Livio, 2002)—that are more likely to be important when consumers are in a more serious, versus frivolous, frame of mind.

Given these prior findings, we propose that the differences in variation in purchase intentions found by Raghubir and Greenleaf (2006) across the relatively serious versus frivolous contexts implies that variation in the product design feature of rectangular ratio will also depend on this context effect. Furthermore, we propose that the variation in design features will be parallel to the variation in purchase intentions. Thus, we propose:

H1: Rectangular ratios found in marketplace offerings in a product subcategory that is used in a relatively more serious context will have less variation than ratios for a subcategory of the same product that is used in a relatively less frivolous context.

Four studies test this hypothesis using actual marketplace offerings. One of the product categories we will study, greeting cards, is similar to the invitation card category that was studied by Raghubir and Greenleaf (2006), while two other categories, newspaper ads and books, extend this inquiry into additional categories. In all studies presented here, we sought categories where:

1. The predominant shape in the product category is a rectangle.
2. The product is two dimensional or primarily seen in two dimensions.
3. Ratios of the product dimensions in the category vary across products and brands.
4. Products in subcategories within the larger product category are used by consumers in different contexts that vary in their relative seriousness versus frivolity.

In all four studies research assistants who were blind to the hypothesis collected the data. For each study we report how we operationalized the relative seriousness/frivolousness of the context using product subcategories or brands or both, then describe the sampling method, and present the results. The analysis is an *F* test of difference in variance across two sets of observations. Summary statistics for all four studies are presented in Table 6.1.

TABLE 6.1 Dimensions and Ratios of Marketplace Offerings, by Context

	Width	Height	Ratio[1]	Std. Dev.	*n*	95% Range[2]
Study 1: Individual and Business Cards						
Individual	5.62	6.44	1.36	0.17	30	1.30–1.42
Business	5.79	6.21	1.43	0.04	30	1.41–1.45
Study 2: Individual Humorous Birthday and Sympathy Cards (n = 40)						
Humorous Birthday	5.26	7.83	1.62	0.33	20	1.48–1.76
Sympathy	5.35	7.75	1.45	0.01	20	1.43–1.47
Study 3: Newspaper Advertisements by Section (n = 118)						
WSJ: All	7.76	11.10	1.61	0.60	36	1.41–1.81
Economy	7.09	9.26	1.48	0.52	20	1.25–1.71
Others	8.91	13.69	1.73	0.69	16	1.38–2.07
SFC: All	6.81	8.57	2.39	2.11	82	1.93–2.86
Less Frivolous Sections	*7.95*	*10.39*	*1.76*	*1.03*	*43*	*1.45–2.08*
Front Page	8.86	10.55	1.78	1.31	22	1.22–2.34
Bay Area	6.88	11.53	1.70	0.26	5	1.46–1.93
Business	9.60	9.11	1.98	1.34	4	0.64–3.32
News	6.16	10.05	1.68	0.50	12	1.39–1.98
More Frivolous Sections	*5.56*	*6.56*	*3.09*	*2.71*	*39*	*2.22–3.96*
Sporting Green	6.69	8.56	3.13	2.76	14	1.66–4.61
Datebook	5.45	3.63	3.94	3.77	9	1.43–6.45
East Bay Friday	4.62	6.45	2.58	1.94	16	1.61–3.55
Study 4: Books						
Children's Books	7.18	8.69	1.31	0.16	30	1.26–1.37
General Science Books	5.94	8.65	1.46	0.10	30	1.43–1.50

[1] Note that ratio may not equal height/width due to differences in orientation in the categories.

[2] 95% confidence interval for mean ratio calculated as mean ratio +/−2 standard error, where standard error = st. dev. / $\sqrt{n}$.

Study 1: Greeting Cards for Individuals versus Businesses

Operationalization of Seriousness of Context

Two subcategories of greeting cards, for businesses and for individuals, were chosen to operationalize the relatively less and more frivolous domains, respectively. The distinctions were based on the manner in which Hallmark categorized the cards on its website.* The cards included wishes for festivals, birthday, anniversary, congratulations, and get well messages.

Sampling Method

Every tenth card within each subcategory (business and individual) was chosen for inclusion in the sample, based on a randomly chosen starting point in a display of greeting cards on the Hallmark website. Thirty cards were chosen from each subcategory.

Results

The dimensions for each card were recorded from the same website, and the ratio of the longer to the shorter side was calculated, as was the variance in this ratio. The variance of the rectangular ratios across the individual greeting cards was significantly greater than this variance across the business greeting cards (variance = .0291 vs. .002; $F(29, 29) = 14.77$, $p < .0001$). This is consistent with the hypothesis that there will be less variation in the ratio of market offerings for the business cards, which is the relatively less frivolous context, compared to the individual cards, which is the relatively more frivolous context, and supports H1.

Study 2: Greeting Cards for Condolence versus Birthdays

Operationalization of Seriousness of Context

Study 2 examined whether H1 would hold within the individual card category for card occasions for individuals that were relatively

---

* http://www.hallmark.com/Website/hallmark_home.html

serious versus relatively frivolous. Condolence (sympathy) and humorous birthday cards were chosen to represent the relatively more serious and relatively more frivolous contexts, respectively. A pretest ($n = 39$) established that birthday cards are perceived to be relatively less serious ($M = 3.33$ on a 1–7 scale anchored at "1 = Not at all" and "7 = Very" serious) than condolence cards ($M = 5.33$, paired $t\,(38) = 6.55$, $p < .001$).

Sampling Method

Twenty cards from each subcategory were selected at random from a Hallmark display in a grocery store in a West Coast city. Cards were selected by choosing a starting point at random and then counting every tenth card, repeating through the selection as necessary to obtain twenty cards per subcategory.

Results

As predicted by H1, the variance of ratios for the relatively more serious condolence cards was smaller than for the relatively less serious birthday cards (variances = .000086 and .1069; $F\,(19, 19) = 1173.8$, $p < .0001$), and its range of ratios was smaller (range = 1.43–1.47 vs. 1.22–2.31 for condolence vs. birthday cards respectively).

Study 3: Newspaper Display Ads

Operationalization of Seriousness of Context

Study 3 examined newspaper display ads appearing in two newspapers on a specific day. We operationalized the seriousness of context for newspapers by choosing a business newspaper, the *Wall Street Journal* (*WSJ*), to represent a relatively less frivolous context, and a family newspaper, the *San Francisco Chronicle* (*SFC*), to represent a relatively more frivolous context.

Further, the SFC is divided into seven different sections that vary along the serious/frivolous dimension. Four of these sections—Front

Page, Bay Area News, News, and Business—are relatively more serious in their content, while three other sections—Datebook (movie and TV listings and articles, social gossip, and horoscopes), Sporting Green, and East Bay Friday—are relatively more frivolous. This gives the opportunity to test H1 both across the two newspapers and across the sections of the *SFC*.

Results of a pretest conducted with undergraduate students in the San Francisco Bay area ($n = 41$) showed that overall newspapers (as a category) are rated 5.23 on a 7-point scale with higher numbers indicating greater seriousness. The *SFC*, as a whole, is rated as less serious than *WSJ* ($M = 4.52$ vs. 6.50, $t(40) = 5.72$, $p < .01$). Further, each of the four sections classified here as relatively serious was rated as more serious ($M = 5.24$, 4.85, 5.30, and 5.16 for Front Page, Bay Area News, News, and Business, respectively), than each of the three sections categorized as less serious ($M = 3.73$, 2.90 and 2.78 for Sporting Green, Datebook, and East Bay Friday, respectively, $p < .05$).

Sampling Method

The number of display ads ($n = 118$) was small enough to permit a census of all advertisements beyond a given size. There were a total of 36 display ads in that day's *WSJ* and 82 ads in the *SFC*. A Friday newspaper (October 19, 2001) was selected in each of the two categories. The section (e.g., Economy, International in *WSJ*), page number, height, and width of each ad were recorded.

Results

The *SFC* ads had a higher variance (range = 1.02–9.56, variance = 4.45) than the *WSJ* ads (range = 1.05–3.70, variance = .36; $F(81, 35) = 12.33$, $p < .01$). Further, ads in the relatively more frivolous sections of the *SFC* had a higher variance (7.36) than those in the less frivolous ones (variance = 1.07 $F(38,42) = 6.91$, $p < .0001$). Therefore, H1 was supported both across different newspapers and across sections of the same newspaper.

Study 4: Books

Operationalization of Seriousness of Context

In a bookstore, the categories "Children's Books" and "General Science Books" were chosen to represent the relatively more and less frivolous contexts respectively. A pretest (n = 39) showed that children's books are rated as less serious than science books (M = 2.54 vs. 5.00, t (38) = 7.64, p < .001).

Sampling Method

Thirty books were selected from each subcategory. We chose a starting point at random and then selected every tenth book title, repeating as necessary to obtain a sample of 30 books. The ratios of the sides of each book's cover were taken from dimensions provided on the Amazon.com website. These dimensions appeared on the same web page that described the book and contained a picture of the cover.

Results

The variance in the ratio of the sides was higher for the children's books (0.025) than for the science books (0.009; F tests for unequal variances, p < .01). The range of ratios of children's books was also wider (1.00–1.64) than the range of science books (1.13–1.57).

To summarize, four studies found convergent evidence that rectangular ratios found in marketplace offerings in a product subcategory that is used in a relatively more serious context have less variation than ratios for a subcategory of the same product that is used in a relatively less frivolous context. This section is illustrative of the manner in which specific research questions can be derived from the conceptual model and tested empirically.

A Proposed Research Agenda

The geometry of products and packages may affect marketplace phenomena that are of interest to marketers and consumer researchers but which have been less studied in the research examining geometry from the perspective of psychology and aesthetics. Next, we discuss an agenda for research on geometry in the marketplace, intended to fill some of the gaps.

Geometry and Competition

Most perceptual experiments do not ask participants which stimuli they wish to see. However, consumers typically form consideration sets of competing products, which omit many products, and then choose from the consideration set. If competing products have different geometric features, marketers need to consider which features tend to motivate consumers to include the product in their consideration set, and then choose that product over competitors in the set. One interesting area for research is to determine how different designs compete. For example, if some products share a geometric feature, does this make consumers more likely to choose a product that shares the common feature, or one that differs from the others? An analogous situation has occurred with personal digital music players. Apple's iPod uses a very simple design, featuring subtly rounded corners and a prominent circle, to differentiate itself from its competitors. Previously Apple differentiated iMac computers by their unusual hemispherical shape. However, not all of the geometric designs in products associated with Steve Jobs, Apple's CEO, have succeeded. In the late 1980s Jobs helped design the NeXT personal computer, a distinctive black cube, which was not commercially successful.

Marketers might also examine how different shapes compete with each other on both an abstract level and when applied to particular products. For example, if an iPod's design features a rectangle with rounded corners and a circle inside, is the best design strategy for a new competing product to use a similar design, or to use a rectangle with different proportions, or introduce an oval or triangular product? Or might an entirely new shape, such as one with two basic shapes superimposed over each other, such as a circle over a rectangle, be more successful? Suppose that the missing part of a shape that the consumer must mentally supply was subtly reproduced on a firm's logo. Would this increase a product's appeal, since the consumer has mentally generated the same shape that the corporation uses?

Mental Processing of Geometry

While considerable research exists on how consumers process information for most product attributes, research on geometric shapes has focused on preferences for these shapes, and not on how people gather information to arrive at those preferences. Research on rectangular preferences has only examined this question occasionally. For example, Ohta (1999) proposed a model of "the decision process of preferred quadrangle shapes" (Ohta, 1999, p. 515) that included stages of "imagining concrete objects" and "transformation of the figure [quadrangle]." He used eye tracking and interviews to obtain a richer perspective on how people process information from simple quadrangle figures. Ohta found that while some participants always treated quadrangles abstractly, others attempted to impose concrete identities on them, such as bathtubs, windows, or even a basketball court. Some participants switched between abstract and concrete modes.

The eye tracking methodology used by Ohta has appeared in several applications in consumer behavior (Lohse & Johnson, 1996; Russo & Leclerc, 1994; Wedel & Pieters, 2000), as have interview techniques. Neither has been applied to study geometry in product design, however. While Ohta limited his study to simple shapes, marketers might examine how people process two- and three-dimensional shapes when they are told what category the product belongs to, or are given other information relevant for consumer behavior. For example, will consumers process geometric shapes differently if they are told that the product is a dish as opposed to a lamp? Suppose it is an expensive dish versus a cheap one, or a product in a relatively new category, such as an e-book, versus a relatively mature product such as a cell phone?

Consumer behavior researchers have also given attention to conscious versus unconscious, or "automatic," processing of information. (Fitzsimons et al., 2002). Based on Ohta's (1999) results, it is apparent that at least some processing of geometric shapes takes place on a conscious level. However, it seems likely that much of this processing is automatic, especially when information on shapes is processed concurrently with information on other attributes.

Reducing Cognitive Effort for Processing Shapes

Consumers often prefer products that reduce the need for cognitive effort. Marketers might want to avoid shapes that require effort to fill in missing pieces or patterns. However, consumers may not prefer that product designers complete patterns that the consumer brain usually must complete. Zeki (1999, ch. 6) discusses how cubist artists tried to show, on a single, painted plane, what a viewer can only see from multiple perspectives. Zeki considers cubism to be unsuccessful, concluding that "The brain of course regularly views objects and people from different angles, but it is able to integrate these different views in an orderly way....The attempt by cubism to mimic what the brain does was, in the neurobiological sense, a failure" (p. 54).

Our point here is not whether or not one should agree with Zeki (he acknowledges that many people would disagree), but rather that his conclusion raises the question of whether design variations intended to do the work of the brain will succeed. For example, Picasso's more demanding cubist works tend to sell for less at auction than his compositions that portray a subject more realistically, such as early works from his Blue and Rose Periods, even though the latter are not the works that made his reputation as a revolutionary artist. Consumer reactions to product designs that simplify processing may be different for more functional or utilitarian products compared to works of art, so we consider the question of how design might facilitate processing of shapes to be far from answered.

PostPurchase Experience

Consumer behavior is also interested postpurchase experience, which is a key determinant of satisfaction, brand loyalty, and word-of-mouth behavior. Studies of geometry in aesthetics and psychology, however, almost all end when the experimental session ends—participants are not asked to take a shape home and report back in a week on their intent to buy or recommend it.

Perhaps the most interesting research opportunity in this respect is whether a product's geometric design creates performance expectations that can affect postpurchase satisfaction. For example, some computer keyboards place the numeric keypad in a second keyboard distinct from the main keyboard, which changes the usual 3:1 keyboard ratio to two rectangular keyboards, one larger and horizontal with a ratio of about 2:1 and a smaller, vertical one with a ratio of about 2:1. While the keyboards are separated for ergonomic reasons—left- and right-handed people can choose where to place the keypad, and the mouse can now be placed closer to the letter keys—consumers might perceive that the unusual rectangular dimensions are also related to other product differences, such as quieter keys.

Second, if a product is used at home, consumers may pay attention after purchase to how it fits with other shapes. A microwave oven with a distinctive oval shape might appeal to consumers in a store, but seem jarring once placed alongside other products in a kitchen. Alternatively, the distinctive microwave might help transform the appearance of other kitchen objects and make them more appealing. General Electric recently introduced a 6-foot wide refrigerator that changes the usual vertical rectangular profile to a square. Such a ratio is quite unusual for a refrigerator. No doubt many customers for this appliance may anticipate that it will radically improve the look of their kitchen, creating high expectations that the refrigerator may not be able to meet for some people. One recent buyer of a 48-inch-wide refrigerator was described as "taken aback at the size when it was delivered several weeks later," and was quoted as saying "I thought, 'What have I done?'" (Schaefer, 2006).

Can changes in design intended to improve consumer perceptions compensate for other product changes that lower utility? One well-known U.S. orange juice company recently replaced some of its 16-ounce "milk carton" cardboard containers with a new plastic container, shaped like a hemisphere placed on top of a cylinder. Less obvious is that the contents were reduced to 14 ounces.

Processing of Product Shapes

If even a small lip is placed around a plain clay pot, its appearance can be much different, due to the increased complexity. As a product becomes more complex, consumers may paradoxically perceive it in a more simplified form. Researchers disagree over whether people tend to perceive an object or shape using simplified interpretations, termed the *simplicity principle*, or using more complex, but more likely, interpretations, termed the *likelihood principle* (Hatfield & Epstein, 1985, see van der Helm, 2000, on reconciling these two principles).

Without taking sides in this debate, we feel that the question of how consumers perceive product designs is worth examining. For instance, in the example of the square refrigerator, consumers using a likelihood principle are likely to be more confused by this design than those using a simplicity principle. Even when product design uses very complicated shapes, it is useful to know how consumers are processing those shapes. For instance, do consumers looking at an iPod perceive the rectangle, the circle, or both? Questions of simplicity versus likelihood may be most important for consumers' first impressions of products, formed before they may know a product's attributes, or even its product category. Marketers may want to know if it is more advantageous to appeal to simplicity or likelihood, or if consumers can be segmented based on which approach they use.

An Integrative Conceptual Model of Consumer Response to Geometry

While we feel that it is useful to study how geometry in design affects factors of interest in the marketplace, many fruitful research opportunities lie with a broader and more integrative conceptual approach that does not draw boundaries between consumer behavior and other disciplines. Here, we present a conceptual model of consumer response to geometry that, while including concepts from consumer behavior, also draws from concepts in art, architecture and aesthetics. This model is intended both as a conceptualization of how consumers respond to geometry and as a starting point to encourage cross-disciplinary work in the area of response to geometry that includes the consumer realm but is not exclusive to it. This model delineates:

1. Primary geometric properties (complexity, curvature, congruence, and completeness)
2. Routes by which they affect consumer judgments (attention, affect, and inferences)
3. Factors moderating their effect (consumer context and individual differences)
4. Types of consumer judgments (perceptual, sensory, cognitive, affective, and conative)
5. Marketing mix implications (for product design, placement, promotion, and pricing)

The model is depicted in Figure 6.1 and summarized below. The model proposes that:

1. Geometric properties affect:
   a. The amount of attention that is directed to an object or figure; and
   b. The production and delivery costs of a product.
2. The extent to which the geometric properties affect attention is moderated by two sets of moderating constructs: the consumer context and individual differences.
3. Attention, in turn, affects both the affect aroused by an object, as well as the inferences drawn about it.
4. The extent to which attention leads to affect is moderated by the consumer context.
5. The extent to which attention leads to different types of inferences is moderated by individual differences.
6. Affect associated with an object also translates into inferences drawn about that object.
7. The level and type of affect, and the types of inferences drawn, together affect consumer judgments.
8. The production and delivery costs of a product (affected by geometric properties) translate into marketplace offerings, contingent on consumer judgments (which are also affected by geometric properties).
9. The model contains feedback, inasmuch as marketplace offerings, in turn, affect the consumer context.

The model is proposed as a set of testable hypotheses delineating constructs and paths that can serve as a guide map for future research interested in examining the implications of geometry for marketplace offerings from a multidisciplinary perspective. It is not comprehensive, but more suggestive of the manner in which the shape and form of objects can affect marketplace offerings through multiple routes. It is conjectural in nature, albeit falsifiable through future empirical testing.

Geometric Properties: A Proposed Categorization

We propose that there are four main categories of geometric features: their *complexity* (including their dimensionality, form, regularity, and clutter), *curvature* (including their circularity, angularity, and convergence), *congruence* (including symmetry, stability, and centrality), and

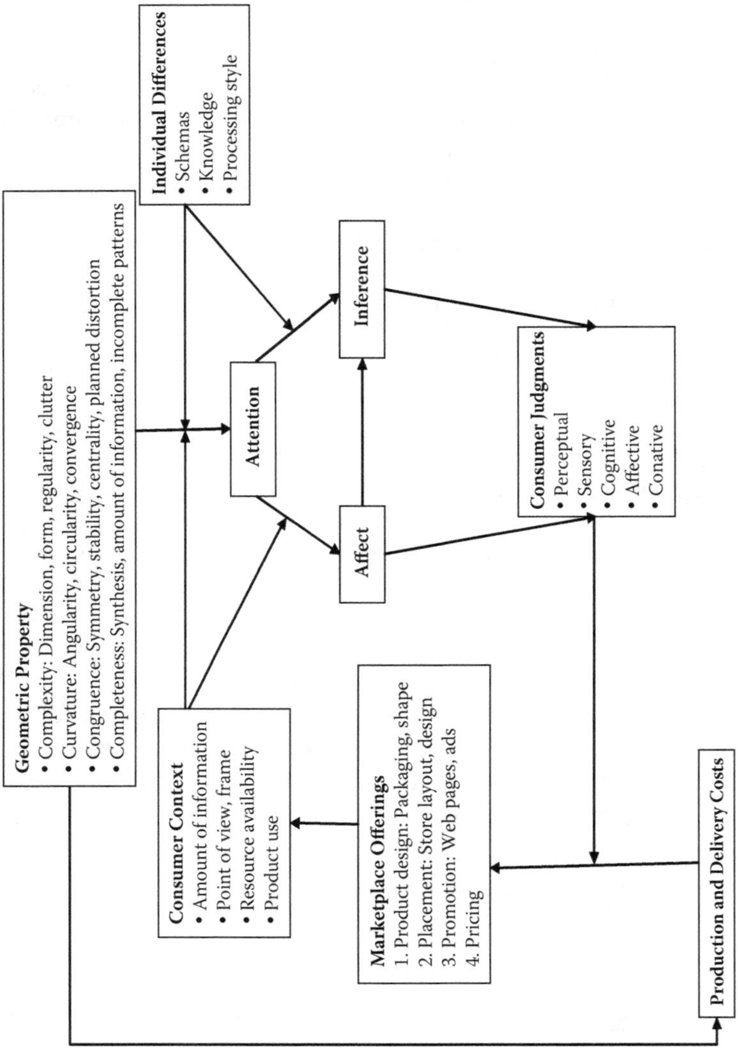

Figure 6.1 An integrative conceptual model of consumer response to geometry.

completeness (including synthesis and amount of information). These primary geometric properties may not be of equal abstraction level. Some argue that curvature is a basic perceptual feature (preattentively attracting attention; Wolfe, 1998), while complexity may be a higher order perceptual dimension encompassing various more specific dimensions. Each of these is briefly defined below:

1. *Complexity:* Complexity pertains to the number of different measures that need to be used to completely describe a shape. We propose that there are four aspects of complexity:
   - ***Dimensionality:*** We propose that two-dimensional shapes (e.g., squares and circles) are less complex than three-dimensional ones (e.g., cubes and spheres), holding other aspects of the shape form constant. A shape that changes form across time can be thought of a four-dimensional shape (e.g., an undulating wave), and is more complex than a three-dimensional shape.
   - ***Form:*** The most common form categories for regular geometric objects are round (circle, sphere, and cylinder), triangular (triangles, pyramids), and rectangular (square, rectangle, and hexahedrons such as the cube and cuboid). Examples of other form classes include the five Platonic Solids: cube, tetrahedron, octahedron, icosahedron, and the dodecahedron. These shapes can be described in terms of their number of vertices (V), faces (F), and edges (E), with these three related as per Euler's Formula $V + F = E + 2$. For example, the tetrahedron has 4 vertices, 4 faces of a triangular shape, and 6 edges, while the dodecahedron has 20 vertices, 12 faces of a pentagonal shape, and 30 edges. We propose that the fewer the faces, vertices, and edges, the less complex the geometric form. By this definition, the sphere with one face, and no vertices or edges, is the least complex form, with both its circumference and volume described by a single parameter: its radius.
   - ***Regularity:*** Regularity pertains to whether a shape follows a strict geometric pattern or whether it deviates from it, thus requiring additional parameters to capture its shape, volume, and circumference. For example, a can is a cylinder that is a regular shape defined by its radius, while most bottles have an elongated neck of a different radius than their body, requiring their volume/circumference to be described using at least two radii, and therefore, being more complex than a simple cylinder.

- ***Clutter:*** The clutter or simplicity of a shape or pattern is defined as the number of lines required to capture it (or the amount of matter in a given space). The greater the lines (matter), the greater the clutter in the shape (space). This concept of clutter derives from feng shui, the ancient Chinese philosophy of wind and water with implications for aesthetics and energy. For example, a pattern that has many lines and shapes is more cluttered than one with fewer lines and shapes. A website with fewer icons is less cluttered than one with many; a store space with fewer displays placed far apart is less cluttered than one which is crowded.

2. *Curvature*
   - ***Angularity:*** Another aspect of geometric shapes is their angularity, ranging from a dot (360 degrees), to a straight line (180 degrees), to obtuse (> 90 degrees), right (90 degrees), and acute (< 90 degrees) angles.
   - ***Circularity:*** The lack of angularity defines the circularity of a geometric shape. The extent to which the circularity is constant through the shape (as in a sphere) or changes (as in a cone) is defined as the complexity of its circularity.
   - ***Convergence:*** The extent to which a shape converges (as does a circle) or diverges (as does a spiral) is another aspect of its geometric shape.
3. *Congruence*
   - ***Symmetry:*** Symmetry is defined as "Exact correspondence in size and position of opposite parts; equable distribution of parts about a dividing line or center."* When the object remains symmetrical when the dividing line or plane is rotated, this is referred to as rotational symmetry. Thus, a circle is rotationally symmetric, while an ellipse is symmetric only along its horizontal and vertical axes. In a geometric sense, we further define symmetry as the ratio of the proportions of the sides of a figure. When they are equal or in a 1:1 ratio, we refer to the figure as symmetric, while when they deviate (e.g., in the ratio of 1:1.618), we capture this under the extent of asymmetry in the figure. For example, this property was explored in greater detail in the empirical section, where we examine marketplace variations in the ratios of rectangular products. A specific example of symmetry is planned distortion, discussed next.
   - ***Planned Distortion:*** Often product designers intentionally distort a shape or package. Although planned distortions have

---

* *The Oxford English Dictionary*, 2nd ed, 1989.

received attention from psychologists and aestheticians, they have received little attention in marketing, yet deserve study. Planned distortions typically reduce actual congruence. Sometimes, however, planned distortions can increase the congruence perceived by the human eye, by correcting for irregularities in human vision. For example, if the sides of an object are truly parallel and straight, they will appear to be bowed slightly inward. If the sides are bowed slightly outwards, a practice known as *entasis*, they will appear parallel. As another example, if the vertical axes of architectural columns are truly parallel, they appear to diverge slightly, which can make a structure appear less attractive, and less solid and able to bear weight. This apparent divergence can be corrected by making the columns tilt in slightly. Both entasis and inward tilt were used in many Doric Greek temples, including the Parthenon. The centerlines of the columns of the Parthenon's front facade tilt inward slightly, and meet approximately 7,000 feet above the ground. Greek Doric architecture employed many other planned distortions, such as tapering columns and slightly domed floors (Lawrence, 1973, ch. 15; Haselberger, 1999, on the use of curvature). Interestingly, later Greek architecture exaggerated many of these planned distortions, such as entasis, so they became an observable characteristic of buildings. Some commentators have criticized this as a "coarsening" of Greek architecture (Lawrence, 1973, p. 171), but other motives for the change are possible. For example, later Greek architects may have exaggerated planned distortion to help establish a design identity distinct from earlier architects. This question is of interest to marketers and consumer behavior researchers as an historic example of planned distortion. Entasis is not just an historic design artifact, however, it is used today in the grille of the Rolls-Royce automobile, and in beverage cans whose sides are slightly bowed out.

- ***Stability:*** The lower the center of gravity of an object, the greater its stability. Thus, conical shapes are more stable than cylinders, and pyramids more stable than cuboids. In a two-dimensional space, the center of the shape would define its stability in an analogous manner.
- ***Centrality:*** The extent to which an object is positioned close to the center of gravity of its frame is defined as its centrality. For example, the placement of a person or product in the center of an array affects perceptions of how good that product/person is, and, therefore, affects the manner in which positive and negative information about that entity are processed: errors

made by people in the center of an array are overlooked as compared to errors made by people at the extremes of an array (Raghubir & Valenzuela, 2006).

4. Completeness
   - ***Synthesis:*** The extent to which subsegments of a shape reflect each other in a symmetrical way and join to form another shape is defined as the synthesis of the shape. For example, the yin and yang reflection within a circle is an example where two disparate halves synthesize into a whole. A square divided into two triangles is another example of two different shapes that synthesize into a square. One of the neatest examples of synthesis is the proof of the Pythagorean Theorem by Bhaskara (an Indian mathematician born in A.D. 1114) where four equal right-angle triangles circumscribe a square within a larger square (see Huntley, 1970, p. 85).
   - ***Amount of Information and Incomplete Patterns and Shapes:*** The extent to which a shape or pattern is complete versus incomplete is defined as the amount of information it contains. Incomplete patterns and shapes are a particularly interesting feature to examine. Research on perceptions of geometric forms has found that if people view only part of an overall pattern, they will mentally fill in the remainder of the missing pattern based on their expectations of what the missing piece looks like. For example, Boselie (1984) finds that the golden ratio is preferred only when different parts of a pattern create this ratio in relationship to each other. Bouleau (1963/1980) presents an analysis of Mondrian's "Painting I" (Museum of Modern Art, New York) that shows how the artist used the golden ratio in a larger overall pattern, only part of which is included in the painting itself (see Boselie, 1992, for a use of Bouleau's analysis of "Painting I"). Research on perceptions of missing pieces of forms and patterns has drawn the distinction between local completions, where mental reconstruction of the missing piece depends only on features near the area that must be reconstructed, and global completions, where this reconstruction depends on overall features, including those distant from the reconstructed area. Researchers have also examined perceptions of complete shapes that are blocked or occluded by another shape (van Lier & Wagemans, 1999). Interestingly, Bouleau's (1963/1980) analysis of "Painting I" assumes that two superimposed shapes are optically (or at least cognitively) transparent, so that they do not block each other, and the viewer simultaneously sees the edges and patterns of both shapes. Pattern incompleteness can affect

the popularity of works of art. In "Eel Spearing at Setauket," (New York State Historical Association, Cooperstown) by the American artist William Sidney Mount, the long handle of the eel spear held by the fishing woman in the bow combines with the boat in which she stands to make two sides of a triangle. The viewer must complete the third side. The completed triangle contributes to the painting's stability—the scene feels calm and unhurried, and we feel assured that the young man in the stern keeping the boat stable with his paddle will maintain control. The woman will not topple. Many Renaissance paintings use subtly pyramidal compositions involving incomplete patterns. Raphael's "Madonna of the Chair" is still a favorite with consumers, and appears on countless plates and wall plaques purchased by tourists visiting Italy.

When patterns are more complete and evident, art may lose its appeal. The boxing pictures that the American artist George Bellows created early in his career, such as "Both Members of this Club" (National Gallery, Washington, D.C.) and "Stag and Sharkey's" (Cleveland Museum of Art), both from 1909, are among his most well-known works, with an unsettlingly honest depiction of brutality and violence that lives up to Bellows's oft-quoted statement that "I don't know anything about boxing. I'm just painting two men trying to kill each other" (Peck, 2001). In 1918, Bellows's became greatly influenced by Jay Hambidge's (Hambidge, 1926/1967) artistic philosophy of "Dynamic Symmetry," which featured an overtly geometric treatment of composition (Braider, 1971). The later boxing pictures that Bellows painted, such as "Dempsey and Firpo" from 1924 (Whitney Museum of American Art, New York) have more obvious geometric patterns. However, this use of almost complete patterns, such as in the triangular stance of Luis Firpo knocking Jack Dempsey through the ropes in the first round, creates a static composition that lacks the visceral feel of the earlier boxing paintings.

Product design often requires consumers to mentally reconstruct missing or occluded shapes and forms. For example, what kind of inferences do people draw about the rest of a car, based on the part that they can see? Beginning with the 1949 Cadillac, and continuing to the early 1960s, car designers, particularly in the United States, placed tailfins on the rear of cars, which were so large that they were visible from the front. The tailfins reduced the need for consumers to mentally reconstruct the rear parts of the car.

Constructs Mediating the Effect of Geometric Properties on Consumer Judgments

We propose that there are three mediating constructs through which geometric properties affect consumer judgments. Attention, which in turn affects both affect and inferences, with affect also exerting an independent influence on inferences. Affect and inferences, then, both influence consumer judgments.

1. *Attention:* The extent to which the human eye is consciously or otherwise drawn to a particular object and the manner in which it processes the information contained in the object. For example, whether an object is noticed or not is a function of the amount of attention directed to it (see Folkes & Matta, 2004, for an example of the manner in which unusual shapes attract more attention than regular ones). Further, the process by which attention is directed pertains to what specific aspect of the object attracts attention more or earlier than others (see Wedel & Pieters, this volume, for a model of attention).
2. *Affect:* The feelings and emotions associated with an object are defined as affect. For example, the extent to which a rectangular product or package cues the feeling of harmony (Raghubir & Greenleaf, 2006), or the yin-yang symbol cues the feeling of peacefulness, would be categorized in terms of the affect generated by a geometric shape. These feelings can also translate into inferences.
3. *Inferences:* The thoughts and beliefs associated with an object are defined as the inferences drawn from the object. For example, the extent to which a circle is perceived to be "warm," a triangle "stable," a square "unexciting," or a kite "fun" may all be captured in terms of the inferences that people draw from the shape of certain items. The inferences can be feeling-laden or affectively-tempered as above, but need not be. For example, an inference of "expensive" or "luxury," for a long-necked bottle as compared to a squat one may be based on preexisting beliefs regarding costs of production or based on the shape priming another figure that is associated with the inference in question.

Factors Moderating the Effect of Geometric Properties on Attention and the Effect of Attention on Affect and Inferences

We propose that the extent to which a geometric property affects attention is a function of the consumer context and the individual within that context. Further, these two sets of factors also influence the extent to which and the manner in which attention translates into affect and inferences.

1. Individual Differences
    - ***Schemas:*** These are defined as preexisting beliefs regarding the relationship between two (or more) constructs. In the context of geometric shapes, a schema could be that "those who sit in the middle are more important," (Raghubir & Valenzuela, 2006), which could lead to inferences regarding centrality of placement on prior perceptions of quality of an entity. These schemas could also affect processing fluency, which could itself bring with it affective and inferential consequences (see Schwarz, this volume).
    - ***Knowledge:*** The extent to which individuals have specific information regarding a product, the less likely it is that they will use other information, such as geometric shapes to draw inferences about the aspects of that product (Alba & Hutchinson, 1987).
    - ***Processing Style:*** The more visual (versus verbal) the processing style and preference of individuals, the greater should be the effect of geometric features on attention and the follow through of attention to inferences (Pham, Meyvis, & Zhou, 2001).
2. Consumer Context
    - ***Amount of Information***: The greater the extent to which information regarding the judgments is readily available in the consumer context (e.g., information about quality, price, etc.), the lower should be the effect of geometric features.
    - ***Point of View:*** The angle of view, including the larger context could also affect the amount of attention and the manner in which it is employed. For example, aerial and frontal views may provide different amounts of information and perspectives on a product (see Meyers-Levy & Peracchio, 1992, for an example of how the angle at which a picture is taken affects judgments regarding the product, with more favorable judgments when the photographer perspective is upwards rather than downwards).
    - ***Frames:*** The visual frame (defined in terms of the same geometric features as the object itself) may also affect the amount of attention directed to an object and the feelings aroused by it. For example, Meyers-Levy and Zhu (this volume) show how ceiling height affects creativity.

- ***Resource Availability:*** The extent to which consumers have the cognitive resources available to make judgments and correct these judgments if required may also affect the manner in which geometric properties translate into consumer judgments (see Raghubir, this volume, for a model of what resource availability leads to what type of information processing method).
- ***Product Use:*** The context in which the consumer uses the product may also affect the consumer impact of geometric features. For example, the relative seriousness versus frivolousness of the occasions for which a product is used or purchased, which was studied earlier in this paper, may also affect the relationship between attention and affect, and may be affected by the range of offerings in the marketplace.

Consumer Judgments

We consider implications of geometric properties for five categories of consumer judgments with examples for each.

1. *Perceptual:* Perception involves visual cues and is a process by which the eye processes information (see chapters this volume by Janiszewski, Pieters & Wedel, Rayner & Castelhano, and Tavassoli).
2. *Sensory:* Sensation involves the processing of information by senses other than sight, including taste, smell, touch, and sound. Open questions are whether the geometric shape of a product would influence its taste, or other sensory properties. For example, does the shape of a perfume bottle affect how consumers believe it smells on them?
3. *Cognitive:* Cognitive judgments include beliefs regarding the product, such as its size. They could be based on perceptual inputs such as its length (see Krishna, this volume for a review).
4. *Affective:* The feelings associated with a shape, moods, and emotions may all be affected by geometric shapes. The ancient concept of *feng shui*, has for many centuries proposed that specific aspects of a spatial arena affect various aspects of the human interacting within that arena, and is commonly used in architectural contexts in Asia (especially China, Korea, Japan, and Taiwan).
5. *Conative:* Finally, actions, such as purchase intentions, and choices could also be affected by geometric shapes (for examples of different actions and choices, see chapters this volume by Chandon, Hutchinson, Bradlow & Young, Cho, Schwarz & Song, Meyers-Levi & Zhu).

Marketing Implications

The main implication of the model is that geometric properties affect marketplace offerings through two routes: directly via costs of production and delivery, and indirectly, via their influence on consumer judgments. While the former is possibly well known to manufacturers and retailers, it is the latter that could lead to either synergistic or counterproductive effects.

1. *Production Costs*: The effect of shape on costs of production is dictated by the shape of the raw material used, and the volume desired. The shape that minimizes wasted material would be the most cost effective. Thus, given a square sheet, squares, rectangles, and triangles would be more cost effective to cut out of the square sheet than circles and ovals. It is possible that the use of the golden ratio in marketplace offerings also traced back to its unique geometric property that cutting a square from a golden rectangle left another golden rectangle. Thus, for manufacturers interested in manufacturing multiple sizes of the same shape of product (such as stationery), the use of the golden rectangle could have been cost effective. The fact that it may also be aesthetically pleasing is a separate issue.
2. *Marketplace Offerings:* Below, we list some possible implications for marketing in terms of tactics involving the "four Ps" of the marketing mix:
   - *Product Design:* packaging and shape
   - *Placement*: store layouts and design
   - *Promotion*: web pages and advertisements: their size, placement, etc.
   - *Pricing:* amount to be charged, volume discounts across different shapes that belong to the same or different product categories.

The extent to which costs of production and consumer judgments translate into actual products, in turn, will affect the consumer context.

To summarize, this section has presented a conceptual framework to examine the effect of geometric features on consumers and marketplace offerings. This framework has taken a broad, integrative approach, using concepts from aesthetics and psychology as well as marketing. Our objective has been to not only pose some testable hypotheses, but also to encourage and promote researchers in all of these fields to take a multidisciplinary approach in studying the impact of geometry on consumers.

Conclusions

Geometry plays a key part in many product designs. Here, we have proposed that consumer behavior research can benefit from studying more closely consumer reactions to geometry. We have provided an empirical example of how such studies can link to the existing literature from aesthetics and psychology to help explain variations in design in the consumer marketplace and how these are affected by context—in this case, the relative seriousness versus frivolity of the occasion a product is used for.

However, research that fully addresses consumer behavior and marketing questions must incorporate issues particular to these fields. We have proposed an agenda for research on geometry in consumer behavior and product design that incorporates some of the issues, such as the competitive nature of consumer choice and the importance of the postpurchase experience. This agenda is not meant to be exhaustive. There are many other issues of concern in consumer behavior and marketing that are usually not investigated in work in psychology and aesthetics.

We have also proposed a broader model of how consumers may be influenced by geometry, which we hope will encourage other researchers to examine these kinds of questions both from a broad perspective that should have the greatest potential to yield new and exciting findings. This model combines concepts from psychology, aesthetics, and marketing, and urges a multidisciplinary approach to the study of geometry's impact on consumers. Although these three fields are often regarded as disparate, they are often very closely linked.

For example, the paintings and works of architecture so often studied in aesthetics, and often used as stimuli in psychology experiments (albeit sometimes in a more abstracted form), were originally created as consumer products. The artists who made them were often very concerned with how the reaction of the marketplace might affect their reputation, their standing among collectors who might purchase their work or individuals and civil and religious entities who might commission future works, and the prices they could command in a competitive marketplace. An oft repeated story that bears out this point is that Michelangelo, upon hearing that admiring visitors believed that his masterpiece, the *Pieta* (a notably pyramidal composition) was sculpted by another artist, stole in at night to where the sculpture was displayed and carved his name on the Virgin's sash. Whether this story is true or was fabricated by Michelangelo's admirers (or detractors?), it illustrates the importance of consumer issues in even the most revered works of art.

In sum, we have studied consumers and geometry by beginning with a more conventional empirical study and broadening to a more conceptual proposal for research in this area, and to an integrative conceptual model of how consumers react to geometry, and how geometry can affect the marketplace. In a time when firms are placing increasing attention on consumer design, we hope that these efforts will encourage researchers to give more attention to geometry as part of the consumer milieu, just as Michelangelo drew attention to his own work half a millennium ago.

Acknowledgments

The authors thank Rishi Chand and Jane Gu for their assistance with survey data collection. The comments of participants at the 2005 IC-1 Conference on Visual Marketing at Ann Arbor, Michigan are gratefully acknowledged. The authors contributed equally to this manuscript, and authorship is alphabetical.

References

Alba, J. W., & Hutchinson, J. W. (1987). Dimensions of consumer expertise. *Journal of Consumer Research, 13*(4), 411–454.

Benjafield, J. (1976). The "golden rectangle": Some new data. *American Journal of Psychology, 89*(4), 737–743.

Bloch, P. H. (1995). Seeking the ideal form: Product design and consumer response. *Journal of Marketing, 59*(3), 16–29.

Borissavliévitch, M. (1958). *The golden number and the scientific aesthetics of architecture.* New York: Philosophical Library.

Boselie, F. (1984). The aesthetic attractivity of the golden section. *Psychological Research, 45*(4), 367–375.

Boselie, F. (1992). The golden section has no special aesthetic attractivity. *Empirical Studies of the Arts, 10*(1), 1–18.

Bouleau, C. (1980). *The painter's secret geometry: A study of composition in art* (J. Griffin, Trans.). New York: Hacker Art Books. (Original work published in 1963.)

Braider, D. (1971). *George Bellows and the Ashcan school of painting.* Garden City, NY: Doubleday.

Fechner, G. T. (1871). *Zur experimentalen aesthetik* [On the experimental aesthetics]. Leipzig: Hirzl.

Fechner, G. T. (1876). *Vorschule der Aesthetik* [Aesthetics introduction]. Leipzig: Breitkopf und Hartel.

Fechner, G. T. (1997). Various attempts to establish a basic form of beauty: Experimental, aesthetics, Golden Section, and square. In M. Nieman, J. Quehl, H. Höge, & C. von Jssietzky, von (Eds. & Trans.), *Empirical studies of the arts* (15th ed., pp. 115–130). Germany: Universität of Oldenburg.

Fitzsimons, G. J., Hutchinson, J. W., Williams, P., Alba, J. B., Chartrand, T. L., Huber, J., Kardes, F. R., Menon, G., Raghubir, P., Russo, J. E., Shiv, B., Tavassoli, N. T. (2002). Non-conscious influences on consumer choice. *Marketing Letters, 13*(3), 269–279.

Folkes, V., & Matta, S. (2004). The effect of package shape on consumers' judgments of product volume: Attention as a mental contaminant. *Journal of Consumer Research, 31*, 390–401.

Ghyka, M. (1977). *The geometry of art and life.* New York: Dover.

Green, C. D. (1995). All that glitters: A review of psychological research on the aesthetics of the golden section. *Perception, 24*(8), 937–968.

Hambidge, J. (1926). *The elements of dynamic symmetry.* New York: Brentano's, reprinted by Dover, New York, 1967.

Haselberger, L. (1999, April). Appearance and essence: Refinements of classical architecture—curvature. *Proceedings of the second Williams Symposium on classical architecture held at the University of Pennsylvania, Philadelphia. Vol. 10.* University Museum symposium series, Philadelphia: University Museum, University of Pennsylvania.

Hatfield, G., & Epstein, W. (1985). The status of the minimum principle in the theoretical analysis of visual perception. *Psychological Bulletin, 97*(2), 155–186.

Herz-Fischler, R. (1987). *The mathematical history of the golden number.* New York: Dover.

Höge, H. (1997). The golden section hypothesis—Its last funeral. *Empirical Studies of the Arts, 15*(2), 233–255.

Holbrook, M. B., & Anand, P. (1992). The effect of situation, sequence, and features on perceptual and affective responses to product designs: The case of aesthetic consumption. *Empirical Studies of the Arts, 10*(1), 19–31.

Huntley, H. E. (1970). *The divine proportion: A study in mathematical beauty.* New York: Dover.

Lawlor, R. (1982). *Sacred geometry: Philosophy and practice.* London and New York: Thames & Hudson.

Lawrence, A. W. (1973). *Greek architecture* (3rd ed.). Harmondsworth, Middlesex, England; Baltimore, MD: Penguin.

Livio, M. (2002). *The golden ratio: The story of phi, the world's most astonishing number.* New York: Broadway Books, Random House.

Lohse, G. L., & Johnson, E. J. (1996). A comparison of two process tracing methods for choice tasks. *Organizational Behavior and Human Decision Processes, 68*(1), 28–43.

McManus, I. C. (1980). The aesthetics of simple figures. *British Journal of Psychology, 71*(4), 505–524.

Meyers-Levy, J., & Peracchio, L. A. (1992). Getting an angle in advertising: The effect of camera angle on product evaluations. *Journal of Marketing Research, 29*(4), 454–461.

Ohta, H. (1999). Preferences in quadrangles reconsidered. *Perception, 28*(4), 505–517.

Peck, G. (2001). George Bellows and the conflicts of his age. Essay in: *With My Profound Reverence for the Victims: George Bellows*, catalogue for exhibit held at the Samuel Dorsky Museum of Art, State University of New York, New Paltz.

Pennick, N. (1980). *Sacred geometry: Symbolism and purpose in religious structures.* San Francisco: Harper & Row.

Pham, M., Meyvis, T., & Zhou, R. (2001). Beyond the obvious: Chronic vividness of imagery and the use of information in decision-making. *Organizational Behavior and Human Decision Processes*, 84, 226–253.

Piehl, J. (1978). The golden section: The "true" ratio? *Perceptual and Motor Skills, 46*, 831–834.

Plug, C. (1976). The psychophysics of form: Scaling the perceived shape of plane figures. *South African Journal of Psychology, 6*, 9–17.

Raghubir, P., & Greenleaf, E. A. (2006). Ratios in proportion: What should the shape of the package be? *Journal of Marketing, 70*, 95–107.

Raghubir, P., & Valenzuela, A. (2006). Center of inattention: Position biases in decision making. *Organizational Behavior and Human Decision Processes, 99*(1), 66–80.

Russo, J. E., & Leclerc, F. (1994). An eye-fixation analysis of choice processes for consumer nondurables. *Journal of Consumer Research, 21*, 274–290.

Schaefer Munoz, S. (2006). Refrigerator heaven: Appliances get massive. *The Wall Street Journal*, April 27, D1.

Shortess, G. K., Clarke, J. C., & Shannon, K. (1997). The shape of things: But not the golden section. *Empirical Studies of the Arts, 15*(2), 165–176.

Svensson, L. T. (1977). Note on the golden section. *Scandinavian Journal of Psychology, 18*, 79–80.

Van Lier R., & Wagemans, J. (1999). From images to objects: Global and local completions of self-occluded parts. *Journal of Experimental Psychology: Human Perception and Performance*, *25*(6) 1721–1741.

Van der Helm, P. A. (2000). Simplicity versus likelihood in visual perception: From surprisals to precisals. *Psychological Bulletin*, *126*(5), 770–800.

Wedel, M., & Pieters, R. (2000). Eye fixations on advertisements and memory for brands: A model and findings. *Marketing Science*, *19*(4), 297–312.

Wolfe, J. M., (1998). Visual search. In H. E. Pashler (Ed.). *Attention*. Hove, East Sussex, UK: Psychology Press.

Zeki, S. (1999). *Inner vision: An exploration of art and the brain*. Oxford: Oxford Press.

7

Are Visual Perceptual Biases Hard-Wired?

Priya Raghubir

Introduction

This chapter proposes a new *hard-wired* model of perceptual judgments as part of a typology of information processing models that span the continuum of controlled to automatic processes. The model proposes that increased attention to a biasing visual stimulus exacerbates rather than attenuates a bias when the additional attention is directed toward the biasing perceptual input rather than toward alternate de-biasing information. After describing the model, visual perceptual biases as they pertain to model predictions are discussed, and are followed by suggestions for testable hypotheses to test remaining model predictions. Data showing visual perceptual biases that appear to be hard-wired are presented at the end. Including such a visual information processing model adds to the current set of information processing models that have been developed in the domain of semantic information processing.

Theoretical Framework of Visual Information Processing

Consumer behavior research in the last decade has demonstrated that visual cues are a salient, vivid, and strong input for choice of route, waiting line, package, and purchase quantity (see Krishna, this volume, for a summary of visual perceptual biases). The notion of bias, however, begs the question whether all individuals are biased or whether some are more biased than others. It also begs the corollary question of whether judgments of biased individuals can be improved, and if so, how they can. At the heart of these questions is the issue of whether an individual can control their use of a biasing stimulus at the time of making a judgment. The issue of the lack of controllability of a bias is important as it implies that training consumers may not be an effective strategy to improve the quality of their decisions, and that consumers may continue to make inappropriate choices in spite of training. In this case, the bias could persist across all types of contexts, whether low or high stakes, and whether fleetingly made or more deliberate.

In this chapter, I propose that certain visual biases are hard-wired. That is, they cannot be controlled even though a person is aware of them, and has the opportunity, ability, and motivation to control them. This hard-wired model is proposed as one process within a larger typology of information processing models that span the continuum of controlled to automatic processes. The five information processing models discussed are:

I. Pre-conscious processing
II. Non-conscious processing
III. Heuristic processing
IV. Systematic controlled processing
V. Hard-wired processing

In two seminal articles, Schneider and Shiffrin (Schneider & Shiffrin, 1977; Shiffrin & Schneider, 1977) argued for a two-stage theory of human information processing. They argue that *automatic processing* is initially activated without necessarily demanding attention, and subsequent to the initial activation, *controlled processing* occurs which requires attention and cognitive capacity. The process is similar to an anchor-and-adjust process where the initial anchor is arrived at using some automatic process, and adjustment is part of a controlled process (see also Gilbert, 1989; Gilbert, Pelham, & Krull, 1988, for applications of a two-stage process in attribution judgments).

Bargh (1989), focusing not so much on how or when automatic processing occurs but on distinguishing it from controlled processes, argues for *conditional automaticity* where a process may have one or more of the automatic criterion (e.g., be outside of awareness, effortless, involuntary, unintentional, and uncontrollable) to be differentiated from a conscious or controlled process. If the primary input to a judgment is outside of the awareness of a consumer, it may continue to exert an effect on the final judgment even if the secondary input to the judgment is a more controlled and conscious process.

Following Bargh (1989), researchers have argued that the use of the biasing stimuli is *uncontrollable* if consumers (a) are aware of the input, (b) are aware of the biasing influence of the input on their judgments, (c) have the cognitive resources to correct for the biasing influence of the input, and (d) are adequately motivated to deploy this input to make an accurate judgment, but still make biased judgments (e.g., Gilbert et al., 1988).

Our proposed hard-wired model is consistent with this set of tests but goes one step further in suggesting that some uncontrollable biases may increase if attention is directed to the biasing stimuli, as the attention is deployed not in correcting a prior automatic anchor, but in redirecting attention to the biasing stimulus. The primary feature of the hard-wired model that distinguishes it from other processes is that increased attention to a biasing stimulus can exacerbate rather than attenuate a bias if the attention is directed toward the biasing input rather than toward alternate de-biasing information. The process is characterized by individuals being aware of the presence of the stimuli, and its influence on their judgments, as well as having the cognitive resources (e.g., time, ability, etc.) available to make an accurate judgment, as well as the motivation to be accurate, *but* the inability to control the influence of the stimulus on their judgments.

A Process Model of How Consumers Process Visual Information

Figure 7.1 depicts the typology of models. It is composed of a set of five questions. "Yes" or "No" responses to the five questions result in five alternative process outcomes. The questions (presented in a linear order, with the possibility of recursion) are:

1. Are consumers aware of the presence of the stimuli? If consumers are not aware of the presence of the stimuli but are influenced by it, then biases would fall into the category of pre-conscious processing.
2. Are consumers aware of the influence of the stimuli on their judgments? If they are aware of the presence of the stimuli, but unaware of the manner in which the stimuli affects their judgments, then this process can be described as non-conscious processing.

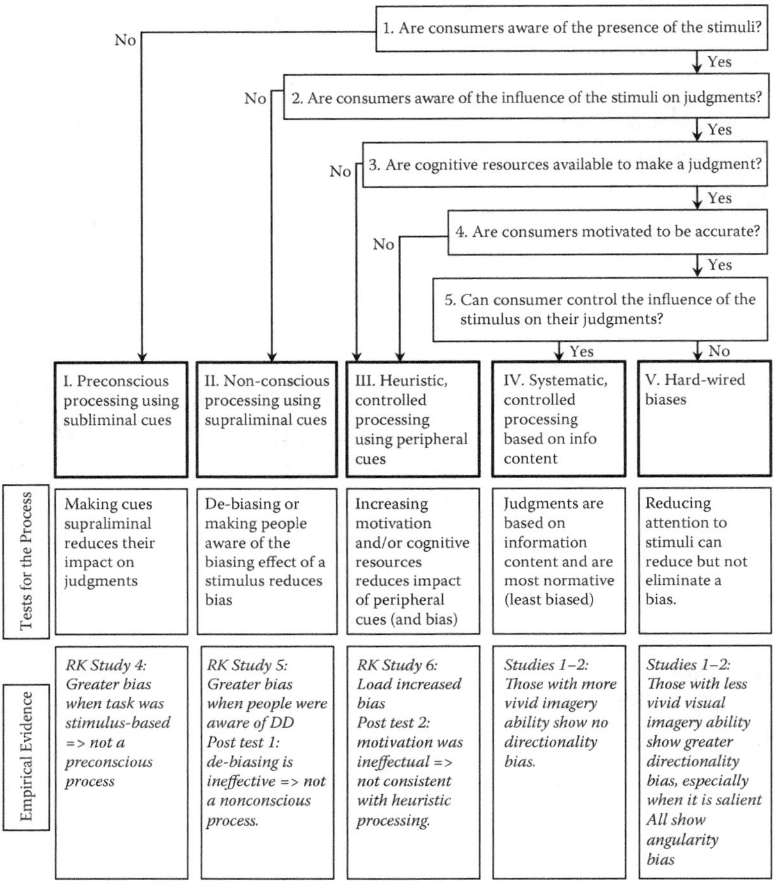

Figure 7.1 A process model and typology of how consumers process information.

3. Are cognitive resources available to make a judgment? When consumers are aware of the cue and its biasing potential, but do not have the ability to make the correct judgment, then they may deliberately process information heuristically, relying on easy-to-use heuristics even if they are biased.
4. Are consumers motivated to be accurate? Lack of ability is one factor that can lead to deliberate heuristic processing. The other is the motivation to be accurate. When the effort required to make an accurate judgment is not warranted by the level of accuracy desired, then people resort to the use of simplifying heuristics: heuristic processing.

5. Can consumers control the influence of the stimuli on their judgments? When people are aware of the cue, its biasing nature, and have the ability and motivation to be accurate they can still be biased depending on whether or not they can control the influence of the stimuli on their judgments. If they can control the influence, then their mode of processing is referred to as systematic controlled processing, and if they cannot, it leads to the proposed mode called the hard-wired bias.

Each of these modes of processing is now described along with the empirical evidence available for them.

A Typology of Information Processing Models

Pre-Conscious Processes Pre-conscious processing (Process I in Figure 7.1) operates outside of consciousness of the presence of the stimulus. Such judgments include subliminal judgments where exposures are at levels that can be detected by the human eye, but not by conscious processes in the brain. This process has been demonstrated in a variety of visual tasks involving preconscious exposure and influence by advertising (Janiszewski, 1988). Such a bias can be reduced when consumers are made aware of the stimulus (e.g., by increasing stimuli exposure times to supraliminal levels that can be detected by the human eye). In the context of subliminal priming, Herr, Sherman, and Fazio (1983) showed that the priming effect was reduced (and, in fact, reversed) when consumers were aware of the presence of the stimuli and could adjust for its possible use in their judgments.

Non-Conscious Processes Among the most studied by consumer researchers are non-conscious processes (Process II in Figure 7.1; see Bargh, 2002; Fitzsimons et al., 2002, for recent reviews of the existence of and implications regarding non-conscious processes in consumer behavior). Such processes are characterized by consumers being aware of the presence of the stimulus (Question 1), but unaware of its influence on their judgments (Question 2). Process II has been demonstrated in a number of consumer behavior domains including impulsive product choice, and the manner in which eliciting purchase intentions affects purchase incidence (e.g., Fitzsimons & Shiv, 2001; Fitzsimons & Williams, 2000; Shiv & Fedorikhin, 1999).

The argument underlying these processes is that given people's lack of awareness of the influence of the stimuli, they are unable to control their reliance on it even if they wish to. This leads them to be biased. Therefore, making consumers aware of the potentially biasing nature of the stimuli can change a non-conscious process to a conscious one. Menon and Raghubir (2003) showed that the use of *ease-of-recall* (the ease with which information comes to mind from memory as opposed to the content of this information) as information to make a judgment was automatic if people had experienced the ease or difficulty of recall prior to its being discredited as a diagnostic input (e.g., through instructions that informed them that the task was easy/difficult), but its effect reduced as consumers became aware of the influence of using recall difficulty to assess the frequency of an event. This argument presupposes that people can control the influence of the biasing stimuli (Question 5), an issue we will turn to when discussing the proposed hard-wired process V.

Conscious and Controlled Processes Heuristic processing (Process III) and systematic processing (Process IV) are both processes that are more conscious and controlled. These processes are characterized by consumers being aware not only of the presence of stimuli, but also aware of the influence of the stimuli on their judgments. When consumers are conscious of the (presence and influence of) stimuli, and can also control the influence of the stimuli on their judgments, then the process is a conscious and controlled one. Prior research has shown that opportunity, ability, and motivation to process information will lead to more systematic or central processing and less heuristic or peripheral cue-based processing and will lead to normatively less biased judgments (Petty & Cacioppo, 1986; Chaiken, 1980). In such conscious and controlled information processing, consumers' effort-accuracy tradeoffs determine whether they will make the effort to process all relevant content-based information to make a judgment. That is, whether they will undertake effortful systematic processing (Process IV), or use peripheral cues and heuristics (rules of thumb) to make a potentially less accurate, but easier judgment (Heuristic Processing: Process III). These two modes of processing apply to judgments that are the product of an information processing task that is controlled and can be made more accurate through directing cognitive resources to the task. For example, increasing the level of attention to a task would increase consumers' cognitive resources available, and, therefore, their ability to make a normatively correct assessment. In the context of attitude judgments, Maheswaran and Chaiken (1991) showed that attitudes were based more on the content of information, rather than on peripheral cues when people were motivated to make a correct judgment. This led to heuristic processing (III) converting to systematic processing (IV).

Hard-Wired Biases: A Proposed Genre of Uncontrollable Processes The heart of the process differentiating the proposed hard-wired model from earlier models is the issue as to whether the mere quantity of attention is either a necessary or a sufficient condition to de-bias individuals. I propose that if additional attention is directed at incorporating hitherto less attended aspects of the stimulus then the increase in attention will lead to better judgments only if the less attended aspects are useful for making a more accurate judgment. For example, if additional attention in a distance estimation task is directed at estimating the length of individual line segments and aggregating these, then the use of this attention will improve the accuracy of the distance estimation task. On the other hand, if the increase in attention is directed at the original biasing aspect of the stimulus, then it would increase the influence of this biasing stimulus in the overall judgment and exacerbate the original bias. The key question is, therefore, not the *amount* of attention that is deployed in the task, but the *manner in which it is directed*: toward or away from the biasing stimulus.

That this process may occur in arenas beyond visual processing is also possible. Recently Dijksterhuis, Bos, Nordgren, and Van Baaren (2006) demonstrated that the greater conscious deliberation prior to making a choice for a complex product (e.g., a home), the worse the choice. They conclude that though deliberate and conscious thought can enhance decision quality for simple choices, it can backfire for more complex ones. They refer to this as the *deliberation-without-attention* effect.

In a similar manner, I suggest that the manner in which attention is deployed differs across types of stimuli and types of consumers. For certain stimuli it is more difficult to direct increased levels of attention to the individual, alternate sources of information that comprise a visual map (e.g., individual segment lengths), making it more likely that the map will be processed as a gestalt whole (see Folkes & Matta, 2004, for a similar argument in the context of volume perceptions).

This process could be the precursor of well-known optical illusions and spatial perception biases in judgments of length, area, volume and number (see Krishna, this volume, for a review of such biases). Biases in visual perception are now discussed in terms of the above framework.

Testable Predictions of the Model There are a few testable predictions that can assist in distinguishing the hard-wired process from other information processing models that have been proposed and tested in the past. Some of these testable and falsifiable predictions in the domain of visual perceptions include:

Visual biases will be greater when information is stimuli-based rather than memory-based.

Individuals higher in need for cognition will be more biased as they will pay more attention to a task.

Individuals with lower visual imagery ability will be more biased as they will direct more attention to the biasing stimulus.

Increasing stakes and motivation levels may increase the extent of the bias rather than reducing it.

Training (i.e., providing instructions to ignore a biasing cue) may backfire as it could lead to greater attention being directed to the biasing cue.

Increased awareness of the bias could exacerbate rather than attenuate the bias, if the awareness leads to greater salience of the biasing cue.

The greater the opportunity to make a normative decision, the greater the possibility of the bias if the opportunity leads to greater attention being directed to the biasing cue.

Empirical Support for the Hard-Wired Model in the Context of the Direct Distance Bias Two studies examine whether people with (a) lower versus higher imagery ability, and (b) a verbal versus visual style of processing are prone to the direct distance bias to a greater extent than their counterparts.

Study 1

Method Study participants were 94 undergraduate students of business who completed the experimental task during a regularly scheduled class for partial course credit.

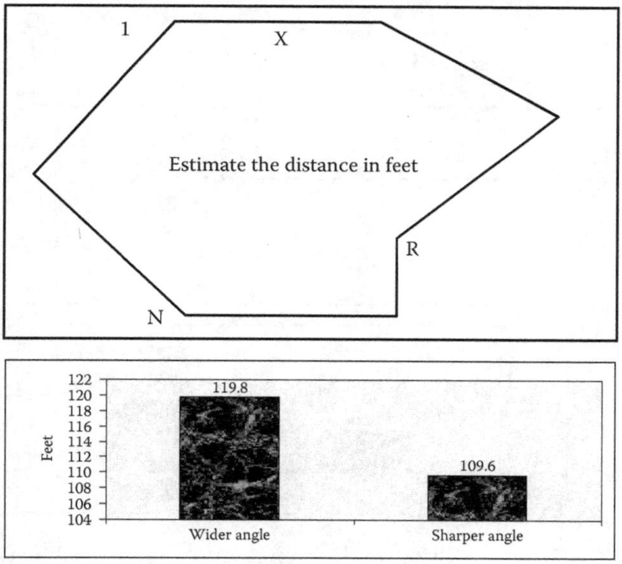

Figure 7.2 Angularity stimuli, from Raghubir and Krishna (1996).

The design was a 2 (Direct Distance: Lower vs. Higher) × 2 (Map: angularity and directionality) × 2 (Individual Difference Factor: Higher/ Lower) mixed design, with individual differences based on a tertile split along the relevant scale.

The stimuli were identical to those used in Raghubir and Krishna's (1996) Study 1. Each participant was given a map that had a pair of paths that manipulated direct distance either through angularity of segments, or through the direction of segments. Thus, angularity and directionality were both manipulated within subjects. The order of administration of the two maps: directionality (see Figure 7.2) and angularity (see Figure 7.3) was counterbalanced, such that half the participants saw the angularity manipulation first, while the other half saw the directionality manipulation first. Note that the pair of paths on each map were of equivalent distance and identical in every respect except for the manipulation. One had a longer direct distance than the other. The left–right orientation of the pair of paths was also counterbalanced: half the participants saw the path with the longer direct distance on the left-hand side and the other half saw it on the right-hand side.

The Vividness of Visual Imagery Questionnaire (VVIQ) scale used was the 16-item scale with four self-reports each of the vividness of

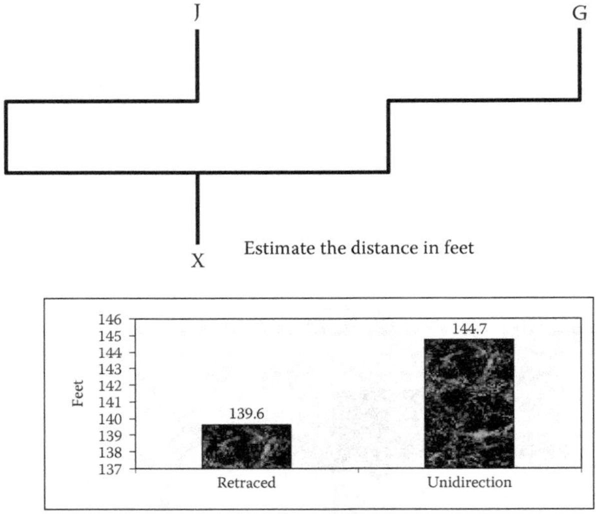

Figure 7.3 Directionality stimuli, from Raghubir and Krishna (1996).

four visual aspects of four visual images (a well-known person, the rising sun, a familiar locale, an imaginary locale), proposed by Marks (1973) and since used by Heckler, Childers, and Houston (1993) among others. Respondents rated how vivid each of the four images were on a 5-point scale, with scale points: 1. Perfectly clear and as vivid as normal vision; 2. Clear and reasonably vivid; 3. Moderately clear and vivid; 4. Vague and dim; and 5. No image at all, you only "know" that you are thinking of the object.

The Style of Processing (SOP) scale used was the 20-item scale developed by Childers, Houston, and Heckler (1985) and shown to be nomologically valid by Heckler et al. (1993). This scale asks for agreement (on a 5-point scale), with 10 statements related to preference for visual style of processing such as "My thinking often consists of mental 'pictures' or images," and "Before I perform an activity, I often close my eyes and picture doing it," and 10 statements related to preference for a verbal style of processing such as "I do a lot of reading."

The dependent measure used was the estimate of the length of the two paths on each of the maps (in feet). In addition, as a manipulation check we measured the amount of attention that subjects paid to the stimuli by asking subjects to rate how much attention they paid to the maps on a 7-point scale anchored at 1 = Paid no attention at all to 7 = Paid a lot of attention.

To rule out that our results were driven by constructs other than attention level, we also measured how motivated participants were while making the judgments, and how interested they were in the judgment task (both measured on a 7-point semantic differential scale anchored at 1 = Not at all, to 7 = Very). We also measured how confident participants were in their estimates to explore whether subject confidence was related to the extent to which they were biased. Confidence in the estimates was measured separately for both maps at the end of the distance estimation task, using a seven-point semantic differential scale anchored at "Not at All/ Very Confident." Both measures were highly correlated ($r = .79$) and were aggregated to form a confidence index.

The scales measuring visual processing preference and visual imagery ability were administered as a filler task between the two maps. Scale reliability was acceptable for both scales (SOP = 0.68, VVIQ = 0.81).

Results We first report the results of manipulation checks aimed at ascertaining that the individual subgroups differ along a scale from their counterparts; scales are independent of each other; subgroups expected to pay more attention to stimuli, in fact do so; and, groups do not differ in terms of other constructs.

Manipulation Checks

Scale Differences When moderation is to be shown using measured variables, an appropriate manipulation check is to assess whether there is adequate variance along the measure within the group, operationalized by examining whether tertile groups significantly differ in terms of their scale values. Accordingly, we conducted one-way ANOVAs using the continuous scale measure as the dependent variable and the tertile category as the independent variable for each of the three scales. These results are reported below. Thirty-two individuals were categorized as high VVIQs (scale score < 2.19 on a 5-point scale where lower scores indicate higher visual imagery ability, $M = 1.81$), and 35 as low VVIQs (scale score > 2.56, $M = 2.82$, $F(1,65) = 203.68$, $p < .001$).

The tertile split along the SOP scale was at the scale values of 3.10 (lower numbers indicating visual processing preference) and 3.30 (higher numbers indicating verbal processing preference). This resulted in 34 individuals categorized as Visual Information processors (M = 2.89) and 39 individuals categorized as Verbal Information Processors (M = 3.55, $F(1,71) = 153.54$, $p < .001$).

Orthogonality of Independent Variables Post hoc we established that the tertile splits along the scales led to orthogonal factors. A cross-tabulation of participants across SOP and VVIQ scales showed orthogonality ($\chi^2(1) = .02$, $p = .89$), replicating Heckler et al.'s (1993) result.

Level of Attention Across Groups We argue that individuals varying on VVIQ and SOP would be differentially prone to the direct distance bias because they vary in terms of the attention they pay to a visual information processing task. To assess whether this is true, we examined differences in the amount of attention paid to the stimuli across groups. We found that verbal information processors reported higher attention levels to the stimuli than did visual information processors (M = 4.83 vs. 4.27, $F(1,67) = 3.44$, $p < .05$). The same pattern was repeated for high VVIQs who reported lower attention (M = 4.19) to the stimuli than lower VVIQs (M = 4.68, $F(1,63) = 2.20$, $p < .07$). The groups did not differ in terms of their level of motivation or interest in the experiment ($p > .40$).

Hypotheses Tests The order of administration and left–right orientation did not affect the results and were ignored for further analysis ($p > .35$). Gender, too, did not exert main or interaction effects ($p > .20$). The first analysis conducted was a repeated measures MANOVA treating the two distance estimates (shorter and longer direct distance) for each of the two maps as two within-subject factors and individual difference as a between-subjects factor. Therefore, the design was a Direct distance × Map × Individual difference (2 × 2 × 2) design, where we were interested in ascertaining whether the individual difference interacted with the direct distance factor. We also expected a main effect of map as distances in the map where paths retraced were longer at 177.77 feet, than distances in the map manipulating angularity which were 153.33 feet.

If the overall 2 × 2 × 2 analysis revealed an interaction between the individual difference variable and the direct distance factor, it was followed by a 2 × 2 (Direct Distance by Map) within-subjects repeated measures ANOVA for each level of the individual difference variable to ascertain if both categories of individuals were prone to the direct distance bias. This was finally followed by a simple effects test for the angularity and directionality bias for each level of the individual variable.

Vividness of Visual Imagery (VVIQ) The 2 × 2 × 2 analysis revealed a significant main effect of direct distance ($F(1,65) = 22.01$, $p < .001$), and the expected interaction with visual imagery ability ($F(1,65) = 2.34$, $p < .06$). This interaction is graphically depicted in Figure 7.4 (left panel). Apart from the map factor that exerted a main effect ($F(1,65) = 26.24$, $p < .001$), all other effects were nonsignificant ($p > .65$).

Individual 2 × 2 analyses for lower and higher VVIQs show that both groups are prone to the direct distance bias, but the size of the bias is greater for lower VVIQs (Higher VVIQs: $F(1,31) = 5.66$, $p < .02$; Lower VVIQs: $F(1,34) = 17.74$, $p < .001$).

Style of Processing (SOP) The 2 × 2 × 2 analysis revealed a significant main effect of direct distance ($F(1,70) = 16.73$, $p < .001$), which was qualified by a significant interaction with style of processing ($F(1,70) = 5.54$, $p < .02$). The Map factor exerted a main effect ($F(1,70) = 25.58$, $p < .001$), and no other effects were significant ($p > .15$).

The form of the interaction was investigated by assessing if both groups were prone to the direct distance bias overall. Results showed that Visual Information Processors ($F(1,33) = 3.44$, $p < .05$) as well as Verbal Information Processors ($F(1,37) = 14.45$, $p < .001$), are prone to the direct distance bias overall. However, individuals with a visual style of processing were not susceptible to the directionality bias ($M = 134.82$ vs. 136.00, $t_{33} = 0.72$, $p = .476$), while those with a verbal style of processing were ($M = 121.24$ vs. 132.21, $t_{37} = 3.52$, $p < .001$). Both groups were, however, susceptible to the angularity bias, though the strength of the effect appears greater for the verbal processors ($M = 102.13$ vs. 109.71, $t_{38} = 2.93$, $p < .005$), as compared to the visual information processors ($M = 103.53$ vs. 107.35, $t_{33} = 1.86$, $p < .05$). This pattern is graphically depicted in Figure 7.4 (right panel).

To examine the robustness of these effects and take them further, a second study was conducted.

Study 2

In Study 1 we found that visual information processors were less prone to the direct distance bias than verbal information processors.

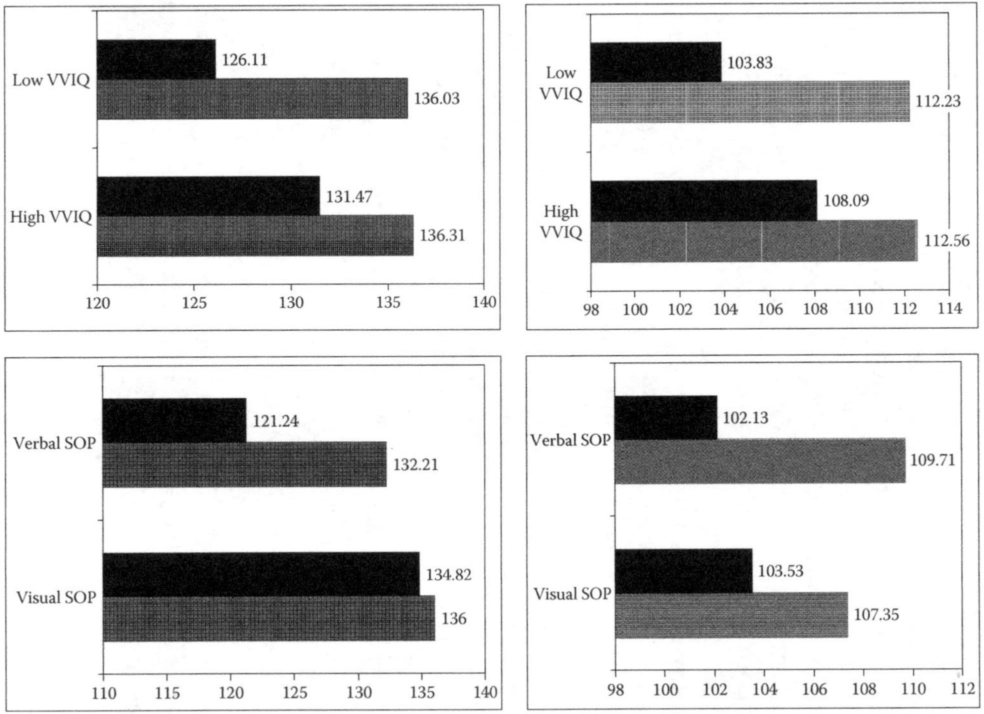

Figure 7.4 Results of Study 1: Results for directionality bias in the left panel and for the angularity bias in the right panel.

This is consistent with the hard-wired model theorizing that visual information processors have better ability to visualize information and are likely to pay less attention to the stimuli at the time of making their distance judgment as compared to verbal information processors. The task used in Study 1 was a stimuli-based task. The map containing the biasing visual cue was present at the time of making a judgment. Therefore, verbal information processors, with a lower visual information processing ability, had recourse to the map while making their judgments. As the direct distance cue overwhelms the perceptual field in a stimuli-based task, we argued that this led to their being more biased than visual information processors, when the judgment task was stimuli based.

This leads to the question of how biased verbal information processors would be as compared to visual information processors if they did not have access to the stimuli at the time of making a judgment. In other words, can the context lead verbal information processors to behave like visual information processors and vice versa? Study 2 examines whether the nature of a task, memory based or stimuli based, affects the extent to which verbal versus visual information processors display the direct distance bias.

Prior research has shown that stimuli-based processing leads to a greater bias than memory-based processing, presumably because when the stimuli is absent, the "other aspects of the spatial configuration should be recalled to the same extent as direct distance. Therefore, the overpowering effect of direct distance as a source of information would be diluted through the inclusion of other nonbiasing perceptual information as a source of information" (Raghubir & Krishna, 1996, p. 28). Therefore, verbal information processors, who do not pay a lot of attention to the stimuli in the first place, are likely to be less biased when the task is memory based than they were when the task was stimuli based, as in a memory-based task they have no recourse to refer to the map at the time of making a judgment, and therefore are less likely to be biased by the presence of the direct distance cue. On the other hand, the absence of stimuli at the time of making a judgment would not reduce the bias for visual information processors. Based on this reasoning, we predict that individual visual versus verbal processing preference will interact with the type of task (memory vs. stimuli based) in determining the direct distance bias, such that visual information processors will be less susceptible to the bias than verbal information processors when the task is stimuli based; but there will be no difference between verbal information processors and visual information processors when the task is memory based.

Method Study participants were 51 undergraduate students of business drawn from the same pool used in Study 1 (excluding those who had participated in Study 1).

The design was a 2 (Direct Distance: Lower vs. Higher) × 2 (Map: angularity and directionality) × 2 (Style of Processing: Visual/ Verbal) × 2 (Task: Memory based vs. Stimuli based) mixed design. The first two factors were manipulated within-subjects as in Study 1 (with order of administration and left–right orientation counterbalanced), style of processing was a measured variable based on a median split along a composite scale, and the task factor was manipulated between subjects.

The stimuli were identical to those used in Study 1 (see Figure 7.2 and Figure 7.3). The procedure was slightly varied. In the stimuli-based condition subjects were specifically asked to turn back to the map while making a judgment whereas in the memory-based condition, subjects were specifically requested to *not* turn back. The actual instructions read:

In this task you will be shown a map drawing. We are interested in studying how university students understand map drawings.

It is very important that when you are presented with a map you take the time to study it closely and pay particular attention to the scale given at the bottom of the map. Please take your time to form an accurate idea of the configuration of the area.

When you turn the page to answer the questions which follow, it is very important that you TURN BACK <DO NOT TURN BACK> to refer to the map. Answer the questions based on the actual drawing of the map in front of you <your memory of the map>.

Study participants estimated the distance of the two paths in each of the maps and then rated their level of confidence in their estimates using the same scale as used in Study 1. The Style of Processing questionnaire task was administered between the two distance estimate tasks. At the end of the task subjects completed a manipulation check asking them whether they had followed the instruction of looking at or not referring to the map at the time of making their judgment. This question reads: "While responding to the questions based on the maps, did you refer to the map presented to you?" Subjects could either respond: "Yes, I looked at the map," or "No, I did not look at the map." We also asked them whether they believed the presence or absence of the map at the time of making a judgment increased or decreased their response accuracy. At the end of the questionnaire all subjects rated how motivated they were, and how interesting they had found the task as in Study 1, and stated their gender and left- or right-handedness.

Results There was no difference across groups in level of motivation, interest, gender, or handedness. These factors are, accordingly, not analyzed further.

Manipulation Checks

Task Manipulation A cross-tabulation of responses to whether subjects had referred to the map versus not while making judgments, with the task they were set revealed the required interaction ($\chi^2(1) = 10.40$, $p < .001$). Only two of 26 subjects in the stimuli-based task cell reported that they had not referred to the map at the time of making a judgment, as opposed to 12 (out of 25) in the memory-based task. Note, however, that there appears to be some stimuli-based processing in the memory-based task. At a minimum, however, the directions were successful at manipulating the extent of stimuli-based versus memory-based processing.

Scale Differences As in Study 1, we conducted a one-way ANOVA using the composite SOP scale score as the dependent variable and the median categorization as one independent variable (Scale median = 3.15 on a 1–5 composite scale). The task factor was used as a second independent variable. This 2 × 2 analysis revealed a significant effect of the SOP categorization ($F(1,45) = 86.67$, $p < .0001$: M: Visual = .86, Verbal = 3.38) and null main and interaction effects of the task factor ($p > .30$). This suggests that the group varied along the SOP dimension.

A repeated measures 2 (map) × 2 (direct distance) × 2 (SOP) × 2 (Task) ANOVA should reveal a significant three-way interaction between style of processing, task, and direct distance. This interaction was indeed significant ($F(1,45) = 3.10$, $p < .05$). The only other significant effects of this analysis were main effects of direct distance ($F(1,45) = 3.93$, $p < .05$), and map ($F(1,45) = 13.13$, $p < .001$), the latter reflecting the differential lengths of the paths used in the two maps ($p > .28$ for all other effects). The interaction is a crossover: verbal information processors are more prone to the direct distance bias than visual information processors when the task is stimuli based. This replicates Study 1 results, where the procedure called for a stimuli-based judgment. However, when the task is memory based, verbal information processors are no more biased than visual information processors.

A 2 × 2 (map by direct distance) repeated measures ANOVA was conducted for each of the four SOP (verbal/visual) by task (stimuli-based/memory-based) cells. These analyses show that when the judgment task is stimuli based, visual processors are not prone to the direct distance bias (*M*: Angularity = 120.00 vs. 120.00; Directionality = 156.53 vs. 154.62: Overall $F(1,12) = .30$, $p = .59$). They are, however, marginally prone to the bias when the judgment task is memory based (*M*: Angularity = 112.46 vs. 117.08; Directionality = 140.85 vs. 143.92: Overall $F(1,11) = 2.41$, $p < .08$).

On the other hand, verbal information processors are prone to the direct distance bias to a significant extent when the task is stimuli based (*M*: Angularity = 109.33 vs. 114.67; Directionality = 128.08 vs. 134.75, $F(1,12) = 5.04$, $p < .05$), but not when it is memory based (*M*: Angularity = 114.82 vs. 117.00; Directionality = 130.36 vs. 131.07, $F(1,10) = .30$, $p = .60$). As they cannot direct attention to the stimuli in a memory-based task, this is consistent with the predictions of the hard-wired model.

Conclusions and Discussion We now examine these visual perceptual biases in the context of the hard-wired model. To do so, we first explore whether any of the other extant models are adequate at explaining the empirical findings reviewed above.

The DD Bias is Not a Pre-Conscious Bias

The proposed framework suggests that for pre-conscious processing increasing the awareness of the stimuli should reduce the bias (Janiszewski, 1988). While examining the effect of the mere presence of the stimuli, RK noted a counterintuitive result: they found that the angularity bias was greater when the judgment task was stimuli based rather than when it was memory based (Study 4). This result implies that the angularity bias is not of the pre-conscious processing genre.

The DD Bias is Not a Non-Conscious Bias

The classic empirical tests for non-conscious processes suggest that increased attention to the influence of a biasing stimulus should de-bias judgments rather than exacerbate the bias in judgments (Bargh, 2002; Fitzsimons et al., 2002). Classic de-biasing techniques in the social judgment arena (e.g., Lord, Lepper, & Preston, 1984) have shown that increasing people's attention to the biasing nature of a stimulus and encouraging them to use alternate sources of information to make a judgment, lead to an attenuation of the bias. This argument presupposes that if the use of the input is outside awareness, bringing it within awareness will lead to normatively appropriate processing.

Increasing awareness of the biasing nature of a stimulus on a judgment and encouraging disregard of it could be successful strategies if biases are consciously controllable. Of course, some biases like the self-positivity bias (Raghubir & Menon, 1998) are extremely strong and difficult to eradicate as they invoke self-esteem. These biases have been shown to be reversible when self-esteem is not at stake, but by the same token as the visual perceptual biases discussed in this chapter, the presence of base-rate information that could attenuate a bias, has been shown to exacerbate it for people whose self-esteem is tied to the belief that they have lower risk than those of other people (Lin, Lin, & Raghubir, 2003).

If biases are uncontrollable due to the way in which visual information is processed (as in the examples used in this chapter) or because they undercut the very basis of a human's self-belief (as in the case of self-positivity), then de-biasing as a strategy may not be adequate or effective. In their Study 5, RK found that the angularity bias was greater when subjects were cued about the use of direct distance as a potential source of information while making a judgment (internal salience), and when it was physically prominent versus not (Study 5). This result suggests that the process does not fit the genre of non-conscious biases as the bias remains even when people are aware of the influence of a biasing stimulus on their judgments.

This result is consistent with the predictions of the hard-wired model which argues that if the direct distance bias is *controllable*, participants who believe that direct distance is reliable should continue to use it and be prone to the direct distance bias, while those who believe it to be unreliable should discontinue their reliance on it and, therefore, not be prone to it. However, if it is *uncontrollable* then participants should not change their reliance on it irrespective of whether they believe it is reliable or unreliable. If the bias is hard-wired and uncontrollable for most people, then there should be no significant difference in bias between people who believe direct distance is a reliable versus an unreliable aid for distance judgments. Said differently, if classic de-biasing does not reduce a bias, it may not be a product of pure non-conscious processing. It should be considered as candidate for the hard-wired process, where the origin of this hard-wiredness could be due to the way in which visual information is processed, due to evolutionary reasons, or due to the manner in which people's self-esteem is inextricably tied to their beliefs. Note that this latter genre of models suggests that the model presented here, while developed for the visual information processing arena, may also apply to certain attitude and judgment domains in the semantic and numerical information processing arenas, such as the *deliberation without attention* model developed by Dijksterhuis et al. (2006) in the context of product choices.

The DD Bias Is Not a Controlled Heuristic Process Bias

A heuristic processing process implies that increasing resources toward a task should reduce a bias especially when people are motivated to respond accurately (Chaiken, Liberman, & Eagly, 1989). RK Study 6 showed that consumers with higher cognitive load were more prone to the angularity bias (70% of participants) versus those in the no load condition, though the latter remained biased (approximately 48% of participants were biased). This implies that the lack of cognitive resources could exacerbate the angularity bias, implying that the bias may belong to the controlled heuristic processing genre. However, the bias was still present in the no load condition. If increased levels of motivation are not adequate at eliminating a bias, this could be because the bias is uncontrollable (given that sample size and size of manipulation are both adequate and the test is properly powered).

Evidence That the Angularity Bias Is a Hard-Wired Bias

The final question in the proposed framework is the issue of whether consumers can control the influence of stimuli on their judgments.

Pham, Meyvis, & Zhou (2001) found that vivid visual imager's judgments were less affected by salient information versus those of less vivid visual imagers. The model is consistent with those of Pham et al. (2001): "those with vivid imagery ability can look beyond the obvious," as imagery vividness attenuates the effects of vivid and salient information.

The tests above focused on the direct distance bias. However, the model proposed may also apply to other visual perception biases such as the use of visual versus verbal information at the time of making a judgment (Janiszewski, 1988). It remains to be tested, however, if these biases are hard-wired in the sense of being individual specific and exacerbated for some when attention to the biasing visual stimuli is increased.

An area for future research identified earlier is whether it is possible that higher levels of motivation may make people more aware of the biasing presence of a stimulus, or increase their sensitivity to its influence on their decisions. A different area for future research would be to examine the role of individual differences such as those explored in this paper on biases in estimates of area, volume, and weight. To what extent are individuals biased by the perceptual salience of a biasing visual cue (such as height or surface area) while making two- and three-dimensional judgments, to what extent do these biases attenuate with formal (geometry) training and reduce as children mature, and to what extent are these biases uncontrollable? Such research would have implications for package design, design of shelf layouts, and pricing.

Acknowledgments

I gratefully acknowledge comments from Aradhna Krishna, participants at the IC-1 conference in Ann Arbor, Michigan, June 2005, and especially Rik Pieters and Michel Wedel on an earlier draft of this chapter.

References

Bargh, J. A. (1989). Conditional automaticity: Varieties of automatic influence in social perception and cognition. In J. S. Uleman and J.A. Bargh (Eds.), *Unintended thought* (pp. 3–51). New York: Guilford Press.

Bargh, J. A. (2002). Losing consciousness: Automatic influences on consumer judgment, behavior, and motivation. *Journal of Consumer Research, 29*, 280–285.

Chaiken, S. (1980). Heuristic versus systematic information processing and the use of source versus message cues in persuasion. *Journal of Personality and Social Psychology, 39*(5), 752–766.

Chaiken, S., Liberman, A., & Eagly, A. H. (1989). Heuristic and systematic information processing within and beyond the persuasion context. In J.S. Uleman & J.A. Bargh (Eds.). *Unintended thought* (pp. 212–252). New York: Guilford Press.

Childers, T. L., Houston, M. J., & Heckler, S. E. (1985). Measurement of individual differences in visual versus verbal information processing. *Journal of Consumer Research, 12*, 125–134.

Dijksterhuis, A., Bos, M. W., Nordgren, L. F., & Baaren, R. B. van (2006). On making the right choice: The deliberation-without-attention effect. *Science, 311*(5763), 1005–1007.

Fitzsimons, G., Hutchinson, J. W., Williams, P., Alba, J. W., Chartrand, T., Huber, J., et al. (2002). Non-conscious influences on consumer choice. *Marketing Letters, 13*, 269–279.

Fitzsimons, G., & Shiv, B. (2001). Nonconscious and contaminative effects of hypothetical questions on subsequent decision-making. *Journal of Consumer Research, 28*, 224–238.

Fitzsimons, G., & Williams, P. (2000). Asking questions can change behavior: Does it do so automatically or effortfully? *Journal of Experimental Psychology: Applied, 6*(3), 249–266.

Folkes, V. S., & Matta, S. (2004). The effect of package shape on consumers' judgments of product volume: Attention as a mental contaminant. *Journal of Consumer Research, 31*, 390–401.

Gilbert, D. T. (1989). Thinking lightly about others: Automatic components of the social inference process. In J. S. Uleman & J. A. Bargh (Eds.), *Unintended thought* (pp. 189–211). New York: Guilford Press.

Gilbert, D. T., Pelham, B. W., & Krull, D. S. (1988). On cognitive busyness: When person perceivers meet persons perceived. *Journal of Personality and Social Psychology, 54*, 733–740.

Heckler, S. E., Childers, T. L., & Houston, M. J. (1993). On the construct of the SOP scale. *Journal of Mental Imagery, 17*(3–4), 119–132.

Herr, P. M., Sherman, S. J., & Fazio, R. H. (1983). On the consequences of priming: Assimilation and contrast effects. *Journal of Experimental Social Psychology, 19*, 323–340.

Janiszewski, C. (1988). Preconscious processing effects: The independence of attitude formation and conscious thought. *Journal of Consumer Research, 15*, 199–209.

Krishna, A. (this volume). Spatial perception biases: An integrative review.

Lin, Y., Lin, C., & Raghubir, P. (2003). Avoiding anxiety, being in denial or simply stroking self-esteem: Why self-positivity? *Journal of Consumer Psychology, 13*(4), 464–477.

Lord, C. G., Lepper, M. R., & Preston, E. (1984). Considering the opposite: A corrective strategy for social judgment. *Journal of Personality and Social Psychology, 47,* 1231–1243.

Maheswaran, D., & Chaiken, S. (1991). Promoting systematic processing in low motivation settings: The effect of incongruent information on processing and judgment. *Journal of Personality and Social Psychology, 61,* 13–25.

Marks, D. F. (1973). Visual imagery differences in the recall of pictures. *British Journal of Psychology, 64,* 17–24.

Menon, G., & Raghubir, P. (2003). Ease-of-retrieval as an automatic input in judgments: A mere accessibility framework? *Journal of Consumer Research, 30*(2), 230–243.

Petty, R. E., & Cacioppo, J. T. (1986). The elaboration likelihood model of persuasion. In L. Berkowitz (Ed.), *Advances in Experimental Social Psychology* (pp. 123–205). Orlando, FL: Academic Press.

Pham, M. T., Meyvis, T., & Zhou, R. (2001). Beyond the obvious: Chronic vividness of imagery and the use of information in decision-making. *Organizational Behavior and Human Decision Processes, 84,* 226–253.

Raghubir, P., & Krishna, A. (1996). As the crow flies: Bias in consumers' map-based distance judgments. *Journal of Consumer Research, 23,* 26–39.

Raghubir, P., & Menon, G. (1998). AIDS and me, never the twain shall meet: The effects of information accessibility on judgments of risk and advertising effectiveness. *Journal of Consumer Research, 25,* 52–63.

Schneider, W., & Shiffrin, R. M. (1977). Controlled and automatic human information processing: I. detection, search, and attention. *Psychological Review, 84,* 1–66.

Shiffrin, R. M., & Schneider, W. (1977). Controlled and automatic information processing: II. perceptual learning, automatic attending, and general theory. *Psychological Review, 84,* 127–190.

Shiv, B., & Fedorikhin, A. (1999). Heart and mind in conflict: The interplay of affect and cognition in consumer decision-making. *Journal of Consumer Research, 26*(3), 278–292.

8

Spatial Perception Research

An Integrative Review of Length, Area, Volume, and Number Perception

Aradhna Krishna

Spatial Perception

Spatial judgments, such as "how big?, how long?, how many?" are an integral part of day-to-day living. In many aspects of everyday behavior, people need to make spatial judgments, such as how long different waiting lines are, how large various fruit or vegetables are, if a carpet will fit nicely in their living room. Since people do not use complex mathematical formulae to make these judgments, systematic biases in these judgments are important to study and document. Research in the area of spatial perceptions has demonstrated many such biases. This research has been done for more than a century in cognitive psychology, environment psychology, and urban planning, but only recently in marketing. This paper is to bring together spatial perception research relevant to marketing in an integrated framework. The framework also shows the links between various seemingly disparate pieces of research being done in marketing related to spatial perceptions.

The review is important both from an academic and a managerial perspective. Because consumer judgment biases also affect consumer behavior, an understanding of this behavior can help managers in decisions concerning packaging, pricing, mall layout, store layout, range of sizes to carry, communicating size information, among other decisions. We also highlight areas for future research in spatial perceptions. As such, the review should facilitate further spatial perception research in marketing and also make managers more aware of spatial perception biases.

We focus on factors that affect *spatial perceptions* and their implications for consumer behavior. Since it is not possible to cover all aspects of spatial perception research in a single survey, we concentrate on length, area, volume, and number perceptions. An exhaustive review of even distance, area, volume, and number perceptions is not possible within one paper—we limit ourselves to research we believe is of importance and interest to marketing researchers and practitioners.

Conceptual Framework

One can think of spatial perceptions as being ordered along dimensionality such that spatial perceptions in one dimension refer to length (or distance) perception, in two dimensions to area perceptions, and in three dimensions to volume perception. Perceptions of number can be along any of one to three dimensions depending on whether one is estimating the number of objects in a line (one dimension), spread out on a flat surface (two dimensions), or spread out in space (three dimensions). We explore how consumers make length, area, volume, and number judgments; the ensuing perceptual biases; and the implication of these biases for marketers (see Figure 8.1).

Figure 8.1 shows the links between various types of *spatial perception biases*, the *consumer action* these spatial perceptions could affect, and the *managerial decisions* the consumer actions would in turn impact. The figure further shows that managerial actions would subsequently impact spatial perceptions, since they will affect the spatial stimuli that consumers observe. We also discuss *individual characteristics* that affect spatial perception biases.

We divide biases in spatial perceptions into three major groups: those pertaining to length and distance, those pertaining to number, and those pertaining to area and volume. Within each group of spatial perception biases, we discuss the different factors that affect them. For example, for volume perception, among other things, we discuss previous literature that shows how elongation of an object affects volume perception. We then elaborate on how biased spatial perceptions among consumers will affect their behavior (*consumer action*).

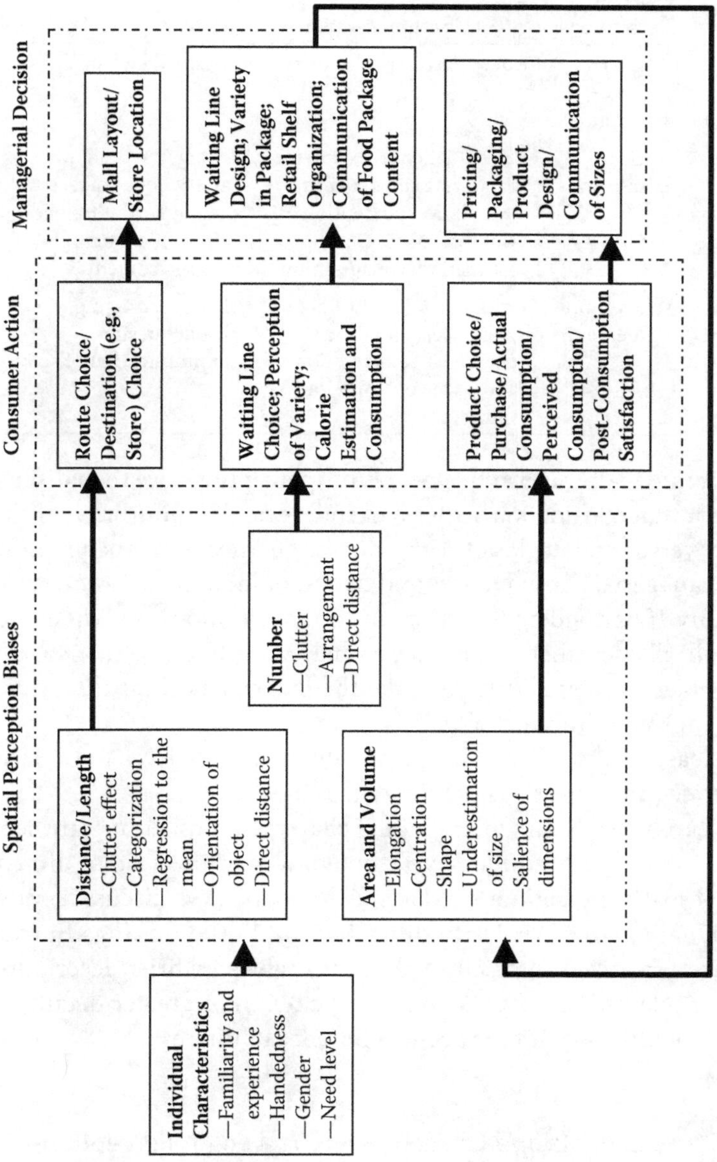

Figure 8.1 Conceptual framework for research on spatial perceptions.

TABLE 8.1 Framework for the Review of Spatial Perception Research

	(i) Spatial Perceptions	(ii) Consumer Action	(iii) Managerial Decision
Part I	Length or distance perceptions	Route/destination choice	Store/mall layout
Part II	Number perceptions	Perceptual count of people in waiting lines, waiting line choice, perception of variety, calorie estimation, consumption	Waiting line design, variety in package, retail shelf organization and communication of food package content
Part III	Area/volume perception	Product choice, product purchase, actual and perceived consumption and post-consumption satisfaction	Pricing, packaging, product design, communication of sizes

Continuing with the example of volume perceptions, we then discuss research that considers whether bartenders tend to pour more into a shorter versus a taller glass. Clearly, answers to these kinds of questions have managerial consequences and thus should influence *managerial decisions*. If bartenders tend to pour too much into short, wide (e.g., highball) glasses, then the managers may want to make them aware of this bias, or better still, to make the bartenders measure out the drink in front of the customer.

For ease of discussion (based on similarity of effects found), we discuss the framework as provided in Table 8.1.

Research pertaining to individual characteristics has mostly been studied for *distance stimuli*, even though it may affect other dimensions of spatial perceptions just as much. As such, we discuss it under Individual Characteristics findings in Part I. The findings in each part are organized into self-explanatory tables. A brief description of some selected findings is given in the text. For greater detail, the reader should consult the specific reference of interest.

Part I: Antecedents and Consequences of Length Perceptions

The table for this part (Table 8.2) is organized by five major factors that have been shown to affect distance perceptions, namely *cluttered*

TABLE 8.2 Distance Perceptions, Route/Destination Choice: Some Findings

	DISTANCE PERCEPTIONS	
CLUTTERED SPACES		
Intervening points	Estimates of distance increase as a function of number of intervening points along the route	Thorndyke 1981
Due to turns	Routes with a greater (vs. fewer) number of right angle turns are estimated as longer	Byrne 1979; Sadalla & Magel 1980; Lee 1963; Newcombe & Liben 1982
Due to intersections	Intersections increase distance estimates along traversed pathways	Sadalla & Staplin 1980
Due to landmarks	The presence of landmarks increases distance perceptions	Allen, Siegel & Rosinski 1978; Lipman 1991
Due to barriers	Distance between two objects estimated as greater when barriers were interposed between them	Kosslyn et. al., 1974
	Routes with barriers are more inaccurately estimated than routes without barriers	Cohen & Weatherford 1980
Theories to explain clutter effect	Information storage model—greater the number of attributes, the larger the mental representation of the space and the larger it appears	Sadalla & Staplin 1980
	Scaling hypothesis—longer distances are underestimated as compared to shorter distances	Dainoff et. al. 1974
	Analog timing model—when one visually scans a route, the scanning procedure activates an internal clock or timer which is stopped at the end of the scan	Thorndyke 1981
DIRECT DISTANCE EFFECT	People use direct distance between two end points of a line to estimate length of the line	Raghubir & Krishna 1996
CATEGORIZATION	People categorize routes into subcategories which bias distance judgments	Allen & Kirasic 1985

continued

TABLE 8.2 (continued) Distance Perceptions, Route/Destination Choice: Some Findings

	DISTANCE PERCEPTIONS	
	People underestimate distance between far objects in the same region and overestimate distance between close objects in different regions	McNamara 1986
	Proximity judgments found to be more accurate when locations were within (vs. across) categories	Allen 1981
OBJECT ORIENTATION	Vertical distances are estimated as longer than horizontal ones	Brosvic & Cohen 1988; Finger & Spelt 1947
REGRESSION TO THE MEAN	Longer distances underestimated and shorter distances overestimated—"Regression to the Mean" effect	McNamara 1986; McNamara, Ratcliff & McKoon 1984; Newcombe & Liben 1982
	Estimation of shorter distances more accurate than of longer distances	Cohen and Weatherford 1980
	Perceived distances are correlated with actual distances	Golledge & Zannaras 1973
	INDIVIDUAL CHARACTERISTICS	
FAMILIARITY AND GOALS	Familiarity does not reduce clutter effect	Sadalla and Magel 1980
	Buildings judged as more familiar rated as closer	Nasar et. al. 1985
	Estimates of urban distances increase with increasing familiarity	Byrne 1979
	Distances covered were overestimated compared with distances to be covered	Brandt & Kebeck 1983
	Estimates of traversed (vs. not) routes were more accurate	Cohen & Weatherford 1980
	Distances into town perceived as longer than distances out of it	Briggs 1972; Golledge & Zannaras 1973
	Distances of outward journeys are overestimated	Lee 1970

TABLE 8.2 (continued) Distance Perceptions, Route/Destination Choice: Some Findings

	INDIVIDUAL CHARACTERISTICS	
NEED	Greater need of object, object appears larger	Brendl, Markman & Messner 2002; Bruner & Godman 1947
MEMORY	Maps based on memorial representation operate similarly to visual maps	Hubbard, Kall & Baird 1989; Raghubir & Krishna 1996
	Routes with easily memorable (vs. difficult to remember) attributes estimated as longer	Sadalla & Staplin 1980
	ROUTE/DESTINATION CHOICE	
	Show importance of the distance parameter in predicting market shares of shopping outlets and entire shopping centers	Haines, Simon & Alexis 1972
	Clustering of destinations affects choice of alternative "trip-chains"	Brooks, Kaufman & Lichtenstein 2004

spaces, direct distance, categorization, regression to the mean, and *orientation of object.*

A lot of attention in the field of spatial perceptions has been given to the effect of cluttering. By *cluttering* we mean the *clutter* or crowding caused by the presence of certain spatial features. Cluttering has been operationalized in many ways. Some of these are the presence of intervening points (Thorndyke, 1981), intersections (Sadalla & Staplin, 1980), turns (Sadalla & Magel, 1980), landmarks (e.g., Allen, Siegel, & Rosinski, 1978), and barriers (Kosslyn, Pick, & Fariello, 1974). Typically, studies in this research domain have been done experimentally with the amount of clutter varying between subjects, and distance perception being measured after subject exposure to the spatial stimuli. The experiments are paper-and-pencil exercises or laboratory studies with clutter manipulated in different ways, for example, by putting an opaque object along a line (Kosslyn et al., 1974).

There are at least three theories proposed to account for the clutter effect. According to the information storage model (Sadalla & Staplin, 1980), cognitive maps are based on attributes of a given space. The greater the number of attributes, the larger the mental representation of the space is. People may judge complex pathways to be longer because they have scanned and stored more information about them. An alternative explanation for the clutter effect is the scaling hypothesis (Dainoff, Miskie, Wilson, & Crane, 1974) that proposes that longer distances are underestimated as compared to shorter distances. Since a spatial feature along a route divides a long segment into two smaller segments, the sum of the distance estimates of these two shorter distances can be expected to be greater than the distance estimate of the initial long segment. Thorndyke (1981) developed the analog timing model to explain the clutter effect. Per this model, when the subject visually scans a route, an internal clock is activated, which is stopped at the end of the scan. The click time indicates elapsed scan time and indirectly the distance. When the scan is performed on a route with many different spatial features, it takes longer and therefore the perceived distance is longer.

Other factors have also been shown to affect perceived distance other than clutter, namely direct distance, categorization, regression to the mean, and orientation of the object. These are discussed in the table as are individual characteristics that affect distance perception biases. Relatively little research has extended the effect of spatial features from the cognitive domain of distance estimation to the behavioral domain of choice. There are only a limited number of studies on route choice, and these have primarily been done using animal subjects (see Poucet, Thinus-Blanc, & Chapius, 1983). However, while there is a paucity of research on route choice involving humans, there exists a rich literature on "store" choice in location models and urban geography. Here consumers' choice of store is modeled as a function of the distance separating the store from the consumer (e.g., Haines, Simon, & Alexis, 1972). Recently, Brooks, Kaufmann, and Lichtenstein (2004) have shown that when consumers evaluate alternative *trip chains* (multiple destinations in a single outing) their choices are not only affected by cost minimization, but also the configuration of the destinations within the trip chains. These studies have used actual metric distance estimates. However as described earlier, perceived distances, though highly correlated with actual distances (Golledge & Zannaras, 1973), may be biased estimates of actual distances. This presents an opportunity for future research in this area.

Our discussion of biased length perceptions and its implications for consumers' route choice has many other implications for design of mall layouts, store layout, store location choice, and traffic monitoring. Small stores would prefer to be in locations where they are *perceived* to be closer to the more popular stores; stores want to give the appearance of having small distances to cover from one end to another; malls want to appear compact so that consumers visit more stores. That this is managerially relevant can be seen from the fact that commercial companies are tracking consumer movements within stores to facilitate store design—currently, experiments are being conducted in stores where consumers are tracked using Radio Frequency Identification Tags (RFIDs) on shopping trolleys (Larson, Bradlow, & Fader, forthcoming). Envirosell, a consulting firm founded by Underhill (1999), videotapes traffic movements within stores with a view toward better store layout and planning.

Part II: Antecedents and Consequences of Number Perceptions

The effect of visual configuration on *numerosity estimation* has been studied for a very long time (see Table 8.3). Much of this research shows that dots are estimated rather than enumerated and that the arrangement and pattern of dots has an important effect on number perception. Recently, there has been research in marketing on relating numerosity perceptions to consumer actions in terms of *waiting line behavior, calorie estimation,* and *consumption*. In Carmon and Kahneman's (1995) studies, subjects interact with a computer program that graphically represents a queue in which the subject's position is indicated. They find that the initial length of the queue decreases real-time affective response and that the frequency of queue movement increases it. Zhou and Soman (2003) show that the number of people waiting behind a customer positively influences her affect and negatively influences her reneging behavior (likelihood of leaving the queue). Thus, they propose and demonstrate that queues of the type "take a number" will have lower affect and higher reneging than linear queues. They also show that the monetary value for a service increases with the number of people waiting behind one in the queue.

The literature on number perception bias would suggest that in addition to waiting line design, number perceptions would also affect migration counts, traffic counts, counts during war, crowd counts, herd count, and various forms of perceptual counts that are done

TABLE 8.3 Numerosity Perceptions, Count of People in Waiting Lines: Some Findings

NUMEROSITY PERCEPTIONS	
A row of dots appears longer than the same empty distance between 2 dots	Oppel 1855
Number estimates are made similar to distance estimates	Luccio & Rodani 1983
Dots are estimated rather than enumerated and arrangement of dots has an important effect on number perception	Atkinson, Francis & Campbell 1976; Bechwith & Restle 1966; Smitsman 1982; Van Oeffelsen & Vos 1982, 1984
Quantification of a small number of objects without counting may be done by pattern recognition	Wolters, Van Kempen & Wijlhuizen 1987
Solitaire illusion (single clusters are estimated as more numerous than an equal number in several clusters	Ginsburg 1978, 1980; Frith & Frith 1972
The incongruity between the length and numerosity of an array increases the time required to estimate	Dixon 1978, Gelman 1969
COUNT OF PEOPLE IN WAITING LINES	
Direct distance effect: people use direct distance between two end points of a waiting line to estimate number of people in the waiting line	Krishna & Raghubir 1997
WAITING LINE DESIGN	
Number of people behind influences affect and value for service, and reneging from the queue	Zhou & Soman 2002
Waiting line's remaining length and speed impacts subjects' affective responses	Carmon & Kahneman 1995
Perceived variety of an assortment is larger and consumption is larger with greater organization, greater shelf size, and lower entropy (how difficult it is to perceive a different type of good)	Kahn & Wansink 2002
Calorie estimation follows a compressive psychophysical power function	Chandon & Wansink 2005

routinely. There are also other kinds of number perceptions that are more relevant to managers which are relatively unexplored. Kahn and Wansink (2004) demonstrate that *perception of variety* increases and consumption increases when the assortment of goods (e.g., jellybeans or beads) is organized versus not (e.g., jellybeans displayed by color or mixed up), with greater size of the assortment (e.g., how many of each type there are), and lower entropy (lower symmetry in number of each type). Chandon and Wansink (2005) focus on calorie estimation. They demonstrate that people's perception of the number of calories in a meal follows a compressive psychophysical power function, so that people are less sensitive about perceiving an increased number of calories as the number of calories in a meal increases.

The studies relating numerosity perceptions to consumer actions have many implications for *managerial action*. Carmon and Kahneman's (1995) results suggest that firms should try and disguise their long waiting lines such as Disneyland does with "snaked" lines. One other implication of Carmon and Kahneman's findings (as they point out) is that operations research results whereby single queues are more efficient than multiple queues may not lead to greater customer satisfaction. Carmon and Kahneman also suggest that a perception of frequent queue movement is important for decreasing negative affect of queues even when the waiting time has been provided. This could be done, for instance, by showing how many people have been served or a sign with "now serving number…." They suggest that future research should study the impact of frequency of this feedback.

Zhou and Soman's (2003) results would suggest that managers should think carefully before using queues of the "take a number" type, which are quite common in gourmet delis and food stores, lumber stores, etc. Their results indicate that these types of queues will have lower affect and higher reneging than linear queues. However, future research needs to extend their results to see if they are valid when customers are able to engage in other activities while waiting (i.e., taking a number lets them estimate the time when they will be served and hence do some other jobs and come back). This is especially important since Carmon (1991) suggests that providing information about waiting duration can decrease dissatisfaction with waiting, whether or not this information can lead to alternate use of time.

Kahn and Wansink's results suggest that consumption increases with greater *variety in package*. Thus, manufacturers of multipacks of candy, chocolate, yogurt, chips, etc., should include greater variety in their multipacks in order to increase consumption. Hence, six different types of chips or yogurt would potentially lead to higher consumption versus two each of three different types. Also, based on Kahn and Wansink's results, there will be an increase in consumption with few, unordered objects (relative to few, ordered ones) and an increase in consumption with many ordered objects (relative to many, unordered ones). Chandon and Wansink's (2005) results on biased calorie estimation suggest that if the department of health wants to *decrease obesity* they need to make consumers aware of their biased calorie estimation. In addition, caloric content should be written more prominently on food packages. They also suggest that (obese) consumers should be told to separate their meals mentally into smaller portions and then estimate the number of calories for each portion, since this would result in less biased estimation.

Part II: Antecedents and Consequences of Area and Volume Perceptions

Research on volume perception focuses on the effect of object shape. On the other hand, literature on area perceptions focuses on both shape effects and size effects (how area perception changes as the size of the object changes while the shape remains the same; see Table 8.4).

Within *shape effects*, research has explored perceptions of different shapes within a form class (e.g., rectangles of different length: breadth ratios) and across different form classes (e.g., square versus triangle). A form class is defined by the number of sides of the figure (circles and ellipses are in the same class, which is different from both the class containing squares and the class of triangles). Regular shapes (e.g., geometric squares, rectangles, pyramids, circles, etc.) are of particular relevance to marketers of frequently purchased consumer products interested in packaging and pricing issues. Findings pertinent to regular shapes include the following.

Shape Effects within Form Class

Piaget (1967, 1968) studied children's perceptions of volume. In a typical Piagetian experiment, colored liquid was poured from a tall

TABLE 8.4 Area and Volume Perceptions, Choice, Consumption, Satisfaction

PERCEIVED AREA AND VOLUME ACROSS DIFFERENT SHAPES WITHIN FORM-CLASS		
VOLUME PERCEPTION	Centration hypothesis: use of height to make volume judgments	Piaget 1960
	Elongation hypothesis: use of height/width ratio to make volume judgment	Frayman & Dawson 1981, Holmberg 1975
AREA PERCEPTION	Psychophysical model of salience of dimensions: use of different dimensions for area judgments is related to their relative salience	Krider, Raghubir & Krishna 2001
PERCEIVED AREA AND VOLUME DUE TO DIFFERENT SHAPES ACROSS FORM-CLASS		
VOLUME PERCEPTION	Mixed results: Cylinders < cuboids (even though taller)	Holmberg 1975
	Cylinders and tetrahedrons > spheres and cubes; cubes < spheres	Frayman & Dawson 1981
	Elongation hypothesis: use of height/width ratio to make volume judgment	Frayman & Dawson 1981, Holmberg 1975
AREA PERCEPTION	Triangles are generally perceived to be larger than circles or squares (but with some exceptions):	
	triangle > circle, square circle > triangle > square triangle = square < circle triangle = circle < squares	Anastasi 1936; Fisher & Foster 1968; Hanes 1950; Warren & Pinneau 1955 Smets 1970 Mansvelt 1928; Wagner 1931
	Inconsistent findings regarding relative size perceptions of circles and squares: Square larger than circle No difference between square and circle Circle larger	Anastasi 1936; Wagner 1931 Croxton & Stein 1932, Warren & Pinneau 1955 Fisher & Foster 1968; Hanes 1950; Mansvelt 1928; Smets 1970

continued

TABLE 8.4 (continued) Area and Volume Perceptions, Choice, Consumption, Satisfaction

PERCEIVED AREA AND VOLUME DUE TO DIFFERENT SHAPES ACROSS FORM-CLASS		
	Circles > squares (or vice versa) depending on length of most salient dimension: when square placed like a kite on a vertex (or on its side), square > (or <) circle	Krider, Raghubir & Krishna 2001
PERCEIVED AREA AND VOLUME DUE TO INCREASING SIZE OF THE SAME SHAPE		
PERCEIVED SIZE IS AN UNDERESTIMATE	The degree of underestimation increases as the object grows larger and is not contingent on the shape of the figure, perceived size = actual size, where e<1	Teghtsoonian 1965
	The exponent range of 0.50–1.00 appears fairly robust across 2D and 3D figures	Baird, Romer & Stein 1970; Ekman 1958, Stevens & Guirao 1963
	2D figures	Baird, Romer & Stein 1970;
	3D figures	Frayman & Dawson 1981; Moyer et. al. 1978
THEORIES PROPOSED FOR PERCEIVED AREA AND VOLUME SHAPE AND SIZE BIASES		
Information selection—people underutilize one or more dimensions in their judgments of size		Verge & Bogartz 1978
Information integration—different rules have been suggested for integrating information, but all dimensions are assumed to be appropriately utilized		Anderson & Cuneo 1978
Psychophysical model of area judgment—dimensions are used per their salience in a multiplicative information integration model		Krider, Raghubir & Krishna 2001
CHOICE, PERCEIVED, AND ACTUAL CONSUMPTION, POST-CONSUMPTION SATISFACTION		
People are willing to pay more for objects perceived to be larger		Krider, Raghubir & Krishna 2001
Larger purchase quantity is made of objects that look smaller		Krider, Raghubir & Krishna 2001

TABLE 8.4 (continued) Area and Volume Perceptions, Choice, Consumption, Satisfaction

CHOICE, PERCEIVED, AND ACTUAL CONSUMPTION, POST-CONSUMPTION SATISFACTION	
Perceived-size consumption illusion: A reversal in perceptions of volume pre- versus post-consumption. More elongated containers lead to greater (smaller) pre-consumption (post-consumption) perceived volume, and to greater actual consumption	Raghubir & Krishna 1999; Wansink & van Ittersum 2003 Folkes, Martin & Gupta 1993; Wansink 1996; Wansink & Park 2001
People consume more if they have larger package sizes	Chandon & Wansink 2002,
If products are more salient, visible, conveniently packaged, hedonic, or conveniently located, then they will be consumed more	Painter, Wansink & Hieggelke 1994, Wansink & Ray 1996
Perceived consumption is overestimated when food is consumed from a convenient location and underestimated if consumed from an inconvenient location	Painter, Wansink & Hieggelke 1994
Reversal of perceived-size consumption illusion when sight versus touch is used for input	Krishna (2006)

cylinder to a shorter and wider cylinder. Piaget found that primary school children appeared to only use the height of the container while making volume judgments—they believed that the volume had reduced when the liquid was poured into a shorter container (Piaget 1967, 1968; Piaget, Inhelder, & Szeminska, 1960). The predominant use of a single dimension, height, to make three-dimensional judgments was termed the *centration hypothesis*. Using the Piaget experiments as a basis, Holmberg (1975) proposed the *elongation hypothesis* whereby the greater the *height/width ratio* of a container, the greater the estimated volume. He found support for this proposition using both cylindrical as well as cuboid shapes. Additional support for the elongation effect was also shown in experiments conducted by Been, Braunstein, and Piazza (1964) and Pearson (1964). They demonstrated that if two cylinders of equal volume are reduced to new identical volumes, one by reducing the height and the other by reducing the width, the cylinder whose height is reduced appears smaller. Raghubir and Krishna (1999) replicated the elongation effect among adults with commonly used packages. Recently, Folkes and Matta (2004) showed that packages that have shapes that are perceived as attracting more attention are also perceived to contain a greater volume of a product than same-sized packages that attract less attention.

Consistent with volume perception, even within area perception, in general, the more elongated a figure (e.g., rectangle vs. square; oval vs. circle), the larger it is perceived to be (Rectangles > Squares: Verge & Bogartz, 1978; Anderson & Cuneo, 1978; Holmberg & Holmberg, 1969).

Shape Effects across Form Class

Holmberg (1975) found that while his elongation hypothesis was true for objects within a form category (i.e., objects of the same geometric shape with differing dimension), the effect broke down while making cross-category predictions: cylinders were estimated as smaller than cuboids even though they were of greater height. A number of studies have also investigated biases in area judgment across figures of different shapes: squares, circles, triangles, and other regular and irregular figures. This research has led to general agreement that figures of the same area but different shape are estimated to be different in area, but the ordinal relation of area estimates across shapes has mixed results. There is no agreement on the *relative size judgements of circles and squares.* Krider, Raghubir, and Krishna (2001) propose that the *relative salience* of the side versus the diagonal of a square should influence which dimension is used for comparing the two figures, and hence, whether the circle or square is judged larger. As predicted, in the side-salient condition, more subjects perceived the circle as being larger than the square and in the diagonal-salient condition, the opposite held true.

As products are often available in different sizes, an important managerial issue is whether consumers can accurately assess size changes (e.g., Does a large pizza look like double the size of the medium one?). Also, is this *size assessment ability* (or lack thereof) contingent on package shape? Attempting to understand how people make size judgments, a group of studies has examined judgments of figures of the same shape, across different sizes. A prototypical study is that by Teghtsoonian (1965) who demonstrated that when subjects are shown objects of the same shape but different sizes, perceived size to actual size follows an exponential rule: Perceived size = Actual size^x, where $x < 1$.

This implies that perceived size is underestimated to a larger extent as the object grows larger. This is consistent with results of many other researchers who have found apparent size to be exponentially related to actual size (see Table 8.4). The exponent values appear to be generalizable across shapes of the same dimensionality. Teghtsoonian (1965) suggested that the exponent of 2-D objects (area estimation task) is around 0.80, whereas that of 3-D objects (volume estimation task) is lower at about 0.60, and that of one-dimensional tasks (length estimation task) is around 1. Overall, the compressive power function bias is consistent in estimates of different size figures. Krider et al. (2001) further show that the value of the exponent is greater when the context increases the salience of a secondary dimension.

Theories Proposed to Explain Shape and Size Biases

The theories that have been developed to explain the above biases are broadly categorized into those which propose that the bias is due to (a) *Information Selection*: people using incorrect information, for example, ignoring one of the dimensions, elongation and centration discussed earlier (see Verge & Bogartz, 1978), or (b) *Information Integration:* an incorrect combinatorial rule to integrate available information (e.g., adding or dividing dimensions, rather than multiplying them; see Anastasi, 1936; Martinez & Dawson, 1973; Warren & Pinneau, 1955). Also, (c) Krider et al.'s (2001) *salience of dimensions model* discussed earlier explains shape and size biases. Raghubir (2006) also provides an alternate theoretical framework for spatial perception biases.

Most of the work on the *consequences of area and volume perceptions for consumers* has been done recently by marketing researchers (see Table 8.4). Krider et al. (2001) show that if a particular product shape is perceived as being larger compared to another (even though the actual size is the same—e.g., a round or square container of ¾ oz. cream cheese), then consumers will also be willing to pay more for the former. These results have been replicated by Yang and Raghubir (2005) in laboratory, field, and scanner data.

Raghubir and Krishna (1999) propose and demonstrate the *perceived-size consumption illusion*: a reversal in perceptions of volume pre- versus postconsumption. They show that the same person perceives the taller glass to contain more, but thinks he or she has drunk more from the shallower glass, when both glasses contain the same amount of fluid and subjects consume the entire amount. They suggest that the reversal is due to a contrast between what is expected and what is experienced. While Raghubir and Krishna demonstrate the effect of the elongation of prepoured drinks on consumption volume, Wansink and van Ittersum (2003) have people pour their own drinks in a series of field experiments. They find that both children and adults pour and consume more juice when given a short, fat glass versus a tall, thin glass, but they perceive the opposite to be true. In a third experiment done with Philadelphia bartenders, they find that the effect of elongation is moderated, but not eliminated, with pouring experience.

Besides beverages, our results also have implications for situations with more dire consequences. Currently, medicine cups (e.g., those provided free with a cough medicine bottle) are not of standard shape or size. If shapes do affect volume perception as we suggest, then consumers, especially older consumers who may not be able to read cup markings easily, may estimate the quantity inaccurately. As such, they may under- or overdose themselves. We would argue for standard shapes, more clear cup markings in a different color (right now, medicine cup markings are merely embossed into the plastic itself on most cups), and warnings to consumers to not try and estimate medicine quantities.

Area and volume research suggests that package shape can impact choice, preference, reservation price, purchase intention, actual and perceived consumption, and postconsumption satisfaction. Thus, these results have major implications for package and product design, range of sizes to carry, and communication of package sizes. For example, clever graphics can lead to a perception of a larger package. If certain dimensions of a package are larger than others (rectangular cartons), these dimensions could be made salient with the use of graphics. Also, not enough companies are focusing attention on how package size information is communicated. A simple example of this is fast food pizza parlors where some parlors give size dimensions in diameter whereas others paste up a picture of the different sized pizzas. Spatial perception research suggests that consumers understand the size increase more readily when presented with pictures of the various sizes, versus when merely presented with the diameters. The research also suggests that offering a discount on two small pizzas may be perceived as more favorable than a discount on one large pizza of the same total area, which may go some way to explaining the success of two-for-one pizza outlets.

Implications for perceived area also apply to the surface area of packages as seen on retail shelves. If consumers want to buy the "biggest" box of detergent within a price range and do not peruse the unit price information (Dickson & Sawyer, 1986), then the shelf facing perceived to have the largest surface area will be chosen. Thus, tall rectangular boxes have two advantages over square ones of equal volume—more fit on a shelf facing, and greater perceived volume. The variation in shapes of cereal boxes suggests that this is not conventional wisdom in the packaging industry.

Conclusions and Areas for Future Research

In line with our framework, future research in spatial perceptions can fall under six different venues (among others), namely:

1. Basic spatial perception research where one is finding completely new spatial perception biases. This would be akin to showing the direct distance bias (Raghubir & Krishna, 1996), what affects perceptions of variety (Kahn & Wansink, 2004) or whether idle time/time away from the goal increases perceptions of total time spent (Soman & Shi, 2003).
2. Testing if established spatial perception biases carry over to other constructs of importance in marketing research. This would be similar to seeing whether the clutter effect carried over to number perceptions, especially to perceptions of number of people in waiting lines (Krishna & Raghubir, 1997). Thus, one could test whether spatial perception effects found for length perceptions carried over for time perceptions, for example, if time perceptions within a mental time category are more accurate than across two mental time categories. Similarly, one could test whether number perception effects carried over for variety perceptions, for example, the solitaire illusion.
3. Testing how spatial perceptions can impact consumer behavior. Kahn and Wansink have studied how variety perceptions affect consumption, and Soman and Shi (2003) have seen the effect of idle time on choice of service. Also, Raghubir and Greenleaf (2006) have shown that certain ratios of sides for products are preferred by consumers and are more likely to be purchased than others (the golden ratio of 1:1.62 vs. 1:1.38). Note that (2) focuses on biases whereas (3) focuses on spatial perceptions, biased or not.

4. Study if spatial perceptions vary across different cultures. Krishna and Zhou (2005) show that people of Asian origin may be less prone to certain spatial perception biases. They test if this difference is due to the fact that some East Asians use a pictorial script or because they take the context into account more than Americans do (see Masuda & Nisbett, 2001).
5. Studying if relative dominance of alternate sensory inputs used to make spatial perception judgments can affect these judgments. Krishna (2006) shows, for instance, that the elongation bias whereby a tall, thin container appears larger than an equi-volume short, fat container is reversed when touch as opposed to vision is dominant for the volume judgment task.
6. Determining how consumer behavior resulting from spatial perception biases should impact managerial decision making. While prior research has suggested avenues for how it may impact managerial decision making, no research to our knowledge has been done from the manager's viewpoint systematically designing a marketing program taking spatial perceptions into account. Needless to say, this would be very valuable research.

Thus, there is a lot of scope and need for future work in the area of spatial perceptions. This review is an attempt to foster this research.

Acknowledgments

Much material for this chapter is from joint research done by Aradhna Krishna and Priya Raghubir.

References

Allen, G. L., & Kirasic, K. C. (1985). Effects of the cognitive organization of route knowledge on judgments of macrospatial distance. *Memory and Cognition, 13*(3), 218–227.

Allen, G. L., Siegel, A. W., & Rosinski, R. R. (1978). The role of perceptual context in structuring spatial knowledge. *Journal of Experimental Psychology: Human Learning and Memory, 4*, 617–630.

Anastasi, A. (1936). The estimation of area. *Journal of General Psychology, 14*, 201–225.

Anderson, N. H., & Cuneo, D. O. (1978). The height + width rule in children's judgments of quantity. *Journal of Experimental Psychology: General, 107*(4), 335–378.

Atkinson, J., Francis, M. R., & Campbell, F. W. (1976). The dependence of the visual numerosity limit on orientation, color and grouping in the stimulus. *Perception, 5*, 335–344.

Baird, J. C., Romer, D., & Stein, T. (1970). Test of a cognitive theory of psychophysics: Size discrimination. *Perceptual and Motor Skills, 30*(2), 495–501.

Beckwith, M., & Restle, F. (1966). Process of enumeration. *Psychological Review, 73*, 437–444.

Been, R.T., Braunstein, M. L., & Piazza, M. H. (1964). Judgment of volume reduction in distorted metal containers. *Journal of Engineering Psychology, 3*, 23–27.

Brandt, A., & Kebeck, G. (1983). Streckenvergleiche im Rokokopark. Ein Beitrag zur Distanzwahrnehmung unter natürlichen Bedingungen [Route comparisons in Rokokopark. A contribution to distance perceiving in natural circumstances]. *5*, 114–124.

Brendl, C. M., Markman, A. B., & Messner, C. (2003). The devaluation effect: Activating a need devalues unrelated choice options. *Journal of Consumer Research, 29*, 463–473.

Brooks, C. M., Kaufmann, P. J., & Lichtenstein, D. R. (2004). The influence of travel configuration on consumer trip-chained store choice. *Journal of Consumer Research, 31*, 241–248.

Brosvic, G. M., & Cohen, B. D. (1988). The horizontal-vertical illusion and knowledge of the results. *Perceptual and Motor Skills, 67*(2), 463–469.

Bruner, J. S., & Goodman, C.C. (1947). Value and need as organizing factors in perception. *Journal of Abnormal and Social Psychology, 42*, 33–44.

Byrne, R.W. (1979). Memory for urban geography. *Quarterly Journal of Experimental Psychology, 31*(Feb), 147–154.

Carmon, Z. (1991). Recent studies of time in consumer behavior. *Association for Consumer Research, 18*, 703–705.

Carmon, Z., & Kahneman, D. (1995). The experienced utility of queuing: Experience profiles and retrospective evaluations of simulated queues (Working Paper). University of North Carolina.

Chandon, P., & Wansink, B. (2002). When are stockpiled products consumed faster? A convenience-salience framework of post-purchase consumption incidence and quantity. *Journal of Marketing Research, 39*, 321–325.

Chandon, P., & Wansink, B. (2005). Obesity and the consumption underestimation bias (Working Paper). University of North Carolina.

Cohen, R., & Weatherford, D. L. (1980). Effects of route traveled on the distance estimates of children and adults. *Journal of Experimental Child Psychology, 29*, 403–412.

Croxton, F. E., & Stein, H. (1932). Graphic comparisons by bars, squares, circles, and cubes. *Journal of the American Statistical Association, 27,* 54–60.

Dainoff, M. J., Miskie, D., Wilson, C., & Crane, P. (1974). Psychophysical measurement of environmental distance. In D. H. Carson (Ed.), *Man-environment interactions: Evaluations and associations EDRA 5 proceedings*. University of Milwaukee, Milwaukee. New York: Dowden, Hutchinson and Ross.

Dickson, P. R., & Sawyer, A. G. (1986). *Point of purchase behaviour and price perceptions of supermarket shoppers* (MSI Rep. No. 86–102). *3,* 42–53.

Dixon, P. (1978). Numerical comparison processes. *Memory and cognition, 6*(4), 454–461.

Ekman, G. (1958). Two generalized ratio scaling methods. *Journal of Psychology, 45,* 287–295.

Finger, F. W., & Spelt, D. K. (1947). The illustration of the horizontal-vertical illusion. *Journal of Experimental Psychology, 37,* 243–250.

Fisher, G. H., & Foster, J. J. (1968). Apparent sizes of different shapes and the facility with which they can be identified. *Nature, 219,* 653–654

Folkes, V. S., Martin, I. M., & Gupta, K. (1993). When to say when: Effects of supply on usage. *Journal of Consumer Research, 20,* 467–477.

Folkes, V., & Matta, S. (2004). The effect of package shape on consumers' judgments of product volume: Attention as a mental contaminant. *Journal of Consumer Research, 31*(2), 390–401.

Frayman, B. J., & Dawson, W. E. (1981). The effect of object shape and mode of presentation on judgments of apparent volume. *Perception and Psychophysics, 29*(1), 56–62.

Frith, C. D., & Frith, U. (1972). The solitaire illusion: An illusion of numerosity. *Perception and Psychophysics, 11,* 409–410.

Gelman, R (1969). Conservation acquisition: A problem of learning to attend to relevant attributes. *Journal of Experimental Child Psychology,* 7, 167–187.

Ginsburg, N. (1978). Perceived numerosity, item arrangement, and expectancy. *American Journal of Psychology, 91*(2), 267–273.

Ginsburg, N. (1980). The regular-random numerosity illusion: Rectangular patterns. *Journal of General Psychology, 103*(2), 211.

Golledge, R. G., & Zannaras, G. (1973). Cognitive approaches to the analysis of human spatial behavior. In W. Ittelson (Ed.), *Environment and Cognition* (pp. 59–94). New York: Seminar Press.

Haines, G. H., Jr., Simon, L. S., & Alexis, M. (1972). Maximum likelihood estimation of central city food trading areas. *Journal of Marketing Research, 9*(2), 154–159.

Hanes, R. M. (1950). Some effects of shape on apparent brightness. *Journal of Experimental Psychology, 40,* 650–654.

Holmberg, L. (1975). The influence of elongation on the perception of volume of geometrically simple objects. *Psychological Research Bulletin, 15*(2), 1–18.

Holmberg, L., & Holmberg, I. (1969). The perception of the area of rectangles as a function of the ratio between height and width. *Psychological Research Bulletin, 9*(6).

Hubbard, T. L., Kall, D., & Baird, J. C. (1989). Imagery, memory and size distance invariance. *Memory and Cognition, 17*(1), 87

Kahn, B. E., & Wansink, B. (2004). Impact of perceived variety on consumption quantity. *Journal of Consumer Research, 30*(4), 519–534.

Kosslyn, S. M., Pick, H. L., & Fariello, G. R. (1974). Cognitive maps in children and men. *Child Development, 45,* 707–716.

Krider R., Raghubir, P., & Krishna, A. (2001). Pizza—pi or squared?: The effect of perceived area on price perceptions. *Marketing Science, 20*(4), 405–425.

Krishna, A. (2006). The interaction of senses: The effect of vision and touch on the elongation bias. *Journal of Consumer Research, 32*(4), 557–566.

Krishna, A., & Raghubir, P. (1997). The effect of line configuration on perceived numerosity of dotted lines. *Memory and Cognition, 25*(4), 492–507.

Krishna, A., & Zhou, R. (2005). *A cross-cultural perspective on spatial perceptions: Does a pictorial script help with spatial judgments.* (Working paper). University of Michigan.

Larson, J. S., Bradlow, E. T., & Fader, P. S. (forthcoming). An exploratory look at supermarket shopping paths. *International Journal of Research in Marketing.*

Lee, T. R. (1963). Psychology and living space. *Transactions of the Bartlett Society, 11.*

Lee, T. R. (1970). Perceived distance as a function of direction in the city. *Environment and Behaviour, 2,* 40–51

Lipman, M. (1991). *Thinking in education.*Cambridge: Cambridge University Press.

Mansvelt, E. (1928). Over het schatten van de grootte van figuren van verschillenden vorm. [On the size judgments of figures of different forms]. *Mededelingen uit het Psychologisch Laboratorium der Rijksuniversiteit te Utrecht, 4*(2), 134–137.

Martinez, N., & Dawson, W. E. (1973). Ranking of apparent area for different shapes of equal area. *Perceptual and Motor Skills, 37*(3), 763–770.

Masuda, T., & Nisbett, R. E. (2001). Attending holistically versus analytically: Comparing the context of sensitivity of Japanese and Americans. *Journal of Personality and Social Psychology, 81*(5), 922.

McNamara, T. P. (1986). Mental representations of spatial relations. *Cognitive Psychology, 18*, 87–121.

McNamara, T. P., Ratcliff, R., & McKoon, G. (1984). The mental representation of knowledge acquired from maps. *Journal of Experimental Psychology: Learning, Memory and Cognition, 10*, 723–732.

Moyer, R. S., Bradley, D. R., Sorenson, M. H., Whiting, J. C., & Mansfield, D. P. (1978). Psychophysical functions for perceived and remembered size. *Science, 200*(4339), 330–332.

Nasar, J. L., Valencia, H., Abidin, O., Chueh, S., & Hwang, J. (1985). *Environment and Behavior, 17*(5), 627–639.

Newcombe, N., & Liben, L. S. (1982). Barrier effects in the cognitive maps of children and adults. *Journal of Experimental Child Psychology, 34*, 46–58.

Oeffelen, van, M. P., & Vos, P. G. (1982). Configurational effects on the enumeration of dots: Counting by groups. *Memory and Cognition, 10*(4), 396–404.

Oeffelen, van, M. P., & Vos, P. G. (1984). Enumeration of dots: An eye movement analysis. *Memory and Cognition, 12*(6), 607–612.

Oppel, J. (1855). Ueber geometrisch-optische Tauschungen [About geometrical-optical illusions]. *Jber.Phys. Ver., Frankfurt*, 34–47.

Painter, J. E., Wansink, B., & Hieggelke, J. B. (2002). How visibility and convenience influence candy consumption. *Appetite, 38*, 237–238.

Pearson, R. G. (1964). Judgment of volume from photographs of complex shapes. *Perceptual and Motor Skills, 18*, 889–900.

Piaget, J. (1967). Cognitions and conservations: Two views. *Contemporary Psychology, 12*, 532–533.

Piaget, J. (1968). Quantification, conservation and nativism. *Science, 162*, 976–979.

Piaget, J., Inhelder, B., & Szeminska, A. (1960). *The child's conception of geometry.* New York: Basic Books.

Poucet, B., Thinus-Blanc, C., & Chapius, N. (1983). Route planning in cats, in relation to the visibility of the goal. *Animal Behavior, 31*(2), 594–599.

Raghubir, P. (2006). Are visual perceptual biases hard-wired? In M. Wedel & R. Pieters (Eds.), *Visual marketing: From attention to action.* Mahwah, NJ: Lawrence Erlbaum, 143–165.

Raghubir, P., & Greenleaf, E. (forthcoming). Ratios in proportion: What should be the shape of the package? *Journal of Marketing, 70*(2), April, 95–107.

Raghubir, P., & Krishna, A. (1996). As the crow flies: Bias in consumers' map-based distance judgments. *Journal of Consumer Research, 23,* 26–39.

Raghubir, P., & Krishna, A. (1999). Vital dimensions: Antecedents and consequences of biases in volume perceptions. *Journal of Marketing Research*, 36(August), 313–326.

Sadalla, E. K., & Magel, S. G. (1980). The perception of traversed distance. *Environment and Behavior, 12*(1), 65–79.

Sadalla, E. K., & Staplin, L. J. (1980). The perception of traversed distance: Intersections. *Environment and Behavior, 12*(2), 167–182.

Smets, G. (1970). When do two figures seem equal in size? *Perceptual and Motor Skills, 30,* 1008.

Smitsman, A. W. (1982). Perception of number. *International Journal of Behavioral Development, 5*(1), 1–31.

Soman, D., & Shi, M. (2003). Virtual progress: The effect of path characteristics on perceptions of progress and choice behavior. *Management Science, 49*(9), 1229–1250.

Stevens, S. S., & Guirao, M. (1963). Subjective scaling of length and area and the matching of length to loudness and brightness. *Journal of Experimental Psychology, 66,* 177–186.

Teghtsoonian, M. (1965). The judgment of size. *American Journal of Psychology, 78,* 392–402.

Thorndyke, P. W. (1981). Distance estimation from cognitive maps. *Cognitive Psychology, 13,* 526–550.

Underhill, P. (1999). *Why we buy: The science of shopping.* New York: Simon and Schuster.

Verge, C. G., & Bogartz, R. S. (1978). A functional measurement analysis of the development of dimensional coordination in children. *Journal of Experimental Child Psychology, 25*(2), 337–353.

Wagner, E. (1931). Das abschatzen von flachen [The judgment of areas]. *Psychotechnisches Zeitschrift, 6,* 140–148.

Wansink, B. (1996). Can package size accelerate usage volume? *Journal of Marketing, 60*(3), 1–14.

Wansink, B., & Ittersum, van, K. (2003). Bottoms up! The influence of elongation on pouring and consumption volume. *Journal of Consumer Research, 30*(3), 455–463.

Wansink, B., & Park, S. (2001). At the movies: How external cues and perceived taste impact consumption volume. *Food Quality and Preference Journal, 12*(1), 69–74.

Wansink, B., & Ray, M. L. (1996). Advertising strategies to increase usage frequency. *Journal of Marketing, 60*(1), 31–46.

Warren, J. M., & Pinneau, S. R. (1955). Influence of form on judgment of apparent area. *Perceptual and Motor Skills, 5*(7), 10.

Wolters, G., Kempen, van, H., & Wijlhuizen, G. (1987). Quantification of small number of dots: Subitizing or pattern recognition. *American Journal of Psychology, 100*(2), 225–237.

Yang, S., & Raghubir, P. (2005). Can bottles speak volumes? The effect of package shape on how much to buy, *Journal of Retailing, 81*(4), 269–282.

Zhou, R., & Soman, D. (2003). Looking back: Exploring the psychology of queuing and the effect of the number of people behind? *Journal of Consumer Research, 29*, 517–530.

9

Perhaps the Store Made You Purchase It

Toward an Understanding of Structural Aspects of Indoor Shopping Environments

Joan Meyers-Levy and Rui (Juliet) Zhu

Introduction

It is often suggested that the design and structural aspects of indoor shopping and consumption environments can affect people's thought processes and responses (e.g., Bechtel, 1997). Nevertheless, our current understanding remains extremely limited about (a) which structural aspects of our environment may be influential, (b) exactly how, why, and when they exert an effect on us, and (c) what consequences these factors have on the many perceptions, judgments, and decisions that we form daily. Two significant factors underlie this gap: the minimal attention paid to structural factors of indoor environments, and the lack of theory-guided investigation that might illuminate answers to these questions. This chapter endeavors to address these barriers and shed light on these questions by drawing on theory and applying it to a wide range of potentially consequential indoor structural elements, particularly ones present in most shopping environments.

Throughout this chapter, we employ the term *structural* quite broadly to refer to all types of (semi-)permanent, tangible elements that often inhabit shopping and consumption environments. We group these structural elements into three categories: architectural factors (e.g., ceilings, windows), free-standing, in-store structures (e.g., display cases, mirrors), and broader contextual factors (e.g., the presence of nearby stores with same- or complementary-category merchandise). We propose that such structural aspects of shopping environments frequently influence not only consumers' cognition and responses, but also the very manner in which they process pertinent information.

Despite this bold proposition, we could uncover little empirical research that investigates this possibility. Undoubtedly, some work has investigated the influence of certain shopping-relevant atmospheric variables such as color (Gorn, Chattopadhyay, Sengupta, & Tripathi, 2004; Meyers-Levy & Peracchio, 1995), odor (Mitchell, Kahn, & Knasko, 1995; Morrin & Ratneshwar, 2003), music (Kellaris & Kent, 1992; Zhu & Meyers-Levy, 2005), consumer crowding (Freedman, 1975; Hui & Bateson, 1991), and noise (Page, 1977; Siegel & Steele, 1980). However, the majority of such studies focus on intangible versus concrete or tangible structural elements. Further, of the few structure-focused studies that we did find (e.g., Ulrich, 1984; Wilson, 1972), virtually none suggested or tested any theoretical explanation for the proposed or observed effects.

To illustrate this, consider some provocative work by Maass et al. (2000) in which individuals were asked to imagine that they were approaching a courthouse with their friend, who was to be tried for stealing goods found in his or her unlocked garage. To aid envisioning this and facilitate spatial perception (Krishna, ch. 8, and Raghubir, ch. 9, this book), participants were shown exterior photos of either an old or a modern courthouse shot at successively closer distances. Findings revealed that participants who were familiar with the viewed building felt greater discomfort when the courthouse was modern versus old. Further, regardless of such familiarity, participants anticipated a higher likelihood of a conviction when the courthouse was modern rather than old. These findings underscore that critical aspects of one's environment may indeed exert an influence on perceptions. Nonetheless, the study neither considered nor examined which particular building features were responsible for participants' differing responses (e.g., the courthouses' differently-sized windows, doors, building materials, etc.).

In summary, this chapter aims to bridge a critical gap in the literature by (a) identifying structural aspects of indoor shopping environments that might affect consumers' responses, (b) applying existing theories to these structural elements to account for how, when and why they might exert an effect, and (c) offering testable propositions intended to spur much needed research in this area and thereby shed light on relevant theoretical and applied matters.

The chapter is organized as follows. We begin by discussing illustrative work that we conducted, which investigates one particular structural property, namely ceiling height. Thus, the next section presents several studies that indicate how ceiling height not only may affect the manner in which consumers process information, but also how they categorize, judge, and remember products. Then we will consider a myriad of structural shopping environment elements and, for each, draw on existing theories that illustrate how theory can spawn viable and testable hypotheses concerning the influence of such elements.

The Effect of Ceiling Height on Processing

Ceiling height has been ranked among the top three architectural details that influence consumers' psychological well-being (Fischl & Gärling, 2004). Moreover, much anecdotal evidence suggests that the ceiling height of indoor environments can produce an array of salutary effects. For example, higher ceilings are suggested to improve the clarity of people's thinking, their energy level, and their health (Bivens, 1997). Perhaps believing in such benefits, airplane manufacturers reportedly employ a variety of techniques that simply foster the illusion of heightened ceilings (Lunsford & Michaels, 2002). Yet, despite such purported benefits, we could find no empirical evidence to suggest whether, how, when or why variation in ceiling height actually matters.

Intrigued by and motivated to explore such issues, we crafted some theorizing and recently embarked on a series of studies involving ceiling (Meyers-Levy & Zhu, 2007). Based on researchers' speculation that rooms with large versus small vertical volume might prime related concepts (e.g., Hall, 1966), we reasoned that, provided individuals are somewhat aware of ceiling height, a high versus low ceiling may prime the concepts of freedom versus confinement, respectively. Moreover, based on an analogous relationship that has been posited in an unrelated body of literature (Kühnen & Oyserman, 2002), we further theorized that, in turn, these two concepts might alter the very type of processing that people use.

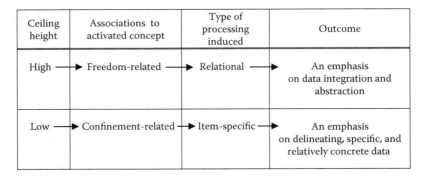

Ceiling height	Associations to activated concept	Type of processing induced	Outcome
High →	Freedom-related →	Relational →	An emphasis on data integration and abstraction
Low →	Confinement-related →	Item-specific →	An emphasis on delineating, specific, and relatively concrete data

Figure 9.1 Model of the mechanism by which ceiling height can affect type of processing.

Specifically, when ceiling height is high and presumably primes the concept of freedom, we conjectured that individuals might engage in predominantly relational processing. This seems to follow because relational elaboration involves processing data *freely* with an eye toward discerning commonalities or, as has been conjectured albeit never tested, higher-order abstractions that are shared by multiple pieces of data (Einstein & Hunt, 1980; Hunt & Einstein, 1981). On the other hand, when ceiling height is low and presumably primes the concept of confinement, we reasoned that item-specific processing might prevail. This would seem to be implicated because item-specific elaboration involves *confining* or restricting one's focus on each isolated piece of data and concentrating on the item's fairly precise, context-specific, concrete attributes. Hence, per this theorizing, we expected that people in a high ceiling room would engage in fairly integrative (i.e., relational) and abstract ideation, while those in a low ceiling room would engage in highly delineating, concrete thinking. With such theorizing in mind (see Figure 9.1 for a summary), we designed several experiments that sought to trace these proposed linkages.

The first experiment examined our initial premise: Provided that ceiling height is reasonably salient, a high versus low ceiling will activate freedom- versus confinement-related concepts. To test this, participants completed a study in rooms that were identical except for their ceiling height; either it was relatively high (10 feet) or low (8 feet). To ensure that participants paid at least passing attention to the ceiling, we enhanced its salience by hanging three Chinese lanterns from it. Three tasks were developed for the study, each allowing detection of participants' relative accessibility of the freedom and confinement concepts. For expediency, we describe only two of the tasks here, those concerning body state and animal preferences.

In a perceived body state task, participants reported their current body state on several items, half that tapped the feeling of freedom (e.g., unrestricted) and half that tapped the feeling of confinement (e.g., encumbered). Because individuals in a high versus low ceiling room were hypothesized to activate the earlier-specified concepts, participants in the higher ceiling room should report an elevated freedom-related body state, but a lower confinement-related body state, whereas these effects should reverse for those in the lower ceiling room. In the animal preference task, participants were asked to select a preferred animal from several animal pairs, where each pair included a wild (free) animal and a similar animal that was domesticated (confined; e.g., tropical versus aquarium fish). Because a high ceiling room should not only activate freedom-related concepts but also the use of abstract ideation, we hypothesized that participants in this condition might process the animal pairs abstractly, rendering them insensitive and indifferent to the specific (i.e., wild or domesticated) attributes of the paired animals. Hence, they should prefer the animals equally. In contrast, a low ceiling should activate confinement-related concepts and prompt the use of item-specific and concrete thinking. If so, participants in this condition should be sensitive to the specific wild or domesticated status of the animals. However, because the presumably primed concept of confinement (versus freedom) may possess somewhat negative connotations when applied to the particular case of animals (i.e., confining animals may seem to defy their preordained natural state), we reasoned that participants in a low ceiling room might respond to this and express a preference for the wild (free) versus domesticated (confined) animal in the pairs.

Our predicted outcomes emerged on each of these (and a third anagram) tasks. Hence, it appears that ceiling height can prime the anticipated concepts.

A second study tested the core of our theorizing: Freedom- versus confinement-related concepts primed by a high versus low ceiling can in turn induce reliance on relational versus item-specific processing, respectively. Yet critically, this should only occur when the salience of the ceiling height is rather high, not low. Because we anticipated that relational versus item-specific processing fosters integrative and abstract ideation rather than delineative concrete thinking, two tasks, one involving categorization and the other judgments, were developed that should be sensitive to these forms of processing. For expediency, we detail only one task here.

For the categorization task, participants received a list of 10 disparate and far-ranging sports. They were asked to identify as many dimensions as they could that were shared by the items (e.g., "all the sports require equipment"). Then, for each dimension, they were to categorize the items into labeled subgroups based on each item's value on that dimension (e.g., given the preceding dimension, they grouped the sports by the type of equipment needed). The type of processing that participants used should be manifested on three indicators. First, individuals in a high versus low ceiling room were expected to identify a larger number of shared dimensions. The logic here is that because these individuals rely primarily on relational versus item-specific processing, this should prompt them to see more connections (i.e., relationships) among the disparate items. Second, those in a high (low) ceiling room should identify dimensions that are more abstract (concrete). This should occur because the relational processing presumably used by those in a high ceiling room should foster greater abstract ideation (Einstein & Hunt, 1980). In contrast, the item-specific processing favored by people in a lower ceiling room should prompt more precise, context-specific thinking, which should spawn more concrete dimensions (Liberman, Sagristano, & Trope, 2002). Third, due to their greater reliance on relational versus item-specific elaboration, participants in a high versus low ceiling room should sort the sports items into fewer subgroups per dimension. This follows because more inclusive (and thereby fewer) categories reflect both more extensive search for shared features or relations (Isen, 1987) and more abstract categorization (Liberman et al., 2002).

All results supported our predictions. More specifically, when ceiling height salience was relatively high (i.e., the lanterns hung from and thus drew attention to the ceiling), participants in the high ceiling condition evidenced more integrative abstract thinking, while those in the low ceiling condition demonstrated greater delineative concrete ideation. But when manipulations rendered the salience of the ceiling low (i.e., the lanterns were near eye level and thereby limited attention to the ceiling), null effects emerged. In addition, we should note that ancillary investigation ruled out the possibility that ceiling-height-induced differences in affect could account for such findings.

Experiment 3 served two purposes. It sought additional evidence for our theory by examining two well-established, "gold standard" indicators of relational and item-specific processing, namely recall clustering during free recall, and cued recall, respectively. It also aimed to offer mediational support for the proposed linkages. To accomplish this, this study: (a) varied ceiling height, but always held its salience constant at a high level; (b) administered the body state assessment task employed previously in experiment 1; and (c) exposed participants to a list of 36 items from six different categories (e.g., birds, occupations), which, after several filler tasks, they were asked to reproduce in both free and cued recall tasks.

Conceptually replicating previous studies that have established people's type of processing by assessing recall clustering and cued recall (e.g., Hunt & Seta, 1984), we hypothesized that participants in the higher ceiling (i.e., relational processing) condition would produce higher recall clustering on a free recall task, yet those in the lower ceiling (i.e., item-specific processing) condition would generate more items during cued recall. Further, we expected to replicate a finding from experiment 1, namely that participants in the higher (lower) ceiling condition would indicate that they presently experienced a higher freedom (confinement) body state. Indeed, the latter observations were important: Because the two body state indices can serve as indicators that people in the high (low) ceiling condition indeed activated the freedom- (confinement-) related concept, they can provide valuable evidence in a mediation analysis. Specifically, in accordance with our theorizing, participants in a high versus low ceiling room should not only exhibit greater recall clustering (signifying primary use of relational processing), but this effect should be mediated by these individuals' heightened freedom-related body state. Analogously, participants in a low versus high ceiling room should exhibit superior cued recall performance (signifying predominant reliance on item-specific processing), yet this outcome should be mediated by their heightened confinement-related body state.

In fact, each of these expectations was confirmed. Thus, experiment 3 provided even more compelling support for the inferences drawn from study 2 and offered mediational support for our theorizing.

Our final study sought to reproduce several of our previously observed outcomes, but did so when ceiling height was held constant yet the freedom- and confinement-related concepts were primed explicitly. Such evidence would powerfully attest to the generalizeability of our basic theory—independent of ceiling height.

It also would provide further mediational support for the theory (for elucidation of this point, see Spencer, Zanna, & Fong, 2005).

In experiment 4, participants were always seated in a low (8 foot) ceiling room and they completed the same tasks used in study 2. Yet, several changes distinguished this study. First, an affect-neutral scenario generation task was administered to activate one of the critical concepts. To prime the freedom concept, participants were asked to describe a situation in which they were in an open and unconfined space that made them feel carefree and boundless. To prime the confinement concept, participants did the same but described a context where they were in a protected and confined space that made them feel cozy and snugly content. Second, the list of sports used in study 2's categorization task was supplemented with a second list (i.e., vehicles). Third, we added a new category membership judgment task in which participants viewed two lists of exemplars from alternative categories (i.e., furniture and clothing). In each list the exemplars were good, moderate, and poor representations of the general category, and participants had to indicate the degree to which each exemplar belonged to that category. We expected that all participants would rate the good exemplars as superior category representations, given their unambiguous superior status. However freedom- versus confinement-primed participants, who should employ predominately relational versus item-specific processing, were expected to regard both the moderate and poor (i.e., more ambiguous) exemplars as better representations of their categories. This follows because relational (item-specific) processing should help individuals perceive more commonalities (unique differences) between such exemplars and the general category.

The findings from experiment 4 upheld all predictions. As such, they provide compelling support for the fundamental tenets of our theorizing and thereby demonstrate that our observed outcomes are not unique effects of ceiling height. Rather, other factors that activate the relevant freedom and confinement concepts, if only using illusory techniques (e.g., the presence or absence of trompe l'oeil sky scenes on ceilings), should produce comparable effects.

Summary

The reviewed series of studies are noteworthy in several respects. Most obviously, they offer seemingly compelling evidence that by varying the structural variable of ceiling height, the vertical volume of space in people's daily consumption and shopping environments may influence *how* they use the information they encounter. Higher volume environments prime thoughts concerning freedom and thereby prompt the use of integrative (relational) as well as abstraction-fostering ideation. In contrast, low volume contexts activate thoughts about confinement and elicit cognitive activity focused on (item-specific) delineation and concrete thinking. Impressively, evidence of this was observed on an assortment of measures, including gauges of product categorization, judgments, and alternative memory indicators.

These observations also are important in several far-ranging ways. First, they raise the possibility that other potentially volume-influencing variables may similarly affect human cognition. Some likely candidates include a room's length or width that (unlike its height) controls horizontal room volume, pastel versus intense colors that seemingly expand or shrink room volume, the presence of low versus high density objects within a given space, and, as we will discuss in greater detail later, the presence versus absence of windows within a room. Second, the findings of the studies underscore a much larger point and one that is central in this chapter: Although they have been largely overlooked in research, structural properties of our environment possess the potential to alter the very nature of our cognition, the ideas that inhabit our minds, and the behaviors that we manifest. Last but by no means least, the studies we have just reviewed demonstrate how by engaging in in-depth and insightful application of existing theories, it may well be possible to both predict and explain how a variety of structural factors in shopping and other milieus critically affect our lives and actions. Our focus in the next section is to do just that.

Theory-Derived Propositions about Structural Factors in Shopping Environment

When shopping for products in a store, consumers typically are exposed to a variety of tangible, semi-permanent or permanent architectural elements (e.g., windows, walls), free-standing in-store structures (e.g., display tables, mirrors), and broader features of the shopping center (e.g., same-category stores within the mall). Although consumer researchers have paid little heed to such elements, we propose that such factors may influence consumers' product responses or behaviors.

In this section, we demonstrate how extant theory can shed light on and enable predictions about which, when, and why such structural factors in shopping environments may influence consumers' perceptions or behavior (see Table 9.1 for a summary of the examined structural elements and the theories used to derive predictions). We discuss all three types of structural factors noted above, starting with architectural elements.

Architectural Factors

Windows Windows are a frequent element of the retail architectural landscape. Although consumers may devote only momentary attention to such windows, there is reason to believe that they may influence consumers' processing of and responses to products (see Ulrich, 1984, & Wilson, 1972, for some relevant intriguing findings, albeit neither theoretically derived nor uniquely explained).

Drawing on the same theorizing discussed earlier in our ceiling height studies (see Figure 9.1 of Meyers-Levy & Zhu, 2007), we propose that the presence or absence of store windows might affect consumers in a similar manner. That is, like retail spaces with high versus low ceilings, the presence versus absence of store windows might prime consumers to think about the concepts of freedom versus confinement, respectively. In turn, the activation of these concepts might shape the type of processing that consumers employ during their shopping. Paralleling our ceiling height findings, the freedom- (confinement-) related thoughts spawned by the presence (absence) of windows may stimulate the use of relational (item-specific) elaboration, which should affect whether consumers' ideation about products is largely integrative and abstract (delineative and concrete).

If the preceding is so, consumers in a store with versus without windows should not only exhibit differences in their categorization, judgments, and memory of products as they did in our ceiling height studies, but they also may manifest differences in creativity and vigilance. For example, assuming that the presence (versus absence) of store windows induces primarily relational (item-specific) processing, consumers in

TABLE 9.1 Structural Elements Proposed to Affect Cognition and Behavior and Suggested Theories that Offer Predictions

Category of Structural Elements	Focal Elements	Selected Theories Suggesting Predictions
Architectural Factors	Ceiling Height	Type of elaboration theory (Hunt & Einstein 1981; Meyers-Levy 1991)
	Windows	Type of elaboration theory (Hunt & Einstein 1981; Meyers-Levy 1991)
	Wall Composition	Priming (Higgins 1996); context effects (Stapel, Koomen, & Velthuijsen 1998)
	Wall Contour	Gender schema theory (Bem 1981)
	Store Layout	Reason introspection (Wilson & LaFleur 1995)
	Architectural Adventure Elements	Perceptual fluency theory (Schwarz, ch. 11, this book)
Free-Standing In-Store Structures	Display Surfaces	Self-construal theory (Markus & Kitayama 1991; Nisbett et al. 2001); context effects (Stapel, Koomen, & Velthuijsen 1998)
	Types of Display Cases	Regulatory focus theory (Crowe & Higgins 1997)
	Arrangement of Display Cases	Gestalt principle of closure (Solomon 2007); process-driven affect theory (Meyers-Levy & Tybout 1989)
	Store Fixture-Product Access Interface	Process-driven affect theory (Meyers-Levy & Tybout 1989; Peracchio & Meyers-Levy 1994)
	Mirror Orientation	Proprioceptive feedback theory (Friedman & Förster 2000; Stepper & Strack 1993)
	Virtual Reality Tools	Self-referencing theory (Burnkrant & Unnava 1989; Meyers-Levy & Peracchio 1996)
	Countertop Displays	Terror management theory (Greenberg, Solomon, & Pyszczynski 1997)

continued

TABLE 9.1 (continued) Structural Elements Proposed to Affect Cognition and Behavior and Suggested Theories that Offer Predictions

Category of Structural Elements	Focal Elements	Selected Theories Suggesting Predictions
	Artwork	Temporal construal theory (Friedman & Liberman 2004; Liberman, Sagristano, & Trope 2002)
Broader Contextual Factors	The Architecture of the Broader Shopping Environment	Resource matching theory (Meyers-Levy & Peracchio 1995)
	Same- and Complementary-Category Stores	Part cuing effect (Alba & Chattopadhyay 1985); type of elaboration theory (Hunt & Einstein 1981; Meyers-Levy 1991)

stores with versus without windows may generate more creative ways of using products, such as buying colorful kitchen trivets, intended to protect furniture from hot dish burns, for use as decorative wall hangings. On the other hand, consumers in a store without versus with windows, who should rely predominantly on item-specific versus relational processing, may be less responsive per se to a sign that indicates a sale, yet more responsive to the precise depth of the price markdowns (e.g., $10 versus only $5). Likewise, these more detail-vigilant item-specific processors may be reluctant to buy a product if it has slight imperfections like smudges, wrinkles, or a snagged thread. Finally, while relational processing shoppers in a store with windows may be more swayed by a product's abstract features, say a lamp's attractive overall design, those in a store without windows (i.e., item-specific processors) may be more influenced by its specific functional attributes, say the lamp's use of halogen (versus standard) bulbs.

Wall Composition Another potentially consequential architectural feature of shopping environments is the composition of a store's internal walls. Although most store walls consist of smooth painted drywall, it is not uncommon to observe walls made of materials like brick, wood paneling, stucco, textured paint or wallpaper, or glass. It seems possible that the composition of a store's walls might affect consumers' perceptions of store products.

Consistent with this notion, extant research suggests that, due to people's common experiences or observations, they often learn or develop shared associations to items (Peracchio & Meyers-Levy, 2005). For example, because brick is made from compacted clay and is commonly used in constructing sturdy homes and fireplaces, people are likely to associate brick with concepts like durability, hominess, and naturalness. On the other hand, because glass is breakable, typically manufactured, and often is a dominant feature in modern décor and buildings, it is likely to be associated with concepts like fragility, modernity, and fabrication (i.e., artificiality).

In light of extant research concerning both priming (e.g., Higgins, 1996) and context effects (e.g., Meyers-Levy & Tybout, 1997), it may be that perceptions of products located near a wall made of such materials could be subject to context effects. This is especially likely if the product itself is ambiguous on the characteristics associated with the wall material (e.g., the product's durability, coziness, and/or naturalness is ambiguous). Numerous theories propose factors that should influence whether a target product will be perceived to possess the associated characteristics of the wall (i.e., an assimilation effect; for example, a product displayed near a brick wall might be viewed as relatively durable, homey and natural) or possess opposite characteristics (i.e., a contrast effect; a product displayed near a brick wall would be viewed as quite fragile, modern and artificial). For example, according to theorizing by Stapel, Koomen, and Velthuijsen (1998), associations to the wall material should be assimilated with perceptions of the target product unless (a) such associations are of high relevance, *and* (b) one elicits thoughts about concrete prototypes that invite comparison (versus abstract concepts that do not). Under the latter high relevance/concrete comparison-inviting conditions, wall associations should foster a contrast effect on product perceptions. This suggests that when dining in a restaurant permeated with airy harmonic music that plausibly promotes abstract thinking, the presence of a brick (glass) wall may enhance patrons' perception of the food being natural and healthy (presented in a delicate or fragile arrangement). On the other hand, if well-defined, articulated, or tersely accented music infuses a media room and promotes concrete thinking, the room's presumably high relevance brick (glass) wall may foster a contrast effect and make the room's projector, TV screen, and sound system appear especially modern and high tech (sturdy and powerful).

Wall Contour A second characteristic of store walls that might affect consumers' responses to products is their contour—whether their expanse is predominantly straight or curved. Drawing on the analogy of the curvature of the male and female body, walls that are mostly straight and broken only by occasional sharp (e.g., right) angles might activate associations to masculinity, while those that are curved may elicit associations to femininity. Combining this notion with those of gender schema theory (Bem, 1981), we hypothesize that consumers' evaluations of products may be influenced by the contour of nearby walls. That is, if the consumer identifies strongly with his (her) gender (Bem, 1981) and thereby favors items associated with masculinity (femininity), consumers may respond more favorably to a gender-neutral product when it appears near a store wall with a contour that corresponds with the consumer's own, versus the opposite, gender. Of course, exceptions may exist: Suppose that the target product category is one that is strongly gendered or tied potently with either masculinity or femininity (e.g., boxing gloves versus dresses, respectively). In this case we speculate that, regardless of their gender schema status, both male and female consumers may respond more favorably to such highly gendered products if they are displayed near walls whose contour is associated with the product's gender (e.g., boxing gloves near a straight wall, and dresses near a curved wall).

Store Layout Although store layout may not be commonly regarded as an architectural factor, we view it as such because it can involve the decision of whether and how to erect dividing walls or barriers as a means of organizing store space and product displays. We also suggest that it may affect how consumers respond to products.

Perhaps the most common store layout is one where goods are grouped together in fairly undivided space based on either their shared taxonomic category (e.g., sofas and chairs displayed together, representing the furniture category) or on their status as variants of a category (e.g., luxury bedding and popular-priced bedding located contiguously in a store). We refer to this as a standard departmental store layout. An alternative, more recent layout scheme is the *store-within-a-store format*. Here certain types of merchandise, for example all goods sold by a particular designer, are arranged in a seemingly separate boutique or store alcove, which is typically controlled by an external company (Kotler & Keller, 2006). In most instances, such boutiques are isolated in a well-bounded niche, designed to exude a distinctive character, and possess a fairly intimate, more personalized feeling (e.g., think of Starbucks coffee shops housed in Barnes & Noble bookstores).

Considering the less stressful and intimate atmosphere of such boutiques, we speculate that consumers shopping in them are likely to engage in fairly thoughtful, well-reasoned cognition, whereas those shopping in stores with a more conventional departmental store layout may rely on more heuristic-based cognition, which is sensitive to off-the-cuff experiential or affective feelings. We combine this proposition with Wilson and LaFleur (1995) theorizing, which concerns the stability of people's judgments and behaviors. Such research indicates that unlike people who consistently base their judgments on how they feel about goods, those who generate reasons for their views often produce a biased set of rationales, ones that are especially accessible at the given moment. Hence, because these reasons are not only momentarily highly accessible but also biased and thereby likely to overrepresent either positive or negative justifications, they tend to be poor predictors of people's subsequent views. This suggests that after such reason-based consumers return home with merchandise from stores that employ the store-within-a-store format (versus a standard departmental layout), they may be more likely to evaluate the merchandise they bought differently, experience postpurchase regret, and engage in more exchanging or returning of merchandise.

Architectural Adventure Elements Striving to better compete with online shopping, many land-based stores have added architectural elements that offer consumers on-premise adventure or entertainment (*Nightline*, 2000). For example, a well-known chain of sporting goods stores provides consumers with the opportunity to test the store's footwear by climbing a 65 foot, 110 ton, in-store climbing mountain or, for the less adventurous, by taking a hike along a faux path, complete with logs and vegetation. Might such vivid in-store drama affect consumers' product evaluations? We believe so.

Perceptual fluency theory suggests that the heightened accessibility or vividness of an event can prompt a sensation of perceptual fluency or ease of retrieval (see Schwarz, ch. 11). However, it is not uncommon for consumers to falsely identify the true reason for such fluency and misattribute it to a false source that merely strikes them as plausible (e.g., a salable product). Plausibly, such perceptual fluency effects might operate when stores install dramatic architectural elements like the aforementioned mountain or nature trail. Hence, we propose that after donning and testing some new shoes by climbing an in-store mountain or hiking a nature path, consumers may misattribute the sensation of fluency or arousal (i.e., exhilaration) engendered by their in-store adventure to the tested new shoes, which may increase their likelihood of purchasing the shoes.

Free-Standing, In-Store Structures

It would be hard to imagine a shopping environment without free-standing structures. Such structures include items like display tables, cases, and countertop displays, which hold, showcase, or otherwise complement the store's offerings. This section applies a number of theories that propose how such structures might influence consumer behavior and responses.

Display Surfaces

Stores often display their products on shelves, tables, or racks that have display surfaces made of materials like wood, glass, metal, or plastic. Because people's associations to items (e.g., construction materials) are often derived from their shared experiences or observations with them (Peracchio & Meyers-Levy, 2005), we reasoned the following: People are likely to associate glass with the concept of modernity, as glass is a dominant material in modern buildings and decor, whereas they associate wood with the concept of naturalness, given its obvious natural origins. Because exposure to display surfaces constructed from such materials may stimulate thought about related concepts, we reasoned that these materials might produce context effects on consumers' product judgments. To assess this, we conducted and will report some studies that not only uphold this notion, but also indicate that the direction of these context effects can vary depending on consumers' self-construal, which affects their mode of information processing.

Research on self-construal theory suggests that a person can think about the self as either fundamentally connected to or separate from others, depending on the self-relevant knowledge that (s)he activates (Markus & Kitayama, 1991). This observation is consequential because evidence shows that the manner in which one construes the self can broaden and apply to how one processes any information that may be encountered (Markus & Kitayama, 1991; Nisbett, Peng, Choi, & Norenzayan, 2001). Along such lines, individuals who activate an interdependent self-construal, hereafter called *interdependents*, perceive the self as an inextricable element of a larger whole that includes others and the prevailing natural background (Markus & Kitayama, 1991). Hence, interdependents generally subject all incoming data to holistic processing that emphasizes the whole rather than an entity's constituent elements (Nisbett et al., 2001). On the other hand, individuals who activate an independent self-construal, henceforth called independents, perceive the self as a unique and autonomous entity, one with distinct boundaries that distinguish it clearly from others and the natural background (Markus & Kitayama, 1991). Following suit, independents apply this orientation more generally by habitually subjecting all incoming information to analytic processing, which involves partitioning data into separate and discrete units.

The use of such self-construal prompted holistic versus analytic processing can be consequential and potentially elicit alternative context effects on people's product judgments. Because holistic processing emphasizes the whole versus its constituent parts, it is likely to foster the assimilation of contextual item associations (e.g., concerning a display table's surface material) with a target product. On the other hand, analytic processing not only deconstructs masses of information into separate well-bounded pieces, but according to Markus and Kitayama (1991), the pieces can serve as standards of comparison that may be "set contrastively both against other such wholes and against a social and natural background" (p. 226). This implies that when analytic processing prevails, associations to contextual items (e.g., the display table surface material) may be employed as a comparison standard and elicit a contrast effect on product judgments.

We investigated these predictions (Zhu & Meyers-Levy, 2007). First, study participants' use of holistic or analytic processing was manipulated by inducing them to activate either an interdependent or independent self-construal. Then participants assessed some products displayed atop either a glass or wood table. Pretests confirmed that people generally associate glass with concepts like modernity and wood with notions like naturalness. The products on display were either neutral and hence could be flexibly interpreted on the aforementioned dimensions (i.e., modernity, naturalness), or they were extreme on these dimensions and most likely immutable. Consistent with our hypotheses, findings showed that the processing that people with alternative self-construals used when thinking about themselves characterized their manner of processing more generally. Thus, when respondents judged the neutral products on the focal dimensions (i.e., their modernity or naturalness), interdependents (independents) employed holistic (analytic) processing and assimilated (contrasted) associations of the display table with the products. But when the products were extreme on the focal dimensions, they were judged similarly, regardless of respondents' self-construal.

Types of Display Cases

Glass display cases represent another in-store structure that is often used to exhibit certain merchandise (e.g., fine jewelry, china, silver). Sometimes cases are highly secure and accessible only with a key. However, at other times they may be open on one side to allow consumers to examine their contents closely. Drawing on prior research findings (Zhou & Pham, 2004), we suggest that these alternative types of display cases may affect consumers' regulatory focus. Locked glass-enclosed cases are likely to induce a prevention regulatory focus owing to their emphasis on security, while open cases may elicit a promotion focus, for they allow consumers to nurture their desires by handling luxury merchandise.

These alternative regulatory foci represent different ways by which consumers may attempt to attain their goals (e.g., Crowe & Higgins, 1997). People who adopt a promotion focus pursue nurturance or achievement goals that concern the presence or absence of positive outcomes. As such, they typically exhibit an eagerness inclination, which is often manifested by considering many different options that potentially satisfy their goal (Crowe & Higgins, 1997). Alternatively, people with a prevention focus concentrate on security or safety goals that concern the presence or absence of negative outcomes. They exhibit an inclination toward vigilance, which may be manifested by considering only a limited number of options that seem to best affirm their goal (Crowe & Higgins, 1997). Thus, based on such theorizing, we hypothesize that because consumers who view products in an open (locked) display case should adopt a promotion (prevention) focus, the breadth of products they consider and purchase is likely to vary. Specifically, we suggest that promotion (prevention) focus individuals will examine more (fewer) products before making a purchase decision. Moreover, if the product is one for which multiple items might be purchased (e.g., place settings of china, crystal goblets, or silverware), promotion (prevention) focus individuals may purchase more (fewer) such items.*

Arrangement of Display Cases

We further suspect that consumers' responses toward products housed in display cases might be influenced by how a store arranges the cases. To illustrate, consider jewelry stores, which typically display their offerings in several glass-enclosed cases. Often these cases are aligned so that each of, say, six abutted cases collectively form a complete shape, a hexagon. Other times they are arranged to imply that shape, but gaps between certain cases interrupt the formation of a complete hexagon. Based on the Gestalt principle of closure (Solomon, 2007) and related theory concerning process-driven affect (e.g., Meyers-Levy & Tybout, 1989), we suggest that these alternative display case arrangements may affect consumers' evaluations of the encased jewelry.

While the closure principle contends that people mentally complete forms that feature missing elements, Peracchio and Meyers-Levy (1994) have qualified this, showing that such mental closure occurs only when their processing motivation is sufficient. Investigations also attest that the very process of resolving the missing elements or incongruity (i.e., instituting closure) can itself be satisfying and spawn

* Consideration of this relationship between one's regulatory focus and the quantity of items identified or considered might prompt one to wonder if reliance on a promotion versus prevention focus stimulates heightened use of relational versus item-specific processing, respectively. In fact, we conducted some research to explore this possibility (Zhu & Meyers-Levy, 2007). Consistent with this view, we found that a promotion focus elicited predominantly relational processing, which led consumers to perceive many commonalities and abstract connections among items. Yet a prevention focus stimulated primarily item-specific processing, causing consumers to focus on specific attributes of each item, independently of all others.

positive feelings, which people often misattribute to plausible albeit invalid sources (e.g., salient products; Meyers-Levy & Tybout, 1989). In the instance of display cases, we suspect that such feelings might be misattributed to the products featured in the display cases. Thus, based on the preceding theorizing, we propose that when consumers' motivation is high (but not when it is low), they may evaluate jewelry more favorably when it is displayed in cases that approximate an incomplete versus a complete shape (e.g., hexagon).

Store Fixture–Product Access Interface

Sometimes store fixtures impede product access, making it difficult for consumers to obtain or examine store merchandise. For example, pegboard hardware may compel consumers to remove numerous items to access a particular desired item. Similarly, home improvement and used book stores often stack merchandise high on shelves, forcing consumers to find and climb a ladder to acquire a desired good. Common sense implies that such fixtures, which hinder consumers' access to products, will heighten consumer frustration and undermine purchase. However, interestingly, growing work suggests that the reverse may occur, provided that consumers are sufficiently motivated to overcome these challenges.

Along such lines, research on process-driven affect holds that provided consumers' motivation or resources are adequate, the very process of grappling with and ultimately resolving such challenges can be rewarding and produce positive affect (Meyers-Levy & Tybout, 1989; Peracchio & Meyers-Levy, 1994). Moreover, this positive affect is often misattributed to consumers' feelings toward a salient product, enhancing the likelihood of product purchase. Accordingly, we posit that among high but not low motivation consumers, store fixtures that hinder product access may elevate product attitudes and heighten purchase.

Mirror Orientation

Mirrors represent another common fixture in shopping environments. Often they are placed in or near dressing rooms, inviting consumers to try on and evaluate merchandise. Depending on their orientation, mirrors often offer either a predominantly vertical or horizontal view of oneself and the environment. Thus, when consumers examine themselves in vertically oriented mirrors, their eyes and heads are likely to move up and down, mimicking a nodding head movement that commonly corresponds with a "yes" response. Yet, when consumers view themselves in horizontally oriented mirrors, their head and eye movement is likely to correspond with the motion that indicates a "no" response. Because these meanings of the motions hold true for Western but not all cultures, our theorizing about mirror orientation may not apply to non-Western cultures.

Research and theorizing concerning proprioceptive feedback suggests that the preceding observation may be consequential. Research shows that certain motor actions humans may perform serendipitously (e.g., adopting a facial stance that mimics a smile versus a grimace; Stepper & Strack, 1993) can provide bodily feedback that corresponds with particular psychological states. Further, people often use such data as if they were informative, drawing on them to determine their overt responses (Friedman & Förster, 2000). Thus, the preceding theorizing prompts the following prediction. Western, but perhaps not Eastern, shoppers who try on goods and view themselves in a predominantly vertically (horizontally) oriented mirror may evaluate the goods more (less) favorably, be more likely to approach (avoid) and consider (reject) other store goods, and ultimately engage in more (fewer) purchases.

Virtual Reality Tools

Increasingly stores offer tools intended to assist consumers in better identifying products that meet their personal needs. For example, L.L. Bean allows customers to create and view offerings on a customized, self-reflective virtual model. Similarly, Best Buy consumers can create personalized virtual facsimiles of rooms in their homes and insert and assess different appliances there. Self-referencing theory, which concerns the process of relating items to oneself (Burnkrant & Unnava, 1989), is germane to these tools and their implications for consumer behavior.

This work suggests that prompting consumers to self-reference or relate products to themselves, as these tools seemingly do, increases consumers' motivation to elaborate on the goods (Burnkrant &

Unnava, 1989; Meyers-Levy & Peracchio, 1996). Moreover, increases in product elaboration from a low to a moderate level generally heighten persuasion and evaluations, as this allows consumers to better understand and appreciate the product's benefits. Yet, as elaboration mounts further to an extreme level, appreciation satiates and now consumers are likely to expend their cognitive resources in ways that undermine persuasion, such as generating counter-arguments or idiosyncratic stray thoughts (Cacioppo & Petty, 1979). Hence, such theory suggests that virtual reality tools should either help or hinder persuasion, depending on consumers' magnitude of self-referencing. Assuming the tools engender moderate levels of self-referencing, product attitudes should be enhanced. However, encouraging such self-referencing further by accompanying the tools with tailored communications that, say, address the consumer by name or by the pronoun *you* (Meyers-Levy & Peracchio, 1996), is likely to prompt undesirable responses.

Countertop Displays

Similar to cause marketing (Marconi, 2002), in-store countertop displays often draw attention to and solicit donations for those affected by ailments (e.g., AIDS, breast cancer) or major disasters (e.g., 9/11, Hurricane Katrina). Not only may such displays remind consumers of such tragedies, but they also may make salient the inevitability of one's own mortality. Terror management theory (TMT; Greenberg, Solomon, & Pyszczynski, 1997) addresses how people cope with such existential anxiety, engendering predictions about how these countertop displays may affect consumers' responses to store products.

TMT holds that people attempt to assuage the terror prompted by the increased salience of their mortality by engaging in activities that affirm socially constructed and consensually validated cultural worldviews (Greenberg et al., 1997). These worldviews serve to heighten people's self-esteem by imbuing order and meaning to their lives and by providing standards of value that promise protection and death transcendence to those who adhere to them. For example, reflecting the influence of such worldviews, heightened mortality salience increases people's attempts to "fit in" by expressing a preference for typical activities (Simon et al., 1997), elevates their support for and commitment to valued (in)groups (Florian, Mikulincer, & Hirschberger, 2002), and promotes heightened regard for socially sanctioned behaviors (Greenberg, Porteus, Simon, Pyszczynski, & Solomon, 1995). These findings translate into predictions about how consumers may respond to mortality salience heightening in-store countertop displays. Consumers exposed to these versus benign displays may be more inclined to purchase conventional or traditional versus faddish products, goods featuring an emblem of an in-group versus an equally prestigious out-group (e.g., one's own versus another equally prestigious school's logo), and goods espoused by a polite and formal versus "hip" and casual salesperson.

Artwork

Many businesses (e.g., restaurants, medical offices, banks) expose patrons to artwork in their waiting or main customer areas. The artwork may be modern or highly futuristic in style, or it may portray commonplace sights that represent the here and now. Such observations are noteworthy in their connections to temporal construal theory (Förster, Friedman, & Liberman, 2004; Liberman et al., 2002). They suggest the possibility that these artwork styles may alter customers' mindset, affecting their construal of the experience and which aspects of the experience influence their satisfaction.

To clarify, research concerning temporal distance and construal has found that thinking about the distant future stimulates abstract ideation (i.e., higher-level, superordinate construals), whereas thinking about the near future or present elicits relatively concrete representations (Liberman et al., 2002). This raises the prospect that consumers' product-related thoughts and priorities may vary depending on whether a venue's artwork stimulates a distant future or more proximate mental orientation. We propose that when surrounded by futuristic versus contemporary or present-day artwork, consumers may elaborate and place more importance on the abstract versus concrete benefits afforded by a good. Thus, in the presence of such artwork, restaurant diners might focus more greatly on the abstract aesthetics and presentation of the food versus the restaurant's accommodations for specialized (e.g., diabetic, gluten-free, vegetarian) diets. Or, medical patients might place greater value on the friendly staff's facilitation efforts versus the doctor's detailed and specific medical recommendations.

Broader Contextual Factors

A third category of potentially influential structural factors present in retail settings relates to the broader context surrounding the store outlet. In this section, we draw on existing theory to generate some plausible predictions concerning such contextual factors.

The Architecture of the Broader Shopping Environment

Architectural elements in the shopping center where a store is located may influence consumers' responses within that store. Consider, for example, Minnesota's Mall of America, which features a sprawl of amusement park rides and a carnival atmosphere in the mall atrium. Mall visitors who enter on the ground atrium level generally cannot ignore these festivities, while those who enter and shop at the mall's upper level stores still are frequently touched by the noise and mayhem. This reverberating impact of the mall festivities suggests that all shoppers' physical and/or cognitive resources may be lowered by the atrium activities.

Resource matching theory speaks to this. It suggests that under high (but not low) motivation conditions, people's performance and judgments are likely to be optimal when the level of resources they apply to a given activity matches, versus falls short of or exceeds, the level required by the task (Meyers-Levy & Peracchio, 1995). When people's supply of resources for a task falls short of what is needed, comprehension and thus appreciation of incoming (product) data suffer. Similarly, when the resources supplied exceed the level needed by the task, people frequently expend their excess resources generating counterarguments or idiosyncratic thoughts, which typically exert a negative influence on responses.

The preceding implies that the demands imposed by contextual mall activity may well affect consumers' responses to products within a given store. If mall activity is extremely minimal, people highly motivated to scrutinize and evaluate goods in a particular category may forgo making a purchase or select an option that is suboptimal for them, because their resources for product scrutiny may exceed those required. Similarly motivated consumers may forgo purchase or make suboptimal choices if mall activity is extremely high, for the latter may drain their existing resources, producing a dearth in their available relative to required resources. However, if mall activity is moderate, motivated consumers should identify and purchase the product that best meets their needs, because in this instance equality ensues between the resources expended and demanded for assessing product options. Finally, such resource-matching-based differences in behavior should be absent among less motivated consumers, who rely uniformly on heuristic influences.

Same- and Complementary-Category Stores

Malls often house multiple retailers of extremely similar goods as well as ones in the same product category (e.g., ubiquitous coffee shops or t-shirt shops). Both research on the part cuing effect (Alba & Chattopadhyay, 1985) and relational versus item-specific types of processing (Hunt & Einstein, 1981; Meyers-Levy, 1991) may be relevant in such situations. The part-cuing literature finds that when trying to recall same-category items, people typically repeatedly access highly familiar or prototypical category members, which interferes with access to less familiar members (Alba & Chattopadhyay, 1985). For example, when considering mall coffee shop options, consumers may repeatedly access memory for the well-known Starbucks or Java Bean shops, but fail to retrieve a new and less familiar coffee proprietor, say one named Tully's. Research on types of processing (e.g., Hunt & Einstein, 1981; Malaviya, Meyers-Levy, & Sternthal, 1999) would suggest that the more familiar, highly accessible shops are repeatedly retrieved in part because the presence of multiple same-category stores itself invites predominantly relational processing rather than a free-recall heightening balance of relational *and* item-specific processing. Further, more linkages probably connect the more versus less familiar vendors with the coffee category, due to insufficient item-specific processing of the newer shops such as Tully's.

Accordingly, we propose the following. If Tully's adopts a logo (e.g., one depicting a steaming coffee cup), corporate colors (e.g., earth tones), and exterior façade that mimic the convention for coffee shops and thereby promote additional relational processing, consumers will likely exhibit the part-cuing effect, displaying poor recall and infrequent visits to Tully's when patronizing the mall. Yet, if Tully's employs a distinctly unique eye-catching logo, colors, and façade, which should promote item-specific processing, the part-cuing effect should lessen and the shop should attract more mall patrons.

Of course at times, heightened relational processing spawned by same-category stores can be advantageous, especially for stores that sell goods in complementary categories. Relevant to this, research on goal derived categories (Barsalou, 1985) contends that seemingly unrelated items may be represented closely in memory within goal derived categories, which represent goods commonly employed to pursue a particular goal. For example, although at first glance music CDs and women's hosiery would appear to belong to and be represented in disparate categories, both products may inhabit the goal derived category of "things one might have need for at parties" (i.e., music for entertainment and hosiery to wear). This leads to a prediction. A female shopper who relies heavily on relational (versus item-specific) processing when browsing a mall's same-category (different-category) stores is more likely upon passing a CD store to suddenly remember to buy hosiery for an upcoming party.

Conclusion

Although structural aspects of shopping environments are likely to have important and wide-ranging implications for consumer behavior, our current understanding of these influences remains extremely limited. This chapter was designed to bridge this gap and encourage research in this critical domain. In this chapter, we have identified numerous indoor structural factors that may affect consumers' responses, illustrated how existing theories invite examination of how, when, and why such factors exert effects, and proposed many testable hypotheses. Our unabashed goal is to motivate consumer research in this understudied field.

Nonetheless, this chapter by no means considers all relevant theories or questions. For example, how might store layout interact with consumers' goals, what consequences may ensue, and what actions might remedy nonoptimal outcomes? To illustrate, consider IKEA stores, which via a one-way traffic flow path effectively force consumers to traverse the huge store's extensive taxonomic category layout of all types of home goods before reaching the checkout kiosks. This layout benefits the store's goal of increasing sales, for it induces relational processing and prompts consumers to consider thematically their needs for all home-related (e.g., kitchen, office, den) products before paying and exiting. However, it defies the goal of consumers who know precisely what they want and wish only to locate and purchase quickly those few particular items. Because these specific-goal-driven consumers may find the IKEA's layout inconvenient, it is possible that they may eschew and spread negative word-of-mouth about IKEA.

We reason that consumers who wish to purchase quickly only precise predetermined goods engage spontaneously in predominantly item-specific processing—despite the relational processing-fostering store layout. Hence, we suggest that IKEA could post unobtrusive yet distinctively illustrative pictorial icons throughout the store that mark short-circuiting pathways to the checkout kiosks, thereby enabling such item-specific shoppers to achieve their goal, but still encouraging less specific-goal-driven, relational consumers to follow the one-way, comprehensive-product path. This is so because the icons' pictorial imagery should be especially conducive to item-specific (versus relational) processing (Meyers-Levy, 1991). Such theory-driven inquiry into the interacting effects of structural variables and other pertinent factors represents merely the tip of the iceberg of potentially fruitful avenues of research in this domain.

References

(Executive Producer). (2000, February). *Nightline:Shopping malls.* [Television broadcast]. New York: American Broadcasting Company.

Alba, J. W., & Chattopadhyay, A. (1985). Effects of context and part-category cues on recall of competing brands. *Journal of Marketing Research, 22*, 340–349.

Barsalou, L. W. (1985). Ideals, central tendency, and frequency of instantiation as determinants of graded structure in categories. *Journal of Experimental Psychology: Learning, Memory, and Cognition, 11*, 629–654.

Bechtel, R. B. (1997). *Environment and behavior: An introduction*, London: Sage.

Bem, S. L. (1981). Gender schema theory: A cognitive account of sex typing. *Psychological Review, 88*, 354–364.

Bivens, R. (1997). Home-builders toy with better designs as baby boomers age. *The Houston Chronicle, 26*, A34.

Burnkrant, R. E., & Unnava, H. R. (1989). Self-referencing: A strategy for increasing processing of message content. *Personality and Social Psychology Bulletin, 15*, 628–638.

Cacioppo, J. T., & Petty, R. E. (1979). Effects of message repetition and position on cognitive response, recall, and persuasion. *Journal of Personality and Social Psychology, 37*, 97–109.

Crowe, E., & Higgins, E. T. (1997). Regulatory focus and strategic inclinations: Promotion and prevention in decision-making. *Organizational Behavior and Human Decision Processes, 9*, 117–132.

Einstein, G. O., & Hunt, R. R. (1980). Levels of processing and organization: Additive effects of individual-item and relational processing. *Journal of Experimental Psychology: Human Learning and Memory, 6*, 588–598.

Fischl, G., & Gärling, A. (2004, July). Enhancing well-being in health care facilities. In B. Martens & A. G. Keul (Eds.), *Evaluation in progress—Strategies for environmental research and implementation. IAPS 18 Conference Proceedings.*

Florian, V., Mikulincer, M., & Hirschberger, G. (2002). The anxiety-buffering function of close relationships: Evidence that relationship commitment acts as a terror management mechanism. *Journal of Personality and Social Psychology, 82*, 527–542.

Förster, J., Friedman, R. S., & Liberman, N. (2004). Temporal construal effects on abstract and concrete thinking: Consequences for insight and creative cognition. *Journal of Personality and Social Psychology, 87*, 177–189.

Freedman, J. L. (1975). *Crowding and behavior.* San Francisco: Freeman.

Friedman, R. S., & Förster, J. (2000). The effects of approach and avoidance motor actions on elements of creative insight. *Journal of Personality and Social Psychology, 79*, 477–492.

Gorn, G. J., Chattopadhyay, A., Sengupta, P., & Tripathi, S. (2004). Waiting for the web: How screen color affects time perception. *Journal of Marketing Research, 41*, 215–225.

Greenberg, J., Porteus, J., Simon, L., Pyszczynski, T., & Solomon, S. (1995). Evidence of a terror management function of cultural icons: The effects of mortality salience on the inappropriate use of cherished cultural symbols. *Personality and Social Psychology Bulletin, 21*, 1221–1228.

Greenberg, J., Solomon, S., & Pyszczynski, T. (1997). Terror management theory of self-esteem and cultural worldviews: Empirical assessments and conceptual refinements. In M. P. Zanna (Ed.), *Advances in experimental social psychology.* San Diego: Academic Press.

Hall, E. T. (1966). *Hidden dimension*. Garden City, NY: Doubleday.

Higgins, E. T. (1996). Knowledge activation: Accessibility, applicability, and salience. In E. T. Higgins & Krugslanski, A. W. (Eds.), *Social psychology: Handbook of basic principles* (pp. 133–168). New York: Guilford Press.

Hui, M. K., & Bateson, J. E. G. (1991). Perceived control and the effects of crowding and consumer choice on the service experience, *Journal of Consumer Research, 18*(September), 174–184.

Hunt, R. R., & Einstein, G. (1981). Relational and item-specific information in memory. *Journal of Verbal Learning and Verbal Behavior, 20* (October), 497–514.

Hunt, R. R., & Seta, C. E. (1984). Category size effects in recall: The roles of relational and individual item information. *Journal of Experimental Psychology: Learning, Memory and Cognition, 10*(July), 454–464.

Isen, A. M. (1987). Positive affect, cognitive processes and social behavior. In L. Berkowitz (Ed.), *Advances in Experimental Social Psychology: vol. 20* (pp. 204–253). New York: Academic Press.

Kellaris, J. J., & Kent, R. J. (1992). The influence of music on consumers' temporal perceptions: Does time fly when you're having fun? *Journal of Consumer Psychology, 1*(4), 365–376.

Kotler, P., & Keller, K. L. (2006). *Marketing management* (12th ed.). Upper Saddle River, NJ: Pearson Prentice Hall.

Kühnen, U., & Oyserman, D. (2002). Thinking about the self influences thinking in general: Cognitive consequences of salient self-concept. *Journal of Experimental Social Psychology, 38*, 492–499.

Liberman, N., Sagristano, M. D., & Trope, Y. (2002). The effect of temporal distance on level of mental construal. *Journal of Experimental Social Psychology, 38*, 523–534.

Lunsford, J. L., & Michaels, D. (2002, November 25). A global journal report: Masters of illusion—plane designers use mirrors, lighting, repositioned bins to make cabins seem roomier. *Wall Street Journal*, B1.

Maass, A., Merici, I., Villafranca, E., Furlani, R., Gaburro, E., Getrevi, A., et al. (2000). Intimidating buildings: Can courthouse architecture affect perceived likelihood of conviction. *Environment and Behavior. 32*, 674–683.

Malaviya, P., Meyers-Levy, J., & Sternthal, B. (1999). Ad repetition in a cluttered environment: The influence of type of processing. *Psychology and Marketing, 16*, 99–118.

Marconi, J. (2002). *Cause marketing*. Chicago, IL: Dearborn Trade Publication.

Markus, H. R., & Kitayama, S. (1991). Culture and the self: Implications for cognition, Emotion, and motivation. *Psychological Review, 98*, 224–253.

Meyers-Levy, J. (1991). Elaborating on elaboration: The distinction between relational and item specific elaboration. *Journal of Consumer Research, 18*, 358–367.

Meyers-Levy, J., & Peracchio, L. (1995). Understanding the effects of color: How the correspondence between available and required resources affects attitudes. *Journal of Consumer Research, 22*, 121–138.

Meyers-Levy, J., & Peracchio, L. (1996). Moderators of the impact of self-reference on persuasion. *Journal of Consumer Research, 22*, 408–423.

Meyers-Levy, J., & Tybout, A. M. (1989). Schema congruity as a basis for product evaluation. *Journal of Consumer Research, 16*, 39–54.

Meyers-Levy, J., & Tybout, A. M. (1997). Context effects at encoding and judgment in consumption settings: The role of cognitive resources. *Journal of Consumer Research, 24*, 1–14.

Meyers-Levy, J., & Zhu, R. J. (2007). The influence of ceiling height: When priming affects the type of processing people use. *Journal of Consumer Research, 34*.

Mitchell, D., Kahn, B. E., & Knasko, S. (1995). There is something in the air: The effects of congruent or incongruent ambient odor on consumer decision making. *Journal of Consumer Research, 22*, 229–238.

Morrin, M., & Ratneshwar, S. (2003). Does it make sense to use scents to enhance brand memory? *Journal of Marketing Research, 40*, 10–25.

Nisbett, R. E., Peng, K., Choi, I., & Norenzayan, A. (2001). Culture and systems of thoughts: Holistic versus analytic cognition. *Psychological Review, 108*, 291–310.

Page, R. A. (1977). Noise and helping behavior. *Environmental Behavior, 9*, 311–334.

Peracchio, L., & Meyers-Levy, J. (1994). How ambiguous cropped objects in ad photos can affect product evaluations. *Journal of Consumer Research, 21*, 190–204.

Peracchio, L., & Meyers-Levy, J. (2005). Using stylistic properties of ad pictures to communicate with consumers. *Journal of Consumer Research, 32*, 29–40.

Siegel, J. M., & Steele, C. M. (1980). Environmental distraction and interpersonal judgments. *British Journal of Social Clinical Psychology, 19*, 23–32.

Simon, L., Greenberg, J., Arndt, J., Pyszcynski, T., Clement, R., & Solomon, S. (1997). Perceived consensus, uniqueness, and terror management: Compensatory responses to threats to inclusion and distinctiveness following mortality salience. *Personality and Social Psychology Bulletin, 23*, 1055–1065.

Solomon, M. R. (2007). *Consumer behavior: Buying, having, and being*, (7th ed). Upper Saddle River, NJ: Prentice Hall.

Spencer, S. J., Zanna, M. P., & Fong, G. T. (2005). Establishing a causal chain: Why experiments are often more effective than mediational analyses in examining psychological processes. *Journal of Personality and Social Psychology, 89*, 845–851.

Stapel, D. A., Koomen, W., & Velthuijsen, A. S. (1998). Assimilation or contrast? Comparison relevance, distinctness, and the impact of accessible information on consumer judgments. *Journal of Consumer Psychology, 7*(1), 1–24.

Stepper, S., & Strack, F. (1993). Proprioceptive determinants of emotional and nonemotional feelings. *Journal of Personality and Social Psychology, 64*, 211–220.

Ulrich, R. S. (1984). View through a window may influence recovery from surgery. *Science, 224*, 420–421.

Wilson, L. M. (1972). Intensive care delirium: The effects of outside deprivation in a windowless unit. *Archives of Internal Medicine, 130*, 225–226.

Wilson, T. D., & LaFleur, S. J. (1995). Knowing what you'll do: Effects of analyzing reasons of self-prediction. *Journal of Personality and Social Psychology, 68*, 1–35.

Zhou, R., & Pham, T. P. (2004). Promotion and prevention across mental accounts: When financial products dictate consumers' investment goals. *Journal of Consumer Research, 31*, 125–135.

Zhu, R., & Meyers-Levy, J. (2005). Distinguishing between the meanings of music: When background music affects product perceptions. *Journal of Marketing Research, 42*, 333–345.

Zhu, R., & Meyers-Levy, J. (2007). Exploring the cognitive mechanism that underlies regulatory focus effects. *Journal of Consumer Research, 34*, 89–96.

Zhu, R. & Meyers-Levy, J. (2007). Evaluations of products viewed on various display surfaces: context effects engendered by self-view and type of processing. Unpublished manuscript.

10

Measuring the Value of Point-of-Purchase Marketing with Commercial Eye-Tracking Data

Pierre Chandon, J. Wesley Hutchinson, Eric T. Bradlow, and Scott H. Young

Introduction

Consumer behavior at the point of purchase is influenced by out-of-store, memory-based factors (e.g., brand preferences) and by in-store, attention-based factors (e.g., shelf position and number of facings). In today's cluttered retail environments, creating memory-based consumer pull is not enough; marketers must also create "visual lift" for their brands—that is, incremental consideration caused by in-store visual attention. The problem is that it is currently impossible to precisely measure visual lift. Surveys can easily be conducted to compare prestore intentions and poststore choices but they do not measure attention. They cannot therefore tell whether ineffective in-store marketing was due to a poor attention-getting ability—"unseen and hence unsold"—or to a poor visual lift—"seen yet still unsold."

Eye-tracking studies have shown that eye movements to brands displayed on a supermarket shelf are valid measures of visual attention and are generally correlated with brand consideration (Pieters & Warlop, 1999; Russo & Leclerc, 1994). However, they have not provided a method for separating the effects of attention and memory on consumer point-of-purchase decisions. More specifically, they have not shown that attention to a brand causes consideration, rather than memory for a considered brand causing visual search for that brand.

In this chapter, we show how commercially available eye-tracking data can be used to decompose a brand's consideration into its memory-based baseline and its visual lift. To achieve this goal, we develop a parsimonious decision-path model of visual attention and brand consideration. We apply this model to eye movements and brand consideration data collected by Perception Research Inc., the leading U.S. provider of eye-tracking studies for marketing research. Our results confirm the importance of visual-based factors in driving brand consideration using a richer and more realistic setting than in existing studies. The two studies also provide new insight into consumer's decision-making process at the point of purchase, and particularly on the interplay between consideration decisions and visual attention to prices and packages. Finally, we show how the decomposition can help decide which brands of a shelf display should be selected for enhanced point-of-purchase (POP) marketing activities.

In the first section of the chapter, we present a framework for the effects of memory and attention at the point of purchase and review the data and methods available to measure these effects. In the second section, we describe the procedure, stimuli, and key descriptive findings of two studies that measured the eye movements and consideration decisions of consumers while they were looking at supermarket shelf displays. In the third section, we introduce a decision-path model of visual attention and consideration decisions and show how this model can be applied to estimate a brand's visual lift and visual responsiveness. There have been significant advances in the modeling of eye-tracking data in recent years (e.g., Pieters, Warlop, & Wedel, 2002; Pieters & Wedel, 2004; Wedel & Pieters, 2000). These studies have developed integrative models of the antecedents and consequences of visual attention to sections of print ads. In the research reported here, we have placed emphasis on parsimony and managerial relevance and have restricted our analysis to the type of data routinely collected by eye-tracking providers (i.e., observational rather than experimental data). In the final section, we discuss how retailers and manufacturers can use the results of estimating the decision-path model to better assess the visual display of brands at the point of purchase.

Concepts and Measures of Point-of-Purchase Marketing

According to the Point of Purchase Advertising Institute, 74% of all purchase decisions in mass merchandisers are made in store

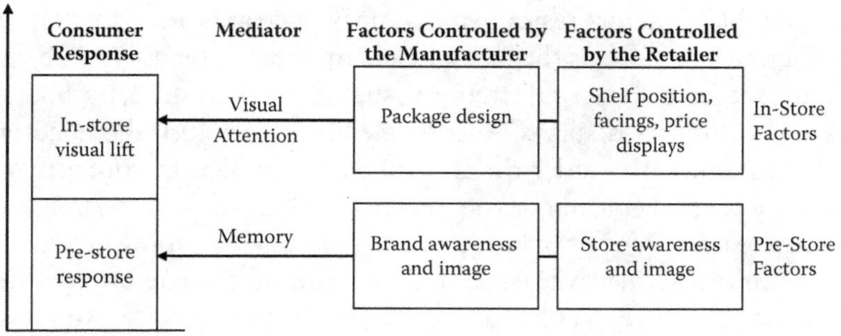

Figure 10.1 A framework of the effects of visual attention and memory at the point of purchase.

(POPAI, 1997). Yet consumers only look at and evaluate a fraction of the hundreds of alternatives cluttering supermarket shelves (Inman & Winer, 1998; Kollat & Willett, 1967). In these conditions, it is not surprising that attracting consumers' visual attention at the point of purchase strongly influences consumer choices. For example, Woodside and Waddle (1975) showed that POP signing multiplies the effects of a price reduction by a factor of six and that it can even increase sales in the absence of price change (see also Bemmaor & Mouchoux, 1991). Other field experiments have documented the influence of shelf space, location quality, and display organization on sales (e.g. Drèze, Hoch, & Purk, 1994; Wilkinson, Mason, & Paksoy, 1982).

The Effects of Memory and Visual Attention at the Point of Purchase

One way to categorize the sources of marketing effects at the point of purchase is to distinguish between memory-based and visual-based* effects (Alba, Hutchinson, & Lynch, 1991). As summarized in Figure 10.1, any observed behavior at the point of purchase (e.g., brand consideration or choice) is influenced by both memory-based and visual factors and, in principle, can be decomposed into a baseline memory-based response and an incremental visual lift. We define memory-based response as the part of consumer behavior

* Usually, the more general term "stimulus-based" is used. However, at the point of purchase the perceptual stimuli are almost exclusively visual in nature and given our focus on visual attention we use the more specific term throughout.

attributable to factors residing in memory, such as brand preferences. We define visual lift as the part of consumer behavior attributable to factors mediated by visual attention, such as shelf location, number of facings, and price displays. As indicated in Figure 10.1, these factors are predominantly under the control of the retailer. In comparison, manufacturers typically devote more resources to and exert greater influence upon the factors influencing memory-based response.

In this research, we measure and model brand consideration rather than brand evaluation or choice because it is more sensitive to visual attention effects than choice, which is likely to be mostly driven by memory-based factors. Also, consideration is directly relevant for manufacturers because most of the variance in final brand choice is driven by inclusion in the consideration set (Hauser & Wernerfelt, 1990) and for retailers because a larger consideration set increases the chances that consumers will make at least one purchase from the category. We operationally define memory-based response as the probability of inclusion in the consideration set when the decision is made purely from memory, and visual lift as the incremental consideration gained from noticing the brand at the point of purchase.

Traditional Methods for Measuring Visual Lift

Most market research methods are not appropriate because they focus on evaluation or choice once the alternatives being evaluated have captured consumer's attention. One exception are field experiments, which measure a brand's visual lift by manipulating its visual salience (the likelihood that it will attract in-store attention) and measuring its impact on sales or consumer shopping behavior (for a review, see Blattberg & Neslin, 1990). Even though field experiments can now be more easily implemented via computerized simulations (e.g., Burke, Harlam, Kahn, & Lodish, 1992), they remain time consuming and costly. Also, by measuring only incremental effects (i.e., one POP condition compared to another) these measures leave unanswered the question of the relative contributions of memory and visual attention to observed rates of consideration and choice.

Another exception is in-store surveys. Compared to field experiments, they do not necessitate the experimental manipulation of visual salience and measure visual lift at the individual level by comparing prestore purchase intentions or memory-based consideration with poststore brand choices or post-hoc recollection of in-store brand consideration (e.g., Hoyer, 1984; Inman & Winer, 1998). However, in-store surveys have several shortcomings. Because they do not have information on visual attention, they cannot tell whether a small difference between pre- and poststore choice is really due to low visual lift (i.e., in-store attention does not increase choice much) or simply to low attention to the brand. Second, visual attention to a brand can trigger the memory-based consideration of other brands (Hutchinson, Raman, & Mantrala, 1994). Because they are purely memory-based, surveys miss this type of stimulus-based consideration and thus may overestimate visual lift. Third, prestore intentions can be influenced by social desirability biases and measuring them before people enter the store can lead to purchases that would not have occurred otherwise (Chandon, Morwitz, & Reinartz, 2005).

Eye-Tracking Studies

Eye-tracking studies provide direct measures of eye movements in a realistic stimulus-based setting and do not require verbalizing prestore memory-based consideration. Eye movements consist of fixations, during which the eye remains relatively still for about 200–300 ms, separated by rapid movements, called saccades, which average 3–5 degrees in distance (measured in degrees of visual angle) and last 40 to 50 ms (for more information, see Rayner's chapter in this volume). Eye-tracking equipment records the duration of each eye fixation and the exact coordinates of the fovea (the central 2 degrees of vision of the visual field) during the fixation with a frequency of 60 readings per second (i.e., one every 17 ms). It then maps the coordinates of the fovea to the location of each area of interest on the picture (e.g., individual brands on a supermarket shelf picture).

Eye-tracking studies are a niche, but fast-growing, segment of the POP market research industry. They are the method of choice for commercial studies of package design and shelf displays (Young, 2000). Commercial eye-tracking studies typically focus on the percentage of subjects "noting" the product (i.e., making at least one eye fixation on the product). More recently, commercial eye-tracking studies have started instructing consumers to imagine that they need to buy from the category and have collected brand consideration data as well as eye-movement data.

Consumer researchers have used eye-tracking data to study how people look at print advertisements (e.g., Pieters & Wedel, 2004; Wedel & Pieters, 2000), yellow pages (Lohse, 1997), and cataloges (Janiszewski, 1998). These studies have shown that eye-tracking data provide reliable measures of attention to stimuli in complex scenes, such as brands on a supermarket shelf (Hoffman, 1998; Lohse & Johnson, 1996; Rayner, 1998). Although attention can be directed without eye movements to stimuli located outside the fovea (the central 2 degrees of vision), the location of the fovea during the eye fixation is a good indicator of attention to complex stimuli because little complex information can be extracted during saccades, because foveal attention is more efficient than parafoveal attention, and because visual acuity deteriorates rapidly outside the fovea.

Two previous studies have specifically demonstrated the value of eye-tracking data for measuring visual attention to products displayed on supermarket shelves. Russo and Leclerc (1994) isolated the sequences of consecutive eye fixations revealing brand comparisons using a method developed earlier (Russo & Rosen, 1975). These sequences of eye fixations revealed that consumers making in-store purchase decisions go through three stages: orientation, evaluation, and verification. Pieters and Warlop (1999) examined the effect of time pressure and task motivation on visual attention to the pictorial and textual areas of products displayed on supermarket shelves. They showed that subjects respond to time pressure by making shorter eye fixations and by focusing their attention on pictorial information. In addition, both studies showed that consideration increases with the number of eye fixations to the brand.

Still, existing studies of eye movements to supermarket shelves have some limitations. First, they do not provide a method for separating the effects of memory-based factors from those of attention-based factors, leaving open the question "Is unseen really unsold?" Second, these studies do not provide much guidance for the allocation of POP marketing activities between the brands of the display. Finally, it is useful to test the robustness of the descriptive findings of these two studies, as they were obtained for relatively simple displays (only one facing per brand, brands well separated from each other, and no price information) and either few brands (six for Pieters & Warlop, 1999) or early eye movement recording techniques (manual coding of eye fixations from videotapes for Russo & Leclerc, 1994). In the next sections, we present the procedure, stimuli, and key descriptive findings of our studies involving eye-tracking and brand consideration data generated by consumers looking at realistically rich shelf displays in two product categories. We then show how a decision-path model calibrated on these data can be used to estimate memory-based consideration and visual lift and thereby accomplish our goals.

Two Eye-Tracking Studies

Procedure and Stimuli

The data used in our analyses were collected in collaboration with Perception Research Services, Inc. (PRS) of Fort Lee, NJ, following the procedure and stimuli typically used in commercial tests of package designs. Adult shoppers were recruited in shopping centers in eight U.S. cities and offered $10 for their participation. They were female heads of household responsible for the majority of their household's grocery shopping. Their ages ranged from 24 to 65, they had at least a high school education and earned a minimum annual household income of $25,000. The final group of respondents included a mix of full-time working people, part-time working people, and full-time homemakers. A total of 309 consumers were recruited, split between the two product categories studied (159 for orange juices, 150 for liquid detergents).

Each person was seated and told that she would see a series of ads like those found in magazines or a series of products like those found in stores. They went through a calibration procedure requiring them to look twice at a blank 35 mm slide with five circles projected on a 4 × 5 feet screen located approximately 80 inches away from the seat. Thus, the 2 degrees of foveal vision covered about 3 inches on the screen. This was less than one shelf facing (which was 3.3 inches for juices and 6 inches for detergents), indicating that consumers could not extract detailed information from different brands from a single eye fixation. Their eye movements were tracked using infrared corneal reflection (ISCAN model #AA-UPG-421), which does not require headgear. Subjects then looked at four or five training displays and at six pictures of individual packages or print ads for an unrelated study. For this unrelated study, subjects were only asked to look at the pictures as they would normally do.

Prior to viewing the last stimulus (i.e., the one used in our studies), subjects were instructed that they would have to say which brands they would consider buying among those shown in the display. The names of the brands considered were recorded during the eye-tracking task by PRS staff as respondents verbalized them. Subjects controlled the amount of time spent looking at the display by pressing a button to go to the following slide (and this time was automatically recorded). After the eye-tracking task, subjects went to a separate room where PRS staff measured brand recall, past brand usage and general questions about shopping behavior in the product category. Each interview lasted approximately 20 to 25 minutes, of which 5 to 10 minutes were spent in the eye-tracking room.

The stimuli were two pictures of supermarket shelves used by PRS in prior studies, one representing orange juices and the other liquid laundry detergents. The two product categories were chosen because of their high level of household penetration (87% for fruit juices and 80% for liquid laundry detergent) and high percentage of sales sold on POP display (respectively, 11% and 25% in 1998, according to Information Resources). The two categories, however, differed on a number of important variables related to visual display and consumer behavior. The picture of orange juices consisted of 16 choice alternatives (which for simplicity we will call "brands" throughout the paper) displayed horizontally on four shelves with a total of 72 facings (see Figure 10.2). There were 10 brands of liquid laundry detergents, each displayed vertically on three shelves with a total of 30 facings (see Figure 10.3). The brands were defined so as to match the classification used in the verbal interviews, and they varied in their level of generality. For instance, Figure 10.2 shows that there are three different brands with the Tropicana umbrella brand name (Tropicana Pure Premium, Tropicana Season's Best, and Tropicana Pure Tropic) because these three alternatives were coded as separate choices in the verbal interviews. In order to expand the range of memory-based and visual lift that would be observed, we created two fictitious brands, Jaffa for juices and Clin for detergents. The packaging of these two brands were patterned after products sold outside the United States. Their price was determined during pretests to position these two brands as regional or store brands. In addition, up to four shelf talkers displaying the brand's logo were added to some brands in some test locations. Because the effects of shelf talkers were small and not reliable across product categories,

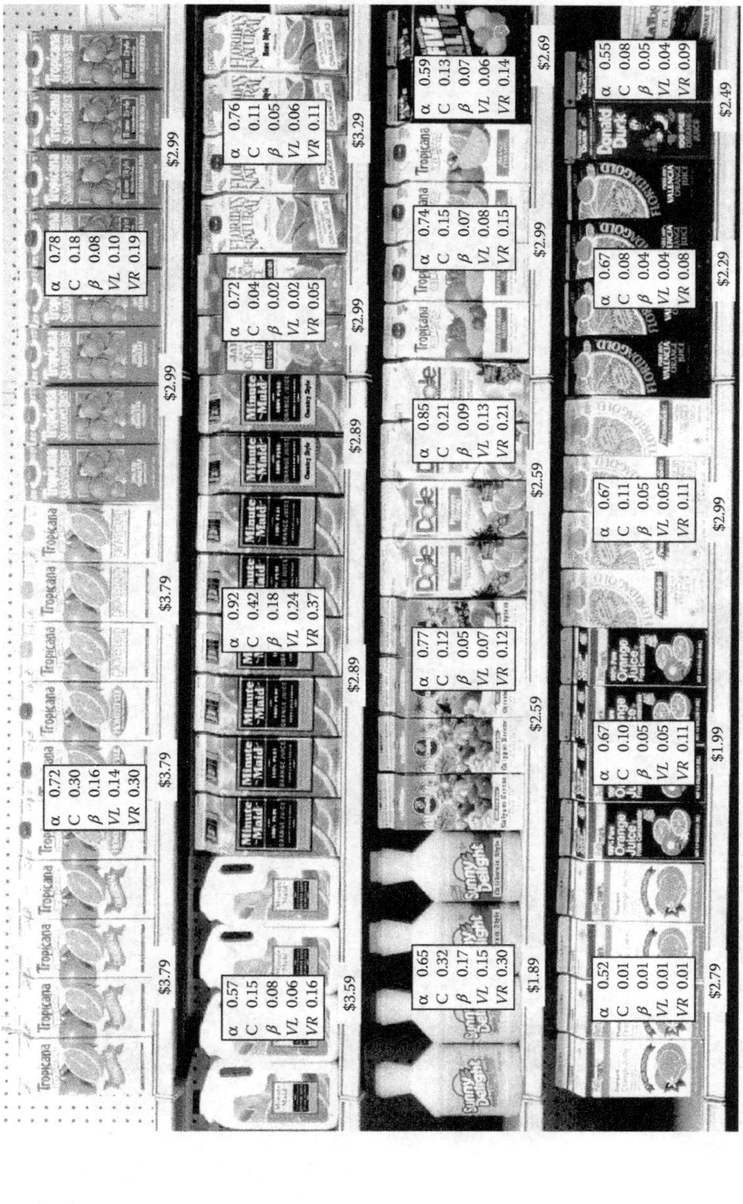

Figure 10. 2 Shelf layout and brand results for juices.

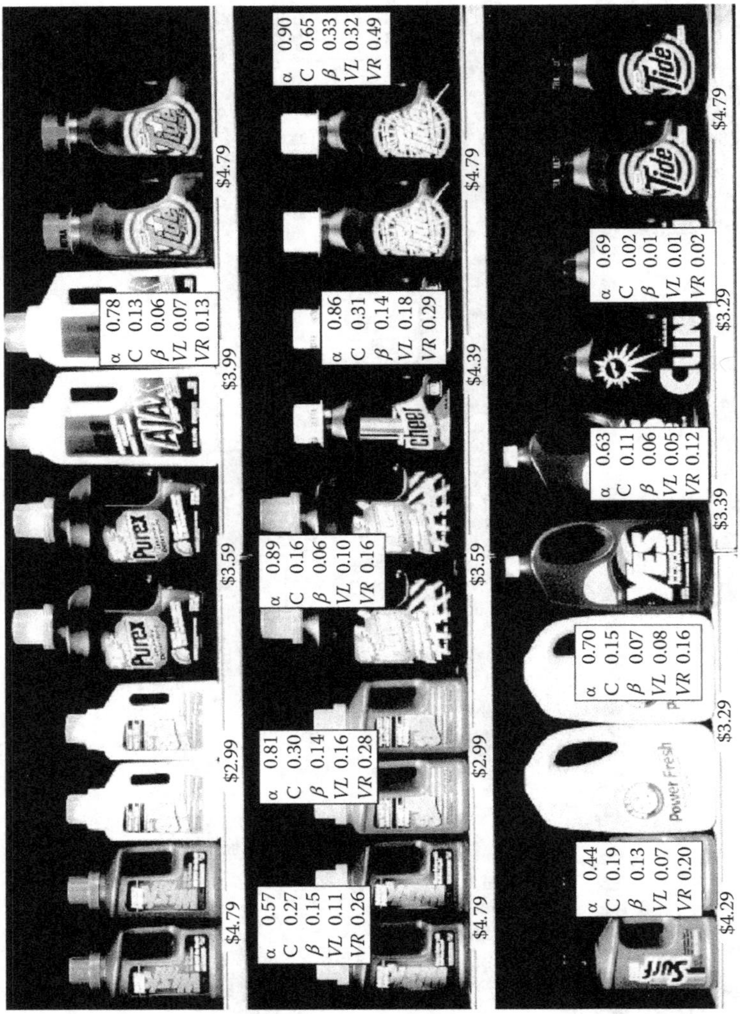

Figure 10.3 Shelf layout and brand results for detergents.

the data were aggregated across the four test locations for juices and the four test locations for detergents.

Detergent brands occupied slightly more shelf space, were priced higher (displayed prices were the regular prices for a food store chain in Philadelphia at the time of the experiment), and were bought less regularly than juice brands (see Table 10.1). In addition, consumers are generally more brand loyal and less likely to buy detergents on impulse (all differences are statistically significant). These differences between juices and detergents suggest that results holding across these two categories are relatively robust.

Descriptive Results

Table 10.1 reports the key results regarding visual attention and brand consideration for juices and detergents. Consumers spent more time looking at the juice display than at the detergents display (25.06 vs. 17.99 seconds, $F(1, 307) = 13.7, p < .001$). These numbers are comparable to the in-store observations reported for detergents by Hoyer (1984) in the U.S. and by Leong (1993) in Singapore (respectively 13.2, $t = .51, p = .71$ and 12.2 seconds, $t = .62, p = .55$). This suggests that consumers were only slightly more involved in the eye-tracking study than in a real shopping situation.

Interestingly, consumers also noted (i.e., fixated at least once) more brands for juices (10.93 vs. 7.09 for detergents, $F_{1,307} = 132.5, p < .001$) but considered the same number of brands in both categories (2.57 brands for juices vs. 2.29 brands for detergents, $F_{1,307} = 1.6, p = .21$). The size of the consideration set for juices is comparable to the number (3.22, $t = .65, p = .72$) reported by Hauser and Wernerfelt (1990) for the same category (Hauser and Wernerfelt do not provide data on liquid laundry detergents). The percentages of participants considering each brand are given in Figures 10.2 and 10.3. Participants noted three to four times more brands than they considered, showing that noting is not a direct proxy for brand consideration. This also indicates that one needs to separately model visual attention and brand consideration if one wants to measure visual lift.

The visual area of each brand was separated into the price tag area and the package area. As shown in Table 10.1, consumers only looked at 4 price tags for juices and at 2.5 price tags for detergents. Virtually

TABLE 10.1 Descriptive Statistics for the Juices and Detergent Studies (Means and Standard Deviations)*

	Juices	Detergents
Visual display characteristics		
Visual area of brand on screen[†] (sq inches)	118.80 (59.42)	189.00 (94.39)
Price[†] ($)	2.80 (.51)	3.88* (.66)
Consumer purchase behavior		
Number of brands used regularly or occasionally[‡]	12.29 (3.70)	6.86** (2.81)
Brand loyalty[‡a]	.52 (.50)	.64* (.48)
Degree of impulse purchasing[‡b]	.37 (.48)	.20** (.40)
Visual attention and consideration		
Time spent on picture[‡] (seconds)	25.06 (21.6)	17.99** (9.35)
Number of brands (pack or price) fixated at least once[‡]	10.93 (3.46)	7.09** (2.23)
Number of packs fixated at least once[‡]	10.54 (3.46)	6.90** (2.17)
Number of prices fixated at least once[‡]	4.04 (2.68)	2.52** (2.00)
Number of brands considered[‡]	2.57 (1.81)	2.29 (1.30)

[†] These are average values across brands (n = 16 for juices, n = 10 for detergents).

[‡] These are average values across consumers (n = 159 for juices, n = 150 for detergents).

[a] Percentage of consumers who state that they "always buy the same brand regardless of price" or "regularly buy one brand unless there is a sale," rather than either "switch between brands" or "buy the cheapest brand."

[b] Percentage of consumers who state that they "usually decide whether or not to buy from the category when they are in the store," rather than "before entering the store."

* $p < .05$, ** $p < .01$.

no brands were fixated on the price area alone, as indicated by the almost negligible increase between the number of packs noted and the number of brands (pack or price) noted (see Table 10.1). Other aspects of the data also demonstrated the predominance of packages in visual attention and generally low levels of price information processing (c.f. Dickson & Sawyer, 1990). For example, consumers almost never noted a product's price if they had not already noted its pack, and when consumers looked at both the pack and the price of the same brand, the pack was noted 6 seconds earlier for juices and 4.7 seconds earlier for detergents. Drawing on these results, all subsequent analyses are based on data aggregated to the brand level (i.e., pack or price).

Although these results show important differences between juices and detergents, the overall picture shows surprisingly similar results when controlling for differences in the number of brands displayed in each category. The proportion of brands noted is very similar across both categories (68% for juices and 71% for detergent). It is also similar to the results reported by Russo and Leclerc (1994) for other categories (69% for ketchup, 61% for applesauce, and 60% for peanut butter). The number of fixations on packs and prices is also remarkably similar across both categories: in both categories, two-thirds of packages are noted (66% for juices and 69% for detergents) and only one quarter of prices are noted (25% for both juices and detergents). Finally, most visual search involves transitions to a different brand rather than within-brand search (92% of observations for juices and 91% for detergents).

Similarly, robust results were obtained when looking at the number of fixations on brands and the average consideration conditional on the number of fixations (see Figure 10.4). For both categories, brands are more likely to be either fixated at least twice (with probability .50 for juices and .55 for detergents) or never fixated (with probability .32 for juices and .29 for detergents) than of being fixated exactly once (with probability .18 for juices and .16 for detergents). Also, for both categories, there is a strong relationship between consideration and the number of eye fixations. On average, making at least two eye fixations added 13 percentage points to the probability of consideration for juices and 10 points for detergents compared to brands that were not fixated on at all. Finally, although infrequent (2.2% of observations for juices and 4.3% of observations for detergents), brands are sometimes included in the consideration set even though they were never fixated

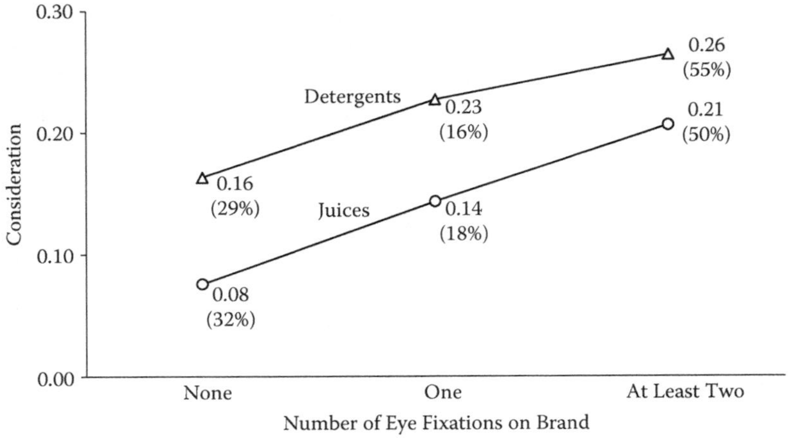

Figure 10.4 Consideration conditional on number of fixations and relative frequency of number of fixations (in parameters). Note: These are average values across brands (defined as pack, price, and, if present, shelf talker).

on. The most likely explanations for this are that some packages are so well known that only peripheral vision is required to identify their presence or that consumers assume their presence based on past experience alone. Further research will be required to address this issue. However, it is consistent with our framework and subsequent model, which postulate that consumers may have a purely memory-based probability of considering a brand before looking at it.

Overall, the descriptive results are largely consistent with in-store observations, supporting the face validity of eye-tracking studies. They show that consumer visual information processing at the point of purchase is limited and mostly driven by packages rather than by prices and that across-brands search is more common than within-brand search. They also provide evidence for both purely memory-based consideration (hence unseen is not always unsold) and for a positive relationship between the number of in-store eye fixations and brand consideration (brands fixated more are more likely to be considered). Of course, these results do not tell whether additional looks yield additional consideration or whether consumers look multiple times at brands that they have already decided to consider (or whether it is some combination of the two). We address this issue in the next section by developing a probability model that links visual attention and brand consideration in both ways.

A Decision-Path Model of Visual Attention and Consideration at the Point of Purchase

The main objective of the decision-path model is to separate the effects of visual factors from memory-based factors as a determinant of brand consideration. In particular, observed likelihoods of consideration for each level of eye fixation are used to estimate a base probability of consideration that is due to out-of-store decision making (i.e., memory-based response) and the incremental consideration probability due to in-store visual attention (i.e., visual lift). Our goal in developing our path-dependent process model was to balance both parsimony and a behaviorally plausible parametric representation. We have thus placed great value on keeping the model simple, estimable using typical commercial eye-tracking data, and helpful and easy to use by managers. To our knowledge, this is the first model of this type in either the marketing or the psychological literatures, so prudence suggests simplicity. Also, the basic data (i.e., the joint frequencies of noting and considering) provide only six possible outcomes (i.e., $df = 5$) for each brand, so brand-level models must be parsimonious. Still, the model presented here provides a multistage decision process for fixation and consideration that is consistent with both the extant literature and our data. The computational approach taken here is general, and hence other tree-like path models can be fit and compared to the one presented here.

Model Specification

We model the POP decision-making process as a sequence of events that alternate between subdecisions to consider the brand and subdecisions to make an eye fixation on the brand (see Figure 10.5). The model assumes that consumers have a memory-based probability of consideration for each brand. This assumption is supported by studies showing that consumers have a long-term consideration set in memory (Shocker, Ben-Akiva, Boccara, & Nedungadi, 1991).

The first decision is a memory-based, prestore consideration that is made before any in-store visual information is assessed (i.e., before the brand is noticed). Next, consumers decide whether or not to

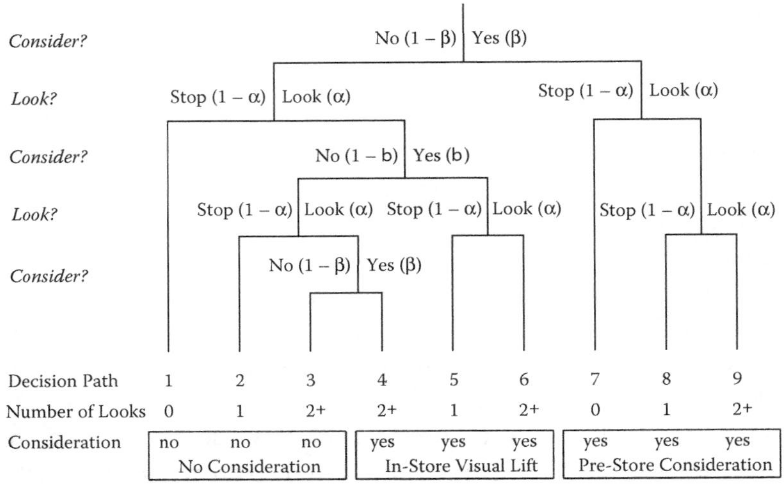

Figure 10.5 A decision-path model of point-of-purchase decision making. Note: α is the probability of an eye fixation on the brand (its visual salience) and β is the probability of considering the brand. In this simple version of the model, β is fixed for each brand and is therefore also the memory-based probability of considering the brand.

look at the brand.* If the brand is not fixated, no new information is acquired, and the consideration decision remains unchanged. If the brand is fixated, the new eye fixation provides a new opportunity to consider the brand. We assume that consideration is irreversible; that is, having considered a brand, consumers might choose to look at it again but they do not "un-consider" it.

Figure 10.5, depicts the nine possible decision paths in the model and the outcomes that would be observed in our data. For brand $_j$, α_j is the probability of making an eye fixation (its visual salience) and β_j is the probability of including the brand in the consideration set. In the simple version of the model depicted in Figure 10.5, β_j is the same whether the occasion of possible consideration is pre- or postfixation. Our data allows us to discriminate between no fixations, one fixation, and two or more fixations. Therefore, we assume

* As with most quantitative models of perceptual and cognitive processes, the represented process greatly simplifies the actual process. It captures certain aspects of decision making (e.g., the temporal flow of looking and consideration), but ignores others (e.g., whether the decisions to look and consider are conscious and deliberate, non-conscious and associative, or some mixture of the two).

that if the brand is not in the memory-based consideration set (which happens with probability $1 - \beta_j$), then the first fixation provides a new opportunity to consider it with probability β_j. Similarly, if the brand is still not considered after the first fixation, subsequent fixations lead to consideration with probability β_j. Each decision path is mutually exclusive of the others and exhaustive of the possible sequences of events. The probability that a specific path occurs is computed as the product of its subdecision probabilities. For example, the probability of being in the first path (i.e., no fixation and no consideration) is $p1_j = (1 - \beta_j) \times (1 - \alpha_j)$. (See Appendix for the probabilities of the nine decision paths).

As can be seen in Figure 10.5, the overall predicted probability of consideration is the sum of the individual probabilities of taking one of the six decision paths leading to positive consideration ($p4_j$ to $p9_j$). Predicted consideration can be expressed as a function of α_j and β_j, as follows:

$$c_j = \beta_j + \beta_j\alpha_j(1 + \beta_j) + \beta_j\beta_j^2(1 - \alpha_j)^2 \qquad (10.1)$$

Model Implications, Visual Lift, and Visual Responsiveness

One immediate implication of the model is that the conditional probability of consideration given fixation increases with the number of fixations (which is consistent with the results reported in Figure 10.4). It is easy to see from Equation 10.1 that the probability of considering the brand is the memory-based consideration probability, β_j (i.e., probability of paths 7, 8, or 9 occurring), plus the incremental consideration provided by the first eye fixation, $\beta_j\alpha_j (1 - \beta_j)$ (i.e., probability of paths 5 or 6 occurring), plus the incremental consideration provided by the second eye fixation, $\beta_j\alpha_j^2 (1 - \beta_j)^2$ (i.e., probability of path 4 occurring). In other words, Equation 10.1 shows that each eye fixation provides a new chance to consider the brand (with probability β_j) provided that the brand is noted (with probability α_j for the first fixation and α_j^2 for the second fixation) and that previous consideration decisions were negative (with probability $(1 - \beta_j)$ for the first fixation and $(1 - \beta_j)^2$ for the second fixation).

A somewhat subtler prediction of the model is that the increase in the conditional probability of consideration as fixation goes from 0 to 1 should be larger than the increase as fixation goes from 1 to 2+. In other words, there are diminishing returns in the gain from each

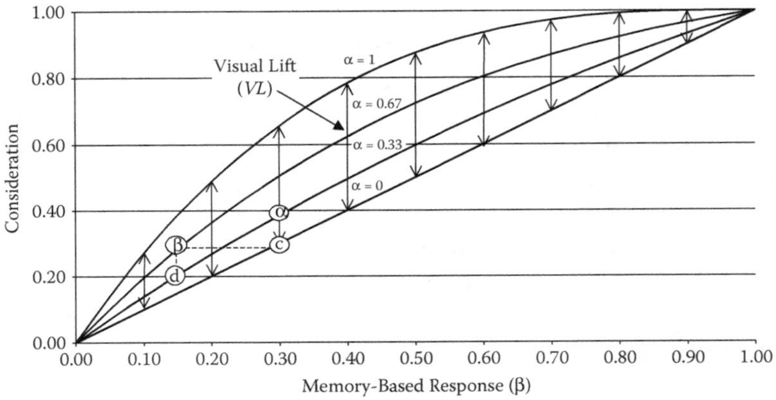

Figure 10.6 Consideration and visual lift as functions of visual salience (α) and memory-based response (β).

additional look. This is because the additional chance of considering the brand after each fixation is the memory-based probability (β_j) weighted by a term smaller than 1 (because $0 \leq \alpha_j \leq 1$ and $0 \leq \beta_j \leq 1$) for the first eye fixation and by an even smaller term for the second fixation (derivation available from the authors). This too is consistent with our data (i.e., .07 vs. .06 for juices and .06 vs. .04 for detergents; see Figure 10.4). Thus, the model is able to capture important qualitative aspects of our empirical data.

One important aspect of the decision-path model is that it also allows for a decomposition of consideration probabilities. It is natural to think of β_j as a measure of memory-based consideration and the increase in consideration due to in-store visual attention as a measure of visual lift. Specifically:

$$VL_j = c_j - \beta_j = \beta_j\alpha_j (1 - \beta_j) + \beta_j\alpha_j^2(1 - \beta_j)^2 \qquad (10.2)$$

Visual lift is jointly determined by the visual salience of the brand (α_j) and by the memory-based consideration of the brand (β_j). This is an important aspect of the model because it shows that simply raising visual salience is not enough. For example, raising visual salience does not create any visual lift in the two extreme cases of zero or 100% memory-based consideration probabilities (e.g., for brands liked by nobody or by everybody). Figure 10.6 plots total brand consideration (c_j) as a function of memory-based response (β_j) for minimum ($\alpha_j = 0$), moderate ($\alpha_j = .33$), typical ($\alpha_j = .67$), and maximum ($\alpha_j = 1$)

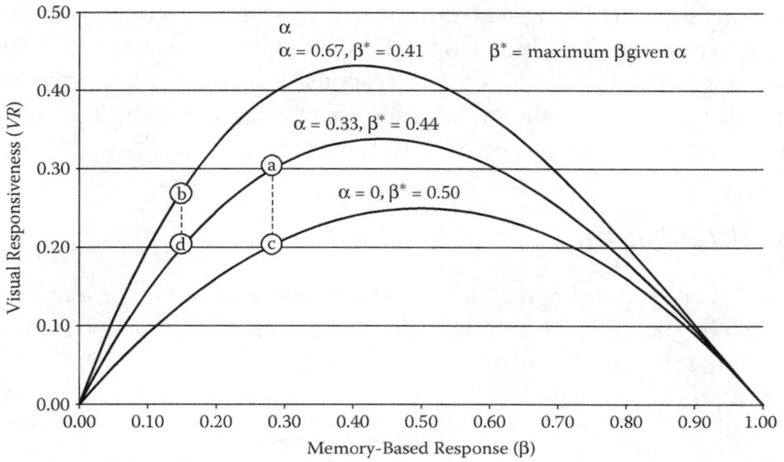

Figure 10.7 Visual responsiveness as a function of visual salience (α) and memory-based response (β).

levels of visual salience. The vertical arrows in Figure 10.6 show maximum visual lift for each level of memory-based response, β_j. As Figure 10.6 shows, visual salience (α_j) increases visual lift for all levels of memory-based response (except of course when $\beta_j = 0$ or $\beta_j = 1$). In contrast, visual lift first increases and then decreases as memory-based response (β_j) increases.

Visual lift, VL_j, provides a natural performance measure because the unit of measurement is incremental probability of consideration, and it reflects the assumption that the effects of visual salience on choice are mediated by inclusion in the consideration set. However, it does not answer the question of which brands should receive incremental POP dollars, a decision directly relevant for manufacturers and retailers. To shed light on this complex decision, we compute another index, visual responsiveness,

$$VR_j = \mathrm{d}c_j/\mathrm{d}\alpha_j, \tag{10.3}$$

which is the same as $\mathrm{d}VL_j/\mathrm{d}\alpha_j$ because $VL_j = c_j - \beta_j$ and β_j is not a function of α_j.

Visual responsiveness, VR_j, is also a function of visual salience (α_j) and memory-based response (β_j) and is plotted in Figure 10.7. From this figure we see that brands with moderate levels of memory-based response provide the best return on POP investments. More specifically, as α_j increases from 0 to 1, the value of β_j with maximum responsiveness (β_j*) shifts from .50 to .39 (derivation available from the authors). We show how visual responsiveness can help marketers decide which brand should be made more visually salient, in theory and for the brands studied here, in the next section.

Model Estimation

As can be seen in Figure 10.6, for any given value of α_j, c_j is a monotonically increasing function of β_j. This function can be inverted to compute β_j from α_j and c_j:

$$\beta = \frac{1}{6\alpha^2}\left[2\alpha(1+2\alpha) + \frac{2\cdot 2^{1/3}\alpha^2\left(-2+\alpha+\alpha^2\right)}{k^{1/3}} + 2^{2/3}k^{1/3}\right], \quad (10.4)$$

where

$$k = -7\alpha^3 - 15\alpha^4 - 3\alpha^5 - 2\alpha^6 + 27\alpha^4 c$$
$$+\sqrt{4\left(2\alpha^2-\alpha^3-\alpha^4\right)^3 + \left(-7\alpha^3-15\alpha^4-3\alpha^5-2\alpha^6+27\alpha^4 c\right)^2}.$$

In principle, this computation could be made even when the empirical values of α_j and c_j come from different sources (e.g., a standard eye-tracking report and a survey measure of memory-based consideration). However, this computation is exact and provides no statistical measures of reliability or validity. Fortunately, the eye-tracking studies described earlier provide richer data. For each brand, our two-parameter model can be estimated via maximum likelihood from the frequencies with which each of the six possible outcomes occur using the equations in (A1) and (A2).*

* We used the Solver add-in of Microsoft Excel to maximize the following equation LL = $\Sigma j\ \Sigma i \ln(I_{i0n_j}p_{0n_j} + I_{i1n_j}p_{1n_j} + I_{i2n_j}p_{2n_j} + I_{i0y_j}p_{0y_j} + I_{i1y_j}p_{1y_j} + I_{i2y_j}p_{2y_j})$ across brands j and consumers i, where I is an indicator function that is 1 for the observed fixation/consideration outcome and 0 otherwise. Using multiple starting values for a subset of the analyses checked the operational robustness of the algorithm. These replications almost always converged to virtually identical solutions, indicating that local maxima were generally not a problem. Also, the correlations between the exactly computed and maximum likelihood estimated values of β_j are very high (.999 for juices and 1.000 for detergents).

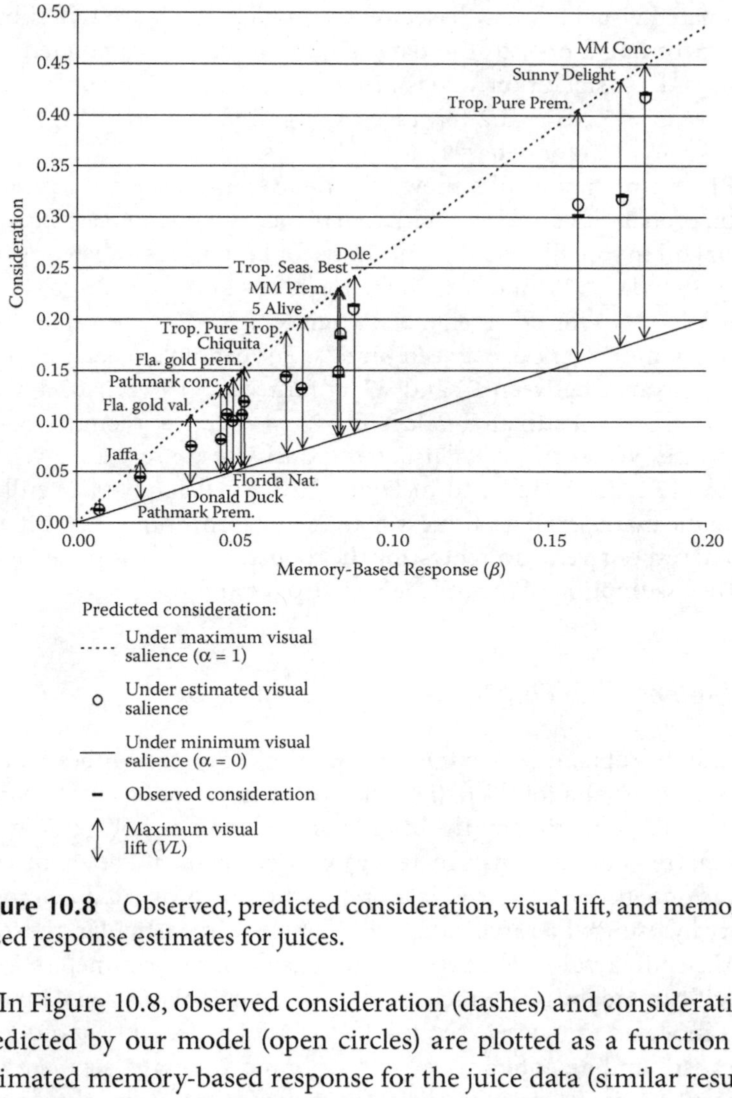

Figure 10.8 Observed, predicted consideration, visual lift, and memory-based response estimates for juices.

In Figure 10.8, observed consideration (dashes) and consideration predicted by our model (open circles) are plotted as a function of estimated memory-based response for the juice data (similar results were obtained for detergents, but are omitted here to simplify the discussion). As in Figure 10.6, the vertical bars represent maximum visual lift. Finally, the dotted line represents the maximal predicted consideration under certain visual attention ($\alpha_j = 1$) and the solid line the (memory-based) minimal level of predicted consideration under no visual attention ($\alpha_j = 0$). The distance from the diagonal to the observed consideration marker (open circle) represents the estimated visual lift, VL_j, based on the model. As Figure 10.8 shows, the fit of our model to the data is quite good. The predicted and observed consideration values are very close (paired t-value = .36, df = 15, p = .57, η^2 = .02 for juices and paired t-value = .71, df = 9, p = .42, η^2 = .04 for detergents).

The estimation results show that, on average, observed consideration probabilities are a combination of memory-based response and visual lift in roughly equal proportions for both juices and detergents (c = .157, β = .076, and VL = .081 for juices and c = .228, β = .114, and VL = .115 for detergents). Of course, these average values hide important differences between brands. For example, visual responsiveness varies between .01 and .37 for juices and between .02 and .49 for detergents. Estimated values of visual salience, memory-based response, visual lift, and visual responsiveness are also given in Figure 10.2, for juices, and in Figure 10.3, for detergents. We illustrate the managerial usefulness of these differences in visual lift and visual responsiveness after testing the robustness of the simple model to the assumption of the independence of α_j and β_j.

Robustness with Respect to Model Specification

To test the robustness of our model, we also estimated a more general version that (a) allowed β_j (i.e., memory-based response) to change as a result of fixating on the brand (i.e., in-store) or not (i.e., out-of-store), (b) allowed all parameters to vary by segment (i.e., nonusers, occasional users, and regular users), and (c) incorporated heterogeneity by using a hierarchical Bayesian model. In particular, the logit of the individual-level fixation and consideration parameters for a specific brand, by a given respondent, in a particular usage segment, was modeled as having a main-effect term for persons, brand, and segment, and an interaction term of brand by usage segment. As is standard in Bayesian models, these parameters were then given Gaussian prior distributions and corresponding conjugate hyperpriors to allow for appropriate uncertainty estimation. The model was fit in the freely available software WinBUGS (www.mrc-bsu.cam.ac.uk/bugs/welcome.shtml); the code and computation details are available upon request from the authors.

For the simple models discussed thus far, the Bayesian parameter estimates replicated the maximum likelihood estimates almost exactly. Also, for most versions of the model, postfixation consideration probabilities were nonzero (and similar in size to prefixation probabilities), rejecting the hypothesis that all consideration is out-of-store and visual lift is zero. However, results for some versions of the model revealed interesting changes in parameter estimates and suggested important limitations to the current data. When fixation probabilities were allowed to differ for not-yet-considered and already-considered brands in the decision-path model, the estimated probabilities were larger for already-considered brands. This resulted in larger estimates of base consideration and smaller estimates for postfixation consideration. These changes reduced visual lift considerably; in some cases, to zero. However, this seems to be the result of a key indeterminacy for observational (i.e., nonexperimental) data such as these. Models with much larger levels of postfixation consideration and visual lift fit the data nearly as well. In fact, distinct bimodality was often observed for these parameters in their posterior distributions. Figure 10.9 shows these distributions for the juices data. The bimodality is particularly evident for occasional users. An important problem for future research is to find ways to resolve this type of indeterminacy.

Implications for POP Marketing

Estimating the Visual Salience of Different Areas of Supermarket Displays

Our results show consistent patterns of visual attention across the different areas of the shelf. As can be seen in Figure 10.2 and Figure 10.3, brands located near the center of the shelf are seen by almost all consumers (e.g., $\alpha = .92$ for Minute Maid® concentrate and $\alpha = .89$ for Purex®). The likelihood of noting the brand then drops very quickly as one moves toward the end of the display (e.g., $\alpha = .52$ for Pathmark Premium and $\alpha = .44$ for Surf®, two brands located at the bottom left end of their respective shelves). In order to explore the factors affecting visual salience, we regressed it onto a binary variable representing bottom shelf (vs. top or middle shelf), a binary variable representing brands located to the left, and another binary variable representing brands located to the right (for juices only; the right location being confounded with Tide for detergents),

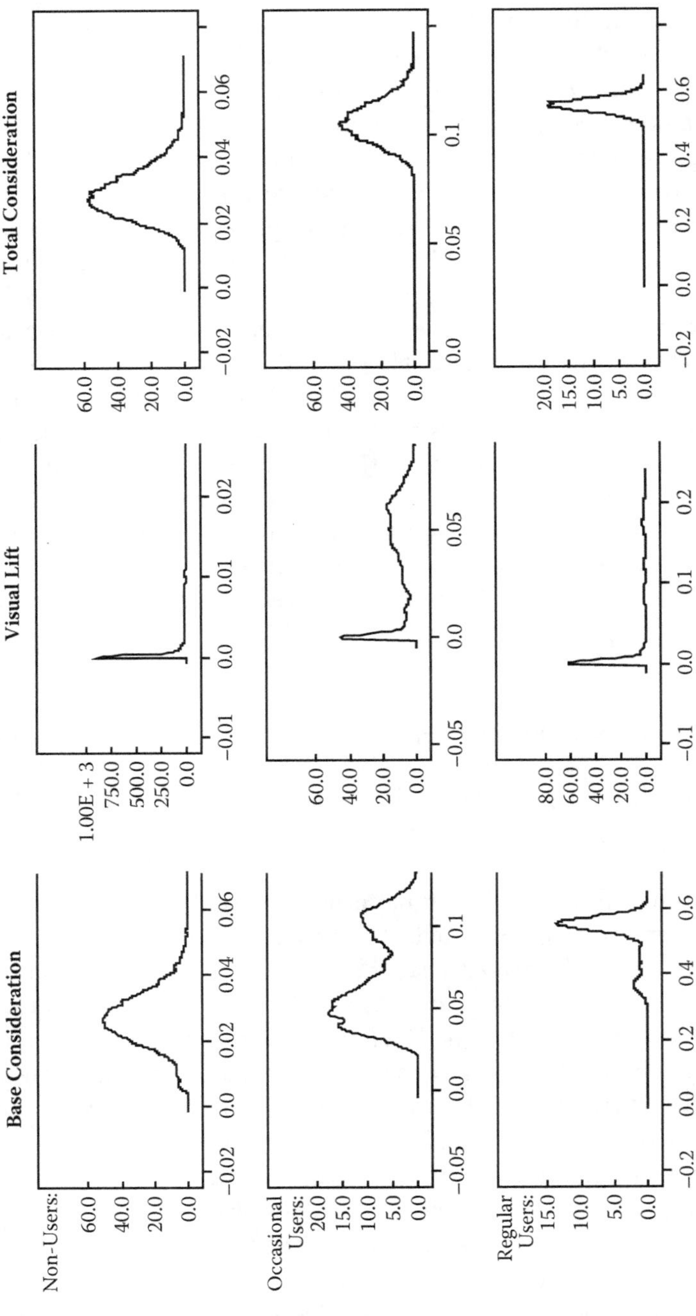

Figure 10.9 Model estimation results using hierarchical Bayes method: Posterior distributions for juices.

and on the number of facings. The coefficients for bottom shelf were: B = −.11, t = −2.50 for juices and B = −.17, t = −2.63 for detergents; for left location: B = −.18, t = −3.43 for juices and B = −.20, t = −3.61 for detergents; for right location: B = −.08, t = −1.94 for juices; and for number of facings: B = −.00, t = −.27 for juices and B = .02, t = .98 for detergents. Thus, there were clear effects of location but little effect of shelf facings.

Of course, our data do not allow to perfectly isolate the effects of these variables and to disentangle them from brand-specific effects. For example, the current displays do not allow testing the visual salience of brands on the top shelf because the top juice shelf contained brands with many facings and the top detergent shelf contained brands located also on the middle shelf. This is clearly an area for future research, involving either the analysis of many varied displays, or an experimental design in which brand, shelf location, and number of facings are orthogonally manipulated. On the other hand, our results suggest that the patterns of visual salience identified here may be fairly robust given that they hold on two categories with considerable differences in visual display and purchase behavior.

Estimating the Effects of Visual Attention Across Brands

Our results reveal large differences across brands for visual lift and responsiveness (see Figure 10.2 and Figure 10.3). Brands with many shelf facings or a central location, like Minute Maid concentrate and Cheer, performed well insofar as visual lift is high compared to memory-based response (β = .18 and VL = .24 for Minute Maid concentrate and β = .14 and VL = .18 for Cheer) and their consideration is near the maximum value possible as estimated by our model (see Figure 10.8). In contrast, brands like Sunny Delight® and Wisk® have high levels of memory-based response (comparable to Minute Maid concentrate and Cheer), but much lower visual lift (β = .17 and VL = .15 for Sunny Delight and β = .15 and VL = .11 for Wisk), and hence much lower overall level of consideration. A similar problem is evident for Surf and Pathmark Premium, which too have substantial room for improvement. We note that all four of these identified "poor performers" are located on the left end of the shelf display, suggesting that this is a low visual lift region of the display. Further analysis is necessary to understand why these brands do not gain as much from each in-store attention as other brands. In any case, one direct use of our measures is to aid managers in identifying potential problem areas in their POP activities.

It is also important to note that the values of memory-based response and visual lift, per se, do not tell the whole story. In order to evaluate the relative POP performance of different brands, one needs to consider visual lift in relation to its maximum value. For example, as can be seen in Figure 10.2 and Figure 10.8, Sunny Delight has slightly higher visual lift than Dole® (.15 vs. .13) but is much farther from its maximum level of visual lift, the difference between memory-based consideration and maximal consideration under perfect visual salience (which is .27 for Sunny Delight vs. .15 for Dole). This analysis shows that Sunny Delight has much more room for improvement than Dole, and thus suggests that it should be selected for improved POP activity (e.g., it should receive a shelf talker); albeit profit considerations are required.

Optimal Allocations of In-Store Visual Salience

In the two categories studied, the brands with highest visual responsiveness are those with highest levels of memory-based response (*VR* = .37 for Minute Maid from concentrate and *VR* = .49 for Tide). This raises the more general question of which brands would benefit the most from additional visual salience, and hence of which brand should receive incremental POP dollars. In practice, manufacturers typically want to improve their weakest brands (e.g., to promote trial of new products). Retailers, in contrast, typically give the most effort to strong brands, with the rationale that they are the most likely to trigger category sales (Drèze et al., 1994). The general optimization problem faced by retailers is very complex because the control variables are many (e.g., shelf locations, numbers of facings, and shelf talkers for each brand in a product category), brands differ (e.g., in brand equity, advertising support, price and profit margin), and the causal impact of POP activities is uncertain and may vary across brands. In this section, we use the decision-path model to abstract away from these complexities and obtain results that shed light on how incremental changes in POP marketing can be optimized.

To simplify the analysis, we first assume that there is a reasonably direct relationship between consideration probabilities and sales and, therefore, profit. That is, we assume the goal is to maximize total consideration across brands and shoppers (and that consideration is statistically independent across brands and shoppers). Second, we assume that visual salience (α_j) is under the control of the manager, but that memory-based response (β_j) is exogenously determined for a finite set of brands that are being managed (i.e., as a retailer's assortment or as a manufacturer's product line). Finally, we assume that cost is linearly related to visual salience.

Given these assumptions, standard economic reasoning dictates that each incremental dollar spent on improving in-store visual salience should be spent where it will do the most good. That is, it should be spent on the brand whose consideration will increase most as a result. Moving beyond small increments to allocating a finite budget across a set of discrete alternatives requires solving some type of "knapsack" problem. Problems of this sort are extremely complex mathematically and are typically solved numerically for specific variations of the problem. One method of solution is to use a *greedy algorithm* that makes a series of small incremental improvements until a local maximum is achieved (Kohli & Krishnamurti, 1995).

Visional responsiveness (VR_j) measures the impact of incremental changes in visual salience (α_j) on brand consideration. As shown in Figure 10.7, for any given level of memory-based response, visual responsiveness increases with the level of visual salience of the brand. Thus, there are marginally increasing returns to visual salience (Implication 1). It is also evident in Figure 10.7 that visual responsiveness is maximal for brands with moderate levels of memory-based equity (Implication 2). It does not pay to increase the visual salience of brands with low memory-based probability of consideration because incremental fixations are likely to lead to negative consideration decisions. Brands with very high memory-based response do not gain much from higher visual salience because they are likely to have already been considered. This result already shows that the common practice of allocating shelf space according to market share (a proxy for memory-based equity) may not be optimal for very strong brands, which are likely to be in the diminishing portion of the VR_j curve in Figure 10.7.

To illustrate these two implications, consider four hypothetical brands depicted in Figure 10.7 as *a*, *b*, *c*, and *d*. The most responsive brand is *a*, so it should receive incremental POP effort. Because increasing the visual salience of *a* will make it even more responsive, it would receive the next increment and so on until it achieved maximum visual salience (Implication 1). Using the same reasoning, subsequent allocations would be made to brand *b* until it achieved its maximum visual salience. Brands *c* and *d* have the same visual responsiveness. However, if the same incremental allocation is made to both brands (e.g., raising visual salience of each by .33, making *c* equivalent to *a* and *d* equivalent to *b*), then the resulting responsiveness of *c* will exceed that of *d*. Thereafter, all subsequent allocations would go to *c* until it reached its maximum. This same logic applies to solutions obtained using a greedy algorithm.

In terms of visual salience and memory-based equity, brand *a* is the strongest in the set. Thus, this example suggests that a "stick-with-the-winner" strategy for making POP allocations should be optimal in many situations. This strategy gives all incremental allocations to the "strongest" brand until it reaches its maximum and then allocates to the next-strongest brand and so on until further allocations are no longer profitable. We contrast this with a "help-the-poor" strategy in which all incremental allocations are given to the "weakest" brand until it reaches its maximum and then allocate to the next strongest brand and so on until further allocations are no longer profitable.

In general, the optimality of the stick-with-the-winner strategy will depend on how brand strength is defined and the relative strengths of the brands in the set over which allocations are made. One natural, but conservative, definition is that one brand is stronger than another if it has higher values of both visual salience and memory-based equity (i.e., a weak ordering on all brands in the (α, β) space). Thus, in our example, *a* is stronger than *c* and *d*, and *b* is stronger than *d*, but the remaining pairs cannot be ranked. Given this definition of strength it is easy to show that if a finite set of brands is strictly ordered by strength and the maximum value of β_j is less than .39, then the stick-with-the-winner strategy will be optimal. No similarly general results emerge if the ordering is not strict or if β_j is greater than .39 for some brands.

To obtain more general results, we explored the concept of brand strength in a series of numerical analyses. In these analyses, a discrete improvement in visual salience was applied to pairs of brands that differed in strength, and the resulting gains in visual lift were compared. In particular, it was assumed that a specific POP action resulted in an independent probability, Δ, that the brand would be noted at each point in the decision path where the base probability,

α_j, was applied. Thus, the new probability of fixation, α_j', was equal to $\alpha_j + \Delta - \alpha_j\Delta$. This is a natural way to represent singular actions such as adding a shelf-talker or end-aisle display for a brand. It also imposes a plausible form of diminishing returns that works against the stick-with-the-winner strategy, making this a conservative test. The gain in visual lift from such a discrete action is:

$$GAIN_j = VE_j' - VE_j$$

$$= \beta_j(\alpha - \alpha_j\Delta)(1 - \beta_j)(1 + (\Delta - \alpha_j\,\Delta + 2\,\alpha_j)(1 - \beta_j)). \qquad (10.5)$$

In our numerical analyses, brand 1 was assumed to be stronger than brand 2 (i.e., $\alpha_1 \geq \alpha_2$ and $\beta_1 \geq \beta_2$). We define gain advantage of brand 1 over brand 2, A_{12}, as

$$A_{12} = GAIN_1 - GAIN_2. \qquad (10.6)$$

Thus, the sign of A_{12} is an indicator of the superiority of the stick-with-the-winner strategy and the size of A_{12} represents the cost of choosing the wrong strategy. A_{12} is a function of 5 parameters (α_1, α_2, β_1, β_2, and Δ), so our approach was to randomly sample parameters and identify regions of the space where A_{12} is predominantly positive or negative.

In our analysis, 2,000 observations were generated by (a) independently drawing Δ, α_1, and β_1 from the uniform distribution on [0,1], (b) drawing α_2 and β_2 conditionally from uniform distribution on $[0,\alpha_1)$ and $[0,\beta_1)$, respectively, and (c) computing A_{12}; of course with the restriction that all probabilities remain between [0,1]. A_{12} was negative for 61% of the observations and had an average value of –.02. Thus, across all possible situations the help-the-poor strategy is slightly favored. Also, the optimal strategy shifts from stick-with-the-winner to help-the-poor as Δ, α_1, and β_1 increase (i.e., the help-the-poor strategy is preferred for POP activities with a large impact on visual salience or when the stronger brand is really strong). A regression of A_{12} onto Δ, α_1, β_1, α_2, and β_2 accounted for 44% of the variance in A_{12} and yielded standardized coefficients of –.19, –.47, –.21, .26, and –.35 for Δ, α_1, β_1, α_2, and β_2, respectively. All coefficients were statistically significant. However, an examination of marginal distributions revealed much stronger and more meaningful results: A_{12} was always negative whenever β_2 (and therefore β_1 also) was greater than .43, indicating that the help-the-poor strategy dominates as long as memory-based equity is at least moderate for both brands. If we operationally define *impulse brands* to be those with memory-based equity less than .43 and *destination brands* as those with memory-based equity greater than .43, then we can generalize these results from pairs to sets of brands as follows: (a) when all brands are impulse brands, use the stick-with-the-winner strategy, and (b) when all brands are destination brands, use the help-the-poor strategy.

Conclusions and Future Research Opportunities

In an era when consumers seem overwhelmed by the number of available products, marketers are investing large amounts of money and effort to ensure that their brands are seen at the point of purchase. Yet, it has been difficult to measure the return on these investments because few data and methods are available to estimate visual lift, the incremental consideration due to in-store visual attention over prestore memory-based consideration. Ideally, marketers would decompose sales into out-of-store, memory-based response and in-store visual lift, similar to the commonly used decomposition of sales into baseline and promotional volumes.

In this paper, we have shown that commercial eye-tracking data, analyzed using a simple decision-path model of visual attention and brand consideration, can provide this type of decomposition. Moreover, our empirical applications and normative analysis show that allocating POP marketing activity according to market shares can be wrong. If all brands have a low memory-based probability of consideration (e.g., for impulse brands), retailers should "stick with the winner" (i.e., focus on the strongest brand until it reaches its maximum and then move to the next-strongest brand and so on until further allocations are no longer profitable). If all brands have a high memory-based probability of consideration (e.g., for destination brands), retailers should use the opposite help-the-poor strategy. Finally, our analyses provide new insights into how consumers make consideration and attention decisions at the point of purchase.

This research opens several areas for future investigation. Showing that in-store visual attention increases brand consideration naturally raises the issue of what influences in-store attention. Future research could examine the effects of factors such as shelf position, the number of facings, and price on fixation and consideration probabilities by testing a series of planograms in which these factors are independently manipulated (for more on the effects of product design and spatial location, see the chapters by Krishna and Raghubir in this volume). This would provide sufficient degrees of freedom to examine temporal dependencies in fixation and consideration probabilities and to incorporate brand and customer heterogeneity. More importantly, this would allow us to better test the direction of the causality between attention and consideration.

Additionally, it would be valuable to know whether visual attention to shelf displays is mainly controlled by automatic and nonconscious processes requiring little or no cognitive capacity, or if consumers are able to locate preselected brands without being distracted by visual factors that are simply too salient to ignore. Another important research issue is determining the extent to which researchers can measure visual attention without needing to collect eye-tracking data. For example, the common Starch scores of exposure actually measure a consumer's recollection of having previously seen the ad. However, it remains to be seen whether asking consumers to recall the brands that they have seen could be used as an indicator of their visual attention to the brand.

References

Alba, J. W., Hutchinson, J. W., & Lynch, J. G., Jr. (1991). Memory and decision making. In T. S. Robertson & H. H. Kassarjian (Eds.), *Handbook of consumer behavior* (pp. 1–49). Englewood Cliffs, NJ: Prentice Hall.

Bemmaor, A., & Mouchoux, D. (1991). Measuring the short term effect of in-store promotion and retail advertising on brand sales: A factorial experiment. *Journal of Marketing Research, 28*(2), 202–214.

Blattberg, R. C., & Neslin, S. A. (1990). *Sales promotion: Concepts, methods, and strategies.* Englewood Cliffs, NJ: Prentice Hall.

Burke, R. R., Harlam, B. A., Kahn, B. E., & Lodish, L. M. (1992). Comparing dynamic consumer choice in real and computer simulated environments. *Journal of Consumer Research, 19*, 71–82.

Chandon, P., Morwitz, V. G., & Reinartz, W. J. (2005). Do intentions really predict behavior? Self-generated validity effects in survey research. *Journal of Marketing, 69*(2), 1–14.

Dickson, P. R., & Sawyer, A. G. (1990). The price knowledge and search of supermarket shoppers. *Journal of Marketing, 54*, 42–53.

Drèze, X., Hoch, S. J., & Purk, M. E. (1994). Shelf management and space elasticity. *Journal of Retailing, 70*(4), 301–326.

Hauser, J. R., & Wernerfelt, B. (1990). An evaluation cost model of consideration sets. *Journal of Consumer Research, 16*, 393–408.

Hoffman, J. E. (1998). Visual attention and eye movements. In H. Pashler (Ed.), *Attention* (pp. 119–154). East Sussex: Psychology Press.

Hoyer, W. D. (1984). An examination of consumer decision making for a common repeat purchase product. *Journal of Consumer Research, 11*, 822–829.

Hutchinson, J. W., Raman, K., & Mantrala, M. K. (1994). Finding choice alternatives in memory: Probability model of brand name recall. *Journal of Marketing Research, 31*, 441–461.

Inman, J. J., & Winer, R. S. (1998). *Where the rubber meets the road: A model of in-store consumer decision-making* (Institute Report 98–122), Cambridge, MA: Marketing Science Institute.

Janiszewski, C. (1998). The influence of display characteristics on visual exploratory search behavior. *Journal of Consumer Research, 25*, 290–301.

Kohli, R., & Krishnamurti, R. (1995). Joint performance of greedy heuristics for the integer knapsack problem. *Discrete Applied Mathematics, 56*, 37–48.

Kollat, D. T., & Willett, R. P. (1967). Customer impulse purchasing behavior. *Journal of Marketing Research, 4*, 21–31.

Leong, S. M. (1993). Consumer decision making for common, repeat-purchase products: A dual replication. *Journal of Consumer Psychology, 2*(2), 193–208.

Lohse, G. L. (1997). Consumer eye movement patterns on yellow pages advertising. *Journal of Advertising, 26*(1), 61–73.

Lohse, G. L., & Johnson, E. J. (1996). A comparison of two process tracing methods for choice tasks. *Organizational Behavior and Human Decision Processes, 68*(1), 28–43.

Pieters, R., & Warlop, L. (1999). Visual attention during brand choice: The impact of time pressure and task motivation. *International Journal of Research in Marketing, 16*(1), 1–16.

Pieters, R., Warlop, L., & Wedel, M. (2002). Breaking through the clutter: Benefits of advertisement originality and familiarity for brand attention and memory. *Management Science, 48*(6), 765.

Pieters, R., & Wedel, M. (2004). Attention capture and transfer in advertising: Brand, pictorial, and text-size effects. *Journal of Marketing, 68*(2), 36–50.

POPAI. (1997). *Consumer buying habits study.* Washington DC: Point Of Purchase Advertising Institute.

Rayner, K. (1998). Eye movement in reading and information processing: 20 years of research. *Psychological Bulletin, 124*(3), 372–422.

Russo, J. E., & Leclerc, F. (1994). An eye-fixation analysis of choice processes for consumer nondurables. *Journal of Consumer Research, 21*, 274–290.

Russo, J. E., & Rosen, L. D. (1975). An eye fixation analysis of multi-alternative choice. *Memory and Cognition, 3*(3), 267–276.

Shocker, A. D., Ben-Akiva, M., Boccara, B., & Nedungadi, P. (1991). Consideration set influences on consumer decision-making and choice: Issues, models, and suggestions. *Marketing Letters, 2*(3), 181–197.

Wedel, M., & Pieters, R. (2000). Eye fixations on advertisements and memory for brands: A model and findings. *Marketing Science, 19*(4), 297–312.

Wilkinson, J. B., Mason, J. B., & Paksoy, C. H. (1982). Assessing the impact of short-term supermarket strategy variables. *Journal of Marketing Research, 19*(1), 72–86.

Woodside, A. G., & Waddle, G. L. (1975). Sales effects of in-store advertising. *Journal of Advertising Research, 15*(3), 29–34.

Young, S. (2000). Putting the pieces together at the point of sale. *Marketing Research, 12*(3), 32.

Appendix

Details of Model Specification

To highlight the tree-like structure of our model for fixation and consideration, we present in Equations (10A.1.1) to (10A.1.9) below, a series of step-by-step probabilities that are not algebraically simplified. Each of these corresponds to a different latent path and their links to observable outcomes are described below in Equations 10A.2.2 to 10A.2.5

$$p1_j = (1 - \beta_j)(1 - \alpha_j), \tag{10A.1.1}$$

$$p2_j = (1 - \beta_j)\alpha_j(1 - \beta_j)(1 - \alpha_j), \tag{10A.1.2}$$

$$p3_j = (1 - \beta_j)\alpha_j(1 - \beta_j)\alpha_j(1 - \beta_j), \tag{10A.1.3}$$

$$p4_j = (1 - \beta_j)\alpha_j(1 - \beta_j)\alpha_j\beta_j, \tag{10A.1.4}$$

$$p5_j = (1 - \beta_j)\alpha_j\beta_j(1 - \alpha_j), \tag{10A.1.5}$$

$$p6_j = (1 - \beta_j)\alpha_j\beta_j\alpha_j, \tag{10A.1.6}$$

$$p7_j = \beta_j(1 - \alpha_j), \tag{10A.1.7}$$

$$p8_j = \beta_j\alpha_j(1 - \alpha_j), \tag{10A.1.8}$$

and

$$p9_j = \beta_j\alpha_j\alpha_j. \tag{10A.1.9}$$

For each person and brand, an observation is one of the six possible events defined by three levels of fixation (0, 1, and 2 or more) and two consideration outcomes (y = yes or n = no). The probabilities for the events observed in our data are easily computed from the path probabilities as follows:

$$p0n_j = p1_j, \tag{10A.2.1}$$

$$p1n_j = p2_j, \tag{10A.2.2}$$

$$p2n_j = p3_j, \tag{10A.2.3}$$

$$p0y_j = p7_j, \tag{10A.2.4}$$

$$p1y_j = p5_j + p8_j, \tag{10A.2.5}$$

and

$$p2y_j = p4_j + p6_j + p9_j. \tag{10A.2.6}$$

11

Images and Preferences

A Feelings-As-Information Analysis

Hyejeung Cho, Norbert Schwarz, and Hyunjin Song

Introduction

Consumer research has long been influenced by the assumptions of microeconomics and its notion of revealed preference (Samuelson, 1938; Savage, 1954). From this perspective, consumers know what they like and want, and their preferences are revealed in the choices they make. As Daniel McFadden (1999), a Nobel laureate in economics, put it, "The *standard model* in economics is that consumers behave *as if* (…) preferences are primitive, consistent and immutable (*preference-rationality*), and the cognitive process is simply preference maximization, given market constraints (*process-rationality*)" (p. 75). In contrast, a large body of psychological research indicates that consumers' preferences are highly malleable and often constructed on the spot (e.g., Bettman, Luce, & Payne, 1998; see Griffin, Liu, & Kahn, 2005, for a recent review). From this perspective, preferences are driven by the information that happens to be most accessible at the time of judgment or choice. Consistent with psychology's general emphasis on the role of declarative information in judgment and decision making, most of this work has focused on declarative information about the target product and its competitors. Presumably, consumers consider the attributes of a product, elaborate on them, and compare them with the attributes of competing products to arrive at an informed judgment. This emphasis on declarative information is true to economists' assumption that only "relevant" attributes of the choice alternatives matter.

Unfortunately, the dominant emphasis on declarative information misses an important point: Reasoning about choice alternatives is accompanied by subjective experiences and these experiences can serve as a source of information in their own right. Moreover, subjective experiences are often a function of incidental variables that are unrelated to "relevant" attributes of the choice alternatives. Experiential sources of information range from affective experiences (such as moods and emotions) and bodily sensations (such as facial expressions and bodily feedback) to metacognitive experiences (such as the ease with which information can be processed or recalled). Each of these subjective experiences can itself serve as a basis of judgment and can qualify the implications of accessible declarative information (for a comprehensive review see Schwarz & Clore, 2007). As a result, a growing body of research shows that we cannot predict consumer judgment and choice by knowing solely *what* is on a consumer's mind, such as by focusing on accessible declarative information. Instead, judgment and choice are always a *joint* function of declarative and experiential information; hence, we need to consider the interplay of feeling and thinking to make sense of consumer behavior.

This chapter highlights some of the lessons learned and brings them to bear on issues of visual marketing. It is organized as follows. The first section introduces the *feelings-as-information* perspective (Schwarz, 1990), which serves as a conceptual framework. The second section shows how the visual context in which a product is presented can elicit affective reactions that consumers misread as their reactions to the product itself. We illustrate this misattribution process in the context of a marketing instrument that has so far received little research attention, namely websites that provide consumers with an opportunity to virtually "try on" a product by displaying it on their own image. The third section reviews how the fluency with which an image can be processed influences perceivers' affective responses and identifies processing fluency as a key determinant of aesthetic experience and preference. Finally, the fourth section turns to a specific feature of images, namely the readability of a print font. We show that the ease with which a print font can be read can have a profound impact on consumer judgment and choice. We conclude with a conceptual integration and identify open issues for future research.

Feelings as Information

Central to the feelings-as-information approach to the interplay of feeling and thinking is the assumption that people draw on their affective, cognitive, and bodily experiences as a source of information (Schwarz, 1990). What these experiences convey depends on the naïve theory that people bring to bear on the task; hence, the same feeling can give rise to different inferences (Schwarz, 2004; Schwarz & Clore, 2007). Like any other piece of information, feelings are not used as a basis of judgment when their informational value for the task at hand is called into question. Accordingly, being aware that the feeling may be due to some unrelated influence eliminates the otherwise obtained effects (e.g., Schwarz & Clore, 1983).

These regularities were first observed in the investigation of mood effects on evaluative judgment. People evaluate nearly anything more positively when they are in a happy rather than sad mood—from their lives as a whole (e.g., Schwarz & Clore, 1983) to consumer products (e.g., Gorn, Goldberg, & Basu, 1993; for a review see Schwarz & Clore, 1988). Following an earlier suggestion by Wyer and Carlston (1979), Schwarz and Clore (1983) proposed that people can simplify the judgment process by asking themselves, "How do I feel about this?" In doing so, they may misread preexisting moods as their apparent response to the target of judgment, resulting in more positive evaluations under positive rather than negative moods. If so, the observed effects should be eliminated when people (correctly or incorrectly) attribute their feelings to a source other than the target. Empirically this is the case and numerous studies demonstrated discounting as well as augmentation effects (for reviews see Pham, 2004; Schwarz, 1990; Schwarz & Clore, 2007).

For example, Schwarz and Clore (1983) observed that survey respondents were in a better mood and reported higher general life-satisfaction when interviewed on sunny rather than rainy days. However, their mood did *not* affect their life-satisfaction judgments when the interviewer pretended to call from out of town and asked as a private aside, "How's the weather where you live?" Answering this question drew respondents' attention to the weather, making them aware that their current feelings may solely reflect a transient influence rather than other, more important aspects of their lives. Supporting this interpretation, drawing respondents' attention to the weather did not change their current mood, but did eliminate the relationship between mood and life-satisfaction—once they realized that their bad mood may be due to the lousy weather, they did not draw on it in evaluating their lives in general. Note that this finding is incompatible with alternative process models that trace the influence of moods to the recall of mood congruent information stored in memory (Bower, 1981) or to mood congruent associations and elaborations (Forgas, 1995). According to such models, sad (happy) moods prime sad (happy) thoughts and it is the content of these thoughts, rather than the feeling itself, that drives the influence on unrelated judgments. If so, mood effects should not be subject to (mis)attribution processes: The implications of any negative aspects of one's life that come to mind while in a bad mood are not discredited because one's current negative mood is due to bad weather.

Later research extended this analysis to other subjective experiences, including specific emotions, bodily sensations, and metacognitive experiences (see Schwarz & Clore, 2007). Throughout, people assume that their current subjective experiences bear on what is in the focus of their attention or why else would they have these experiences now, at this moment? This perceived relevance of experiential information parallels the *aboutness principle* that Higgins (1998) identified for declarative information, that is, the assumption that any thoughts that come to mind are "about" the issue we focus on. Perceiving one's thoughts and feelings as relevant to the task at hand is the default. In contrast, the attribution of one's current thoughts or feelings to an unrelated influence requires attention and awareness of the potential influence (Schwarz, 2001). Hence, people often misinterpret incidental thoughts and feelings as informative responses to what they are thinking about, as the studies reviewed below will illustrate.

Image and Affect: When I Like My Picture, I Like the Product

Consistent with the "How-do-I-feel-about-it?" heuristic, Gorn and colleagues (1993) observed that consumers evaluated a set of stereo speakers more favorably when the music played for demonstration purposes put them in a happy rather than sad mood. Presumably, they misread their affective reaction to the music as being their reaction to the speakers. Supporting this interpretation, the impact of the music was eliminated when participants' attention was drawn to the music played to them (for reviews of related work see Pham, 2004; Schwarz & Clore, 2007). In general, consumers find it difficult to distinguish between their reaction to the context in which a product is displayed and their reaction to the product itself.

We tested this hypothesis in a domain in which the display is intended to provide information that is directly relevant to the consumer's consumption experience, namely the recent development of virtual product presentation technology that allows consumers to virtually "try on" a product by displaying it on their own image. This virtual product trial technology is increasingly used by retailers who offer cosmetics (e.g., lorealparisusa.com, maybelline.com), clothing (e.g., landsend.com), eyeglasses (e.g., eyeglasses.com) and similar products. Note that such displays differ from advertising that attempts to shape the image of a product by associating it with particular lifestyle contexts. Here, the display does not associate the product with lifestyle cues but merely displays it on an image that consumers select to determine how the product would look on them. Of interest is whether consumers' evaluation of the product is affected by the particular image on which they try it on (for a related discussion of the role of pictorials in advertising see McQuarrie, this volume).

In one experiment (Cho & Schwarz, 2006), earrings were virtually presented on female participants' own digital photos, using special software. Half of them evaluated the earrings presented on their own *smiling* photo, whereas the other half evaluated the same earrings presented on their own *nonsmiling* photo. Figure 11.1 shows an example. At the end of the study, each participant was shown her nonsmiling and smiling image side by side, without any earrings. Eighty-three percent of the participants preferred their smiling portrait over their nonsmiling portrait. Would this preference for their own smiling images also be reflected in a higher liking of the earrings displayed on these images?

Empirically, this was the case. Participants evaluated any given set of earrings more favorably when it was displayed on their own smiling rather than nonsmiling faces. One practical implication of this finding is that marketers would want to encourage their customers to upload their favorite picture of themselves. If the customer happens to pick a less appealing picture that is easily available, the product will appear less appealing as well.

In a related experiment, we manipulated consumers' image preference in a different way. Drawing on the observation that repeated

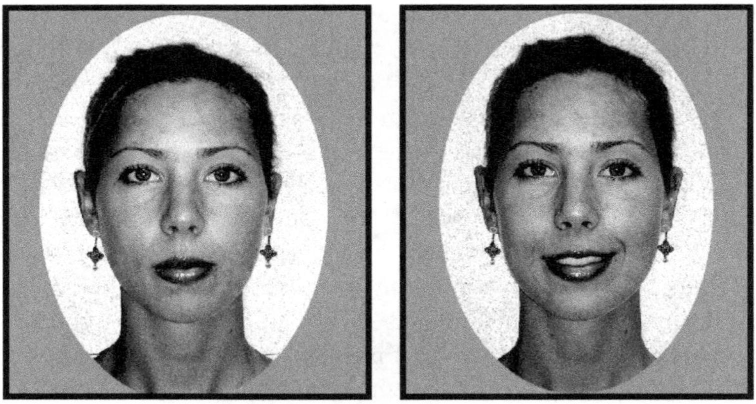

Figure 11.1 Jewelry presented on a consumer's own nonsmiling or smiling image (from Cho and Schwarz 2006).

exposure to a stimulus facilitates increased liking (Zajonc, 1968), Mita, Dermer, and Knight (1977) proposed that people would prefer their mirror image over their regular image. After all, we see ourselves more often in the mirror than on a photo, making the mirror image the more familiar one—and we often wonder if we "really look like this" when we see pictures of ourselves (although this may change with the development of digital photography and more frequent exposure to one's own pictures). To test if people prefer a product when it is shown on their mirror image rather than their regular image, we took a picture of each female participant and created her mirror image by horizontally flipping her original regular photo image. Figure 11.2 shows an example. At the end of the experiment, each participant was shown both images side by side (without a product) and indicated her preference.

Replicating the above results, participants again evaluated any given set of earrings more favorably when it was presented on their preferred image: those who preferred their regular photo image over their mirror image also preferred the earrings shown on their regular image over the earrings shown on their mirror image, and vice versa for those who preferred their mirror image over their regular image. A particularly interesting aspect of this finding is that participants were not aware of the fact that they had been exposed to two different images of themselves during the product evaluation task.

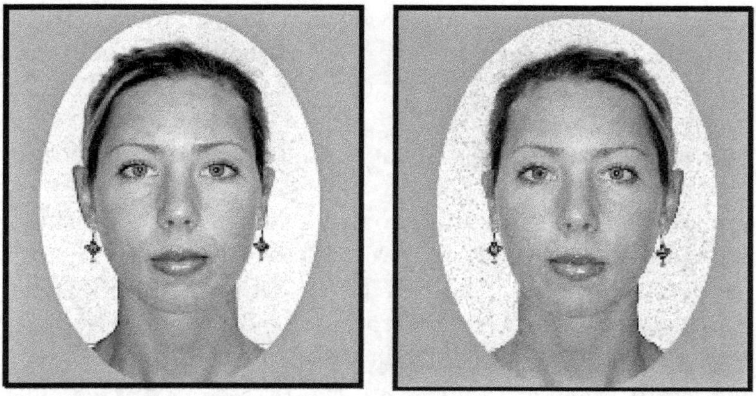

Figure 11.2 Jewelry presented on a consumer's own regular (left) and mirror (right) image (from Cho and Schwarz, 2006). Note: For clearer contrast between the mirror and regular image, identical earrings are shown in the illustration above. In the actual experiment, different but equally attractive earrings were presented and counterbalanced across participants.

Nevertheless, their product preferences were significantly influenced by their differential affective reactions to their own image.

In combination, these and related findings (see Cho & Schwarz, 2006) illustrate that the context in which a product is shown can profoundly affect product evaluation, even when the context is not designed to shape the image of the product through its association with lifestyle cues. Presumably, the key purpose of virtual product presentation technology is to provide consumers with an opportunity to see how the product would look "on them." Yet we have only one window on our experience and hence find it difficult to isolate our affective reactions to different components of an image. Accordingly, consumers are likely to misread their affective reaction to their own liked or disliked picture as being their reaction to what is in the focus of their attention, namely the product that they are to evaluate. This results in a more favorable product evaluation when the product is displayed on a more favorable image.

From a marketing perspective, these findings suggest that consumers should be encouraged to upload their most favorable pictures when they use virtual product presentation technology. The choice of a conveniently available, but less flattering picture is likely to have adverse consequences for their assessment of the product. To date, none of the websites we sampled pays attention to this contingency.

Image, Fluency, and Affect: Beauty Is in the Processing Experience

The above mirror-image study took advantage of the well known mere exposure effect (Zajonc, 1968), that is, the observation that a frequently seen stimulus is preferred over a novel one. Recent research traced the influence of repeated exposure to a more general process that is highly relevant to the evaluation of images, namely the fluency with which a stimulus can be processed (see Winkielman, Schwarz, Fazendeiro, & Reber, 2003, for a review). A wide range of variables can influence the experience of processing fluency. Some of these variables affect the speed and accuracy of low-level processes concerned with the identification of a stimulus' physical identity and form; they influence *perceptual fluency* (e.g., Jacoby, Kelley, & Dywan, 1989). Relevant examples include figure–ground contrast, the clarity with which a stimulus is presented, the duration of its presentation, or the amount of previous exposure to the stimulus. Other variables influence the speed and accuracy of high-level processes concerned with the identification of stimulus meaning and its relation to semantic knowledge structures; these variables influence *conceptual fluency* (e.g., Whittlesea, 1993). Relevant examples include semantic predictability, the consistency between the stimulus and its context, and the availability of appropriate mental concepts for stimulus classification. Empirically, both types of fluency tend to show parallel influences on judgments (for a review see Winkielman, Schwarz, Fazendeiro, & Reber, 2003) and can be subsumed under the general term *processing fluency*. Processing fluency can be assessed with objective measures, like processing speed and accuracy, as well as subjective measures, like subjective impressions of effort, speed, and accuracy.

The experience of processing fluency is hedonically marked and high fluency gives rise to a positive affective reaction that can be captured with psychophysiological measures. For example, Winkielman and Cacioppo (2001) assessed participants' affective responses to fluent stimuli with facial electromyography (EMG). This methodology relies on the observation that positive affective responses increase activity over the region of the zygomaticus major (smiling muscle), whereas negative affective responses increase activity over the region of the corrugator supercilli (frowning muscle; e.g., Cacioppo, Petty, Losch, & Kim, 1986). As expected, high fluency was associated with stronger activity over the zygomaticus region (indicative of positive affect), but was not associated with activity of the corrugator region (indicative of negative affect). Similarly, Monahan, Murphy, and Zajonc (2000) observed that repeated exposure to initially neutral stimuli improved participants' self-reported mood, again reflecting positive affective reactions to fluently processed stimuli.

Consistent with the feelings-as-information logic (Schwarz, 1990), the positive affective response elicited by high processing fluency gives rise to positive evaluations of fluently processed stimuli. Indeed, a growing body of research indicates that any variable that facilitates fluent processing will also facilitate positive evaluations. For example, Reber, Winkielman, and Schwarz (1998) presented participants with slightly degraded pictures of everyday objects and manipulated processing fluency through a visual priming procedure. Depending on conditions, the target picture was preceded by a subliminally presented, highly degraded contour of either the target picture or a different picture. As predicted, pictures preceded by matched contours were recognized faster, indicating higher fluency, and were liked more than pictures preceded by mismatched contours. Moreover, participants were unaware of the fluency manipulation, thus eliminating the possibility of strategically responding to pictures preceded by different primes.

Extending this work, Winkielman and Fazendeiro (reported in Winkielman, Schwarz, Fazendeiro & Reber, 2003) showed participants unambiguous pictures of common objects and manipulated processing fluency through semantic primes. In the high fluency condition, the picture (e.g., of a lock) was preceded by a matching word (e.g., "lock"), in the moderate fluency condition by an associatively related word (e.g., "key"), and in the low fluency condition by an unrelated word (e.g., "snow"). As predicted, pictures preceded by matching words were liked more than pictures preceded by related words, which, in turn, were liked more than pictures preceded by unrelated words. Follow-up studies indicated that these fluency effects do not require that the concept primes immediately precede the target pictures. Instead, the same pattern of effects was obtained when participants studied a list of concept primes well before they were exposed to the pictures. Lee and Labroo (2004) obtained similar findings in the consumer domain and found, for example, that consumers reported more positive attitudes toward ketchup when they were previously exposed to a closely related product (mayonnaise) rather than an unrelated one (vitamins). Presumably, the closely related product facilitated processing of the target product, much as related semantic primes facilitated processing of the target pictures in Winkielman and Fazendeiro's study.

Numerous other variables that affect processing fluency produce parallel effects, from figure–ground contrast and presentation duration (e.g., Reber et al., 1998) to the prototypicality of the stimulus (e.g., Halberstadt & Rhodes, 2000; Langlois & Roggman, 1990). Moreover, the influence of many variables addressed in the psychology of aesthetics (see Arnheim, 1974; Tatarkiewicz, 1970), like figural goodness, symmetry, and information density, can be traced to the mediating role of processing fluency: All of these variables facilitate stimulus identification and elicit more positive evaluations.

Based on these and related findings, Reber, Schwarz, and Winkielman (2004) proposed that aesthetic pleasure is a function of the perceiver's processing dynamics: The more fluently perceivers can process a stimulus, the more positive is their aesthetic response. This proposal provides an integrative account of diverse variables and traces their influence to the same underlying process. First, image variables that have long been known to influence aesthetic judgments, like figural goodness, figure–ground contrast, symmetry, and prototypicality, exert their influence by facilitating or impairing fluent processing of the stimulus. Second, perceiver variables, like a history of previous exposure or a motivational state to which the stimulus is relevant, similarly exert their influence through processing fluency. Third, previously unidentified contextual variables—such as visual or semantic priming—operate in the same fashion and also affect preference through their influence on processing fluency. Such contextual variables play no role in traditional theories of aesthetic appreciation or in lay intuitions about aesthetic appeal and are uniquely identified as determinants of aesthetic pleasure by Reber and colleagues' (2004) fluency account.

This fluency theory of aesthetic appreciation has important implications for visual marketing. Most obviously, it suggests that marketers are well advised to design images that allow for fluent processing. Traditional design variables, like figural goodness, symmetry, and figure–ground contrast, are relevant in this regard and are usually observed. In addition, repeated exposure to an image will increase the fluency with which it can be processed, resulting in more favorable evaluations, as known since Zajonc's (1968) identification of the mere exposure effect. Less obvious, fluent processing can also be facilitated by the context in which an image is presented, as illustrated by the observation that previous exposure to related visual material (Reber et al., 1998), semantic concepts (Winkielman, Schwarz, Reber & Fazendeiro, 2003) or related products on a supermarket shelf (Lee & Labroo, 2004) can increase processing fluency and the favorable evaluation of products. These contextual variables provide new and promising avenues for visual marketing, which have so far not been systematically exploited.

Image, Fluency, and Effort: When Preference Is in the Print Font

In addition to eliciting a positive affective response (Winkielman & Cacioppo, 2001), fluent processing is experienced as easy and effortless, whereas disfluent processing is experienced as difficult and effortful. This experience of ease or difficulty can again serve as information that consumers systematically use in making a variety of judgments and decisions.

For example, previous research showed that consumers are likely to defer a purchase decision when they find it difficult to choose among competing products. This is not surprising when the difficulty arises from relevant attributes of the choice set, e.g., because all alternatives are similarly attractive or unattractive (e.g., Dhar, 1997). Yet the same effect can be observed when the experienced difficulty is solely due to visual presentation variables that impede fluent processing. One such variable is the quality of the print font, which can make it easy or difficult to read a product description (for a discussion of the processes involved in reading text, see Rayner & Castelhano, this volume). For example, Novemsky, Dhar, Schwarz, and Simonson (forthcoming) presented consumers with descriptions of two cordless phones and asked them to select the one they prefer, giving them the option to defer choice if they had no clear preference. As expected, more than twice as many participants deferred choice when the font was difficult rather than easy to read. Apparently, participants mistook the difficulty of reading the material as reflecting the difficulty of making a choice. Supporting this interpretation, the influence of processing fluency on choice was eliminated when participants' attention was drawn to the quality of the print font, thus alerting them that the experienced difficulty was not due to the nature of the choice alternatives themselves.

Much as people may mistake the difficulty of processing product information as indicative of the difficulty of making a choice, they may mistake the difficulty of processing instructions as indicative of the difficulty of performing the described behavior. For example, Song and Schwarz (2007) provided participants with a description of an exercise routine, printed in an easy or difficult to read font (see Figure 11.3 for an example).

As predicted, participants inferred that the exercise routine would flow more naturally and take less time when the font was easy to read, resulting in a higher reported willingness to make the exercise part of their daily routine. Similarly, participants of a second study inferred that preparing a Japanese lunch roll would require more effort and skill when the recipe was printed in a difficult to read font—and were less inclined to prepare that dish at home. Throughout, participants mistook the fluency of reading the instructions as indicative of the fluency with which the described behavior could be performed. Importantly, participants in both print font conditions had read the instructions carefully and did not differ in their ability to recall relevant elements of the instructions at the end of the study.

These findings again highlight that minor aspects of the visual display can have a profound influence on judgment and choice. On the applied side, they illustrate that easy to read instructions are at least as important as the actual ease of product use, given that instructions can often be perused prior to the purchase decision. Even semantically clear and easy to follow instructions may discourage consumers from a purchase when they are printed in a tiny font to fit small packaging.

Implications for Visual Marketing

As our selective review illustrates, consumers' preferences and choices can be profoundly influenced by incidental variables that are unrelated to the features of the choice alternatives. Consumers like the same set of earrings more when it is displayed on their smiling

- Tuck your chin into your chest, and then lift your chin upward as far as possible. 6–10 repetitions
- Lower your left ear toward your left shoulder and then your right ear toward your right shoulder. 6–10 repetitions
- Turn your chin laterally toward your left shoulder and then rotate it toward your right shoulder. 6–10 repetitions
- Stand tall, feet slightly wider than shoulder-width apart, knees slightly bent. Keep the back straight at all times.
- Swing both arms continuously to an overhead position and then forward, down, and backwards. 6–10 repetitions
- Swing both arms out to your sides and then cross them in front of your chest. 6 repetitions
- With your hands on your hips and feet spread wider than your shoulders, make circles with your hips in a clockwise direction for 10–12 repetitions. Then repeat in a counterclockwise direction.
- Extend your arms out to your sides and twist your torso and hips to the left, shifting your weight onto the left foot. Then twist your torso to the right while shifting your weight to the right foot. 10–12 reps on each side

- *Tuck your chin into your chest, and then lift your chin upward as far as possible. 6–10 repetitions*
- *Lower your left ear toward your left shoulder and then your right ear toward your right shoulder. 6–10 repetitions*
- *Turn your chin laterally toward your left shoulder and then rotate it toward your right shoulder. 6–10 repetitions*
- *Stand tall, feet slightly wider than shoulder-width apart, knees slightly bent. Keep the back straight at all times.*
- *Swing both arms continuously to an overhead position and then forward, down, and backwards. 6–10 repetitions*
- *Swing both arms out to your sides and then cross them in front of your chest. 6 repetitions*
- *With your hands on your hips and feet spread wider than your shoulders, make circles with your hips in a clockwise direction for 10–12 repetitions. Then repeat in a counterclockwise direction.*
- *Extend your arms out to your sides and twist your torso and hips to the left, shifting your weight onto the left foot. Then twist your torso to the right while shifting your weight to the right foot. 10–12 reps on each side*

Figure 11.3 Exercise instructions in easy-to-read (left) and difficult-to-read (right) print font. Note: The instructions were adapted from an exercise website (www.brianmac.demon.co.uk/dynamic.htm).

rather than nonsmiling face (Cho & Schwarz, 2006) and find a picture of a lock more attractive when they previously read the word "lock" or "key" (Winkielman, Schwarz, Fazendeiro & Reber, 2003). Moreover, they are more likely to defer a choice when the decision "feels" difficult because the print font is hard to read (Novemsky et al., forthcoming), and conclude that preparing a Japanese recipe requires more skill (Song & Schwarz, 2007). All of these examples share that consumers' judgment is not solely based on declarative information about features of the choice alternatives. In fact, the declarative information was always identical in the above studies and merely consumers' subjective experiences varied across conditions, due to different visual presentation formats.

Because people have only one window on their subjective experiences, they find it difficult to distinguish experiences elicited by incidental variables (such as background pictures or print fonts) from experiences elicited by the focal object of interest: In most cases, they assume that their experience is "about" whatever is in the focus of their attention. Hence, they draw on their experience as a relevant source of information in evaluating the focal object, unless the incidental source of the experience is highly salient or their attention is drawn to it (for a comprehensive review see Schwarz & Clore, 2007). Thus, the positive response to one's smiling face is misread as a positive response to the earrings one is to evaluate (Cho & Schwarz, 2006). Similarly, the positive affect elicited by fluent processing (Winkielman & Cacioppo, 2001) is misread as a positive response to the image processed (Winkielman et al., 2003), turning one's own processing dynamics into a determinant of perceived beauty (Reber et al., 2004). Along the same lines, the difficulty experienced when processing a hard to read product description is misread as the difficulty of making a choice, prompting a choice deferral (Novemsky et al., forthcoming), and a recipe that is difficult to read will surely be difficult to prepare (Song & Schwarz, 2007).

Accordingly, theories of consumer judgment and choice need to take the role of experiential information into account and marketers need to consider relevant variables in their design of marketing materials. Even very desirable product features will be less appreciated when the product description is difficult to process, for example, because a tiny print font is chosen to fit small packaging or because a fashionable color choice results in a poor figure–ground contrast. Importantly, such variables affect preferences even when the relevant product information is correctly understood and recalled (e.g., Song & Schwarz, 2007). To facilitate a favorable product evaluation, all images and materials should be designed to foster fluent processing by optimizing the image and context variables reviewed above (Reber et al., 2004). Beyond facilitating the correct acquisition of declarative information, materials that can be fluently processed will have the added benefit of facilitating a positive affective response and avoiding the negative consequences of experienced processing difficulty.

Similarly, marketers who use virtual product presentation technology are well advised to make its use as easy as possible. Difficulty of use will not only limit the utilization of the technology, but also run the risk of inducing a negative experience that colors the perception of the product, paralleling the impact of poor print fonts. Moreover, consumers should be encouraged to upload their most favorable pictures, rather than a less flattering one that happens to be conveniently at hand. As our results indicate, consumers react to the overall image and dislike the product when they dislike their picture (Cho & Schwarz, 2006).

While much remains to be learned, the available research highlights that we cannot understand the constructive nature of consumer judgment and choice without taking the interplay of feeling and thinking into account.

References

Arnheim, R. (1974). *Art and visual perception: The new version*. Berkeley, CA: University of California Press.

Bettman, J., Luce, M. F., & Payne, J. (1998). Constructive consumer choice processes. *Journal of Consumer Research*, *25*(3), 187–217.

Bower, G. H. (1981). Mood and memory. *American Psychologist, 36*(2), 129–148.

Cacioppo, J. T., Petty, R. E., Losch, M. E., & Kim, H. S. (1986). Electromyographic activity over facial muscle regions can differentiate the valence and intensity of affective reaction. *Journal of Personality and Social Psychology*, *50*(2), 260–268.

Cho, H., & Schwarz, N. (2006). When good pictures make for good products: Consumer misattribution effects in virtual product presentation. *Advances in Consumer Research*, *33*, 637–638.

Dhar, R. (1997). Consumer preference for a no-choice option. *Journal of Consumer Research*, *24*(2), 215–231.

Forgas, J. P. (1995). Mood and judgment: The affect infusion model (AIM). *Psychological Bulletin, 117*(1), 39–66.

Gorn, G. J., Goldberg, M. E., & Basu, K. (1993). Mood, awareness, and product dvaluation. *Journal of Consumer Psychology, 2*(3), 237–256.

Griffin, D., Liu, W., & Kahn, U. (2005). A new look at constructed choice processes. *Marketing Letters, 16*(3/4), 321–333.

Halberstadt, J., & Rhodes, G. (2000). The attractiveness of nonface average: Implications for an evolutionary explanation of the attractiveness of average faces. *Psychological Science, 11*(4), 285–289.

Higgins, E T. (1998). The aboutness principle: A pervasive influence on human inference. *Social Cognition, 16*(1), 173–198.

Jacoby, L. L., Kelley, C. M., & Dywan, J. (1989). Memory attributions. In H. L. Roediger & F. I. M. Craik (Eds.), *Varieties of memory and consciousness: Essays in honor of Endel Tulving* (pp. 391–422). Hillsdale, NJ: Erlbaum.

Langlois, J. H., & Roggman, L. A. (1990). Attractive faces are only average. *Psychological Science, 1*(2), 115–121.

Lee, A. Y., & Labroo, A. A. (2004). The effect of conceptual and perceptual fluency on brand evaluation. *Journal of Marketing Research, 41*(2), 151–165.

McFadden, D. (1999). Rationality for economists? *Journal of Risk and Uncertainty, 19*(1), 73–105.

Mita, T. H., Dermer, M., & Knight, J. (1977). Reversed facial images and the mere-exposure hypothesis. *Journal of Personality and Social Psychology, 35*(8), 597–601.

Monahan, J. L., Murphy, S. T., & Zajonc, R. B. (2000). Subliminal mere exposure: Specific, general, and diffuse effects. *Psychological Science, 11*(6), 462–466.

Novemsky, N., Dhar, R., Schwarz, N., & Simonson, I. (forthcoming). Preference fluency in consumer choice. *Journal of Marketing Research.*

Pham, M. T. (2004). The logic of feeling. *Journal of Consumer Psychology, 14*(4), 360–369.

Reber, R., Schwarz, N., & Winkielman, P. (2004). Processing fluency and aesthetic pleasure: Is beauty in the perceiver's processing experience? *Personality and Social Psychology Review, 8*(4), 364–382.

Reber, R., Winkielman, P., & Schwarz, N. (1998). Effects of perceptual fluency on affective judgments. *Psychological Science, 9*(1), 45–48.

Samuelson, P. A. (1938). A note on the pure theory of consumer's behavior. *Economica, 5*, 61–71.

Savage, L. J. (1972). *The foundations of statistics*. New York: Dover. (Original work published 1954.)

Schwarz, N. (1990). Feelings as information: Informational and motivational functions of affective states. In E. T. Higgins & R. M. Sorrentino (Eds.), *Handbook of motivation and cognition: Foundations of social behavior* (pp. 527–561). New York: Guilford Press.

Schwarz, N. (2001). Feelings as information: Implications for affective influences on information processing. In L. L. Martin & G. L. Clore (Eds.), *Theories of mood and cognition: A user's handbook* (pp. 159–176). Mahwah, NJ: Erlbaum.

Schwarz, N. (2004). Metacognitive experiences in consumer judgment and decision making. *Journal of Consumer Psychology, 14*(4), 332–348.

Schwarz, N., & Clore, G. L. (1983). Mood, misattribution, and judgments of well-being: Informative and directive functions of affective states. *Journal of Personality and Social Psychology, 45*(3), 513–523.

Schwarz, N., & Clore, G. L. (1988). How do I feel about it? Informative functions of affective states. In K. Fiedler & J. P. Forgas (Eds.), *Affect, cognition, and social behavior* (pp. 44–62). Toronto: Hogrefe International.

Schwarz, N., & Clore, G. L. (2007). Feelings and phenomenal experiences. In E. T. Higgins & A. W. Kruglanski (Eds.), *Social psychology: A handbook of basic principles* (2nd ed., pp. 385–407). New York: Guilford Press.

Song, H., & Schwarz, N. (2007, January). *If it's easy to read, it's easy to do: Processing fluency affects the prediction of behavioral fluency.* Presentation at the Eighth Society for Personality and Social Psychology Annual Conference, Memphis, TN.

Tatarkiewicz, W. (1970). *History of aesthetics.* The Hague, The Netherlands: Mouton.

Whittlesea, B. W. (1993). Illusions of familiarity. *Journal of Experimental Psychology: Learning, Memory, and Cognition, 19*(6), 1235–1253.

Winkielman, P., & Cacioppo, J. T. (2001). Mind at ease puts a smile on the face: Psychophysiological evidence that processing facilitation elicits positive affect. *Journal of Personality and Social Psychology, 81*(6), 989–1000.

Winkielman, P., Schwarz, N., Fazendeiro, T., & Reber, R. (2003a). The hedonic marking of processing fluency: Implications for evaluative judgment. In J. Musch & K. C. Klauer (Eds.), *The psychology of evaluation: Affective processes in cognition and emotion* (pp. 189–217). Mahwah, NJ: Lawrence Erlbaum.

Winkielman, P., Schwarz, N., Fazendeiro, T., & Reber, R. (2003b). Cognitive and affective consequences of visual fluency: When seeing is easy on the mind. In L. Scott & R. Batra (Eds.), *Persuasive imagery: A consumer response perspective* (pp. 75–89). Mahwah, NJ: Lawrence Erlbaum.

Wyer, R. S., Jr., & Carlston, D. E. (1979). *Social cognition, inference, and attribution*. Hillsdale, NJ: Lawrence Erlbaum.

Zajonc, R. B. (1968). Attitudinal effects of mere exposure. *Journal of Personality and Social Psychology*, *9*(2), 1–27.

12

Rethinking Visual Communication Research

Updating Old Constructs and Considering New Metaphors

Chris Janiszewski

Introduction

Consider the following facts about visual communication. First, an analysis of print media trends shows that a larger and larger percentage of print advertising is purely image-oriented (McQuarrie chapter; Pollay, 1985; Stephens, 1998). Second, the video component of a television commercial communicates the advertiser's message much more effectively than the audio component (Bryce & Olney, 1988). Third, there is overwhelming evidence that visual merchandising (e.g., shelf design, merchandise arrangement, building architecture) has a significant impact on retail sales (Turley and Milliman, 2007). All of these examples suggest images (e.g., pictorial information, video images, shopping environments, etc.), not words, best communicate meaning to an audience. If this is the case, one must wonder why research on visual communication in general, and images in specific, is such an infrequent occurrence, at least as compared to research on verbal communication.

The relative dearth of research on visual communication is likely a function of its perceived value. Information processing theory makes a number of implicit assumptions that suggest there is nothing to be gained by a research program on visual communication (Crowther-Heyck, 1999). If it is assumed that people "process information," and it is also assumed that the mechanisms used to process information are identical for any piece of information, then insight gained from the study of text-based information processing should be no different than insight gained from the study of image-based information processing. Information is information, regardless of its form. In effect, implicit assumptions about information processing mechanisms suggest that the study of image-based information is redundant with the study of text-based information.

Assumptions about information processing theory also influence assessments of the value of researching specific processes. For example, attention is often viewed as an information reception activity. It is a necessary condition for information processing, but it is irrelevant to higher order activities like elaboration, inference, and creative thought. Switching stimuli from text, where attention is often uniform, to images, where attention is less uniform, simply creates an opportunity for information loss (i.e., adds noise to the system). Similarly, perception is often viewed as an information definition activity. It defines the inputs into the information processing system, but it is irrelevant to processes that support higher order activities. Images are often more ambiguous (i.e., can support multiple interpretations or meanings) than text passages, hence images create more variance in definitions across respondents and more noise in a specific theory test. As each of these illustrations demonstrates, investigations of imagery are often underappreciated because they are perceived as a less controlled approach to the study of information processing.

The preceding analysis suggests that a greater appreciation of visual communication research may require a recasting of the assumptions that underlie information processing theory or a reframing of the research agenda. With this in mind, I will discuss three approaches to increasing the impact of visual communication research. First, one could broaden the scope of the constructs used to investigate information processing by arguing that these constructs have additional explanatory power for image-based processing. Second, one could argue that there are visual communication issues that deserve research attention. For example, it could be argued that the act of meaning creation is as relevant as the more commonly studied act of information analysis. Third, one could propose a new metaphor that highlights the differences between visual communication research and information processing research. To the extent this metaphor is compelling, it may motivate additional research in the area. Each of these approaches represents an independent strategy for increasing the impact of visual communication research, although there is some overlap in scope and focus.

Option 1: Reframing the Constructs

Three constructs are fundamental to information processing theory, yet receive little attention in the consumer behavior literature. Attention, perception, and comprehension are most often seen as preliminary subroutines in the sequential processing of information. Expanding the uses of these processes may create opportunities for novel visual communication research.

Attention

Visual attention (henceforth attention) has traditionally been defined as an information processing support activity. Attention is an attempt to improve the precision of a representation through repeated sampling of the environment. Yet attention need not be relegated to the role of providing information content (see the Pieters & Wedel and the Rayner & Castelhano chapters for additional critiques of the traditional view of attention).* The act of attention itself is information. The premise that *attention is information* can be illustrated by the awareness that often accompanies an orienting response. When attentional sampling increases, owing to a sudden change in the environment (e.g., stimulus event) or environmental ambiguity (e.g., the attended event does not yield sufficient meaning), the processing system orients (i.e., increases the rate of sampling). In stable environments, people do not orient to well-defined events or to irrelevant events. Instead, people often orient to the mildly ambiguous (i.e., material for which more than one interpretation exists). If orienting is unsuccessful (i.e., the ambiguity is not resolved), the person becomes aware of the difficulty of assigning meaning to the event. In other words, the characteristics of the attentional activity provide information that encourages

* Fernandez-Duque and Johnson (2002) provide an interesting discussion of alternative metaphors of attention.

a subjective awareness of interest, perplexity, or unease. The increase in attentional effort is meaningful to the processing system.

If awareness is contingent on changes in attentional effort, then it is not unrealistic to hypothesize that the characteristics of attention can serve as information for other experiences and decisions. In the case of ambiguous stimuli, high rates of attentional sampling may inform a person about a potential danger or a curiosity that requires additional investigation. In the case of a nonambiguous stimulus, high rates of attentional sampling may be used as evidence about the interestingness, appeal, or value of the experience. The interesting research questions concern *if* and *how* these inferences about attention are made. Unlike an overly structured, text-based processing task, an image-based processing task allows considerable flexibility concerning how to execute the task and how to interpret the processing experience. Visual imagery is likely to provide many more opportunities for a person to make inferences about the act of attention.

Perception

Perception has traditionally been viewed as an act of meaning selection (Marcel, 1983). A perceiver has to select the most meaningful or most relevant perception from the array of perceptions that are available given the stimulus environment (Cesario, Plaks, & Higgins, 2006). Perceptual selection is equivalent to a late attention filter in the information processing system (Johnston & Heinz, 1979; Johnston & Wilson, 1980). An alternative framing of the perception construct is to view it as a production activity (Janiszewski, 2007). A person produces a perception that is useful for the current task.

Reframing perception as a production activity raises an interesting issue. What are the factors that encourage people to produce any one perception relative to another? A useful analogy may be language production. Language is generated to communicate meanings with another individual. The words a person chooses to communicate an idea to individual A and to individual B will vary, even though the goal of the communication may be identical across the two individuals. The choice of words and pace of the explanation can also be adjusted for an individual communication partner based on feedback about the success of the communication.

If perceptual production is similar to verbal production, then who is the communication partner in a perceptual system? One possibility is to think of perception as an interaction between the person and the environment. A person generates meaning in order to interact with the environment in a beneficial way. Yet, unlike language production where the goal is to express meaning to another person (i.e., communicate intent), in perceptual production the goals are to (a) express meaning to oneself (i.e., experience) or (b) assess the intent of the environment.* People strive to express meanings that will provide the most rewarding, most informative, or least ambiguous interaction with the environment. People also anthropomorphize the environment and the events in it, assuming that animals, machines, locations, and systems (e.g., weather) are behaving with intent. An assumption of environmental intent may not be accurate, but it does allow a person to communicate with the environment (and derives meaning) in the same way a person communicates with people (and derives meaning). Given this view of perception, visual communications could be thought of as interactive communications in which the audience produces self-relevant intent within the context of the imagery. Recasting visual communication is providing an opportunity to produce an experience, and understanding how imagery can encourage a viewer to adopt certain behaviors that express intent to others is a relevant research agenda.

Comprehension

Comprehension integrates a current perceptual experience with prior perceptual experiences (i.e., memory) to enhance and extend meaning.† Comprehension has been studied using an objective approach and a subjective approach (Mick, 1992). The objective model is most popular with positivist researchers because it assumes a constant, culturally based meaning. The subjective model is most popular with postpositivist researchers because it highlights the diversity of comprehension across individuals (Mick & Buhl, 1992). The

* I advocate a Gibsonian perspective. The environment is not an entity and it does not have intention. The environment affords inferences of intention. Tomasello (1999) provides an insightful discussion of this issue.

† To relate perception and comprehension, perception is the static experience of a meaning whereas comprehension is the dynamic linking of a sequence of meanings.

subjective view is certainly more representative of the experiences of people that process imagery, yet it also seems to acknowledge a heterogeneity of experience across people that makes the study of comprehension difficult. In the traditional information processing framework, comprehension creates an input into higher order processes. It is easier to make inferences about the mechanics of these higher order processes if the inputs are assumed to be uniform across experimental participants.

Although it may be procedurally convenient to view comprehension as a process that creates an input into higher order processes, it is also interesting to view comprehension as a process that creates an output that is interesting in its own right. Meaning is fundamental to branding and positioning, yet the study of meaning creation is often viewed as under the purview of the practitioner. It is as if the heterogeneity of meaning is taken as evidence that meaning creation is an error-laden process. Most academic researchers do not attempt to account for random error, so variability in the meaning of an event, product, or brand is inherently uninteresting.

An alternative to the view that meaning heterogeneity exemplifies random error is the view that meaning heterogeneity can be predicted. At the most fundamental level, one might attempt to predict the amount of meaning heterogeneity (i.e., explain the source of the ambiguity). A more aggressive research agenda would be to understand why each specific meaning is generated. We know that different people generate different meanings because they live in different cultures and have had different life experiences. We also know that the same person will often generate a different meaning for a recurrence of the same event because of different contextual factors. Yet, this does not imply that meanings cannot be predicted. Meanings are generated because they are useful (i.e., they perform a function). To the extent we can understand the task a consumer is trying to accomplish, we should be able to understand the meanings that are acceptable or relevant to that task. As in perception, where many potential interpretations of the environment are ignored in favor of one interpretation, many meanings of an item can be ignored in favor of one meaning. The meaning that helps the person advance toward a current task or goal is the meaning that is most likely to be generated.

If the goal of cognition is to enable a person to interact with the environment in a beneficial way, then meaning becomes a temporarily constructed tool that allows people to achieve their goals. The relativism of meaning should be predicted by the goals the perceiver is trying to accomplish during his interaction with the environment (DeGrandpre, 2000). Given this view, information is not the fundamental unit of analysis in the cognitive system. The task-environment interface is the unit of analysis and the type of meaning generated becomes the dependent measure of interest. Thus, wherein meaning is an independent variable in most investigations of information processing, meaning is the dependent variable in this alternative approach to investigating comprehension.

Option 2: Information Transmittal versus Meaning Creation

One of the most fundamental questions of human existence is, "Why are we here?" If I were to constrain the possible answers to (a) to act or (b) to experience, most if us would acknowledge that humans act, but that acts are a means to an end. Humans act in order to accumulate a lifetime of experiences. Cognition is an evolutionary system that manages these experiences. The implication is that we should investigate the experiences people seek to create in addition to the processes that support the creation of these experiences. Put another way, both the information and the processing are important components of cognition.

If the advertising, consumer research, and psychology literatures were to focus on meaning creation (i.e., information), there would be additional research agendas in the literature. First, there would be considerably more emphasis on motivational goals and task goals. Currently, there is a resurgence of goal research, but the emphasis is more on goal completion and goal conflict than on the broader question of how goals shape psychological experience. Second, there would be a greater emphasis on the contributions of social identity, environmental context, and culture to meaning creation. Third, there would be more emphasis on the evolution of experience (i.e., how one's experiences change over a lifetime). This evolution of experience could refer to a person, an object, and an act, or an environment. The research objective would be to understand why experience with any stimulus becomes richer or more subdued over time.

There are also some less obvious consequences of studying meaning and psychological experience. First, there might be more interest in finding commonalities in the behaviors that generate meaning.

In other words, why are some behaviors strong carriers of meaning whereas other behaviors are not? For example, why does product use encourage the consumer to form a "relationship" with some brands, but not others (Fournier, 1998)? Does the intensity of experience associated with these behaviors signal something about the behavior, the context in which the behavior is performed, or the current goals of the individual? Second, there might be an attempt to understand myopic behavior (e.g., obsessive-compulsive disorder, collecting behavior, risk-seeking tendency) and eclectic behavior (e.g., variety seeking, procrastination) from a meaning creation perspective. What encourages a person to want to continue to generate (avoid generating) the same meaning? Third, why do certain behaviors become valued (devalued) with repeated execution? Can behavioral consistency be seen more as a function of the meanings it supports as opposed to a series of rewards and punishments provided by the environment? After all, some people do repeatedly engage in a variety of negative-outcome behaviors.

Although many of these issues may seem "one step away" from the study of visual communication, all of these issues are inherently intertwined with the images people see on a day-to-day basis. Imagery activates goals and provides examples of behaviors that can lead to experiences that satisfy the goals. In many cases, people have to be taught about the experiences that should be associated with a certain behavior. Imagery allows advertisers to show the intent and experience of others. Imagery also provides a means to manage the evolution of the experiences associated with a product or brand. Iconic brands (e.g., Coca-Cola, Ford, McDonald's) have to continually update the experiences associated with their products so as to coincide with the experiences desired by each generation of consumers. Finally, imagery can be used to reinforce the meaning of the ownership or consumption experience in a person's life (Belk,1988; Deighton, 1984). Although a marketer does not necessarily want a consumer to be obsessive-compulsive about his brand, fervent loyalty is not necessarily a bad thing. The management of the meaning experiences associated with a brand would seem to be a fundamental component of brand loyalty.

Option 3: Changing the Cognitive Metaphor

The traditional information processing theory relies on a computer metaphor. Information enters the computer as input, it is processed according to the constraints of the task at hand (i.e., subroutines are accessed and executed), and an output is generated. This metaphor places a premium on understanding the processes (i.e., subroutines) executed by the mind (i.e., computer). Alternative cognitive metaphors are the sculpture and construction metaphors. The sculpture metaphor is a top-down metaphor in which the environment (a block of marble) and the individual (the sculptor) combine to create meaning (a sculpted piece). This metaphor is aligned with the Gibsonian claim that the environment is rich with "information" and that much of this information must be discarded to create a coherent perception. The construction metaphor is a bottom-up metaphor in which the environment (material) and the individual (builder) combine to create meaning (a constructed piece). This metaphor is aligned with the Helmholtzian claim that perceptions are built from individual pieces of information within the environment.

The sculpture and construction metaphors emphasize the interaction between what the environment affords and what the individual can imagine. In each case, meaning will be a function of the characteristics of the environment and the perceiver's history of experience (i.e., prior meanings). The sculpture and construction metaphors also implicitly assume that the underlying goal of the environment–person interaction is to produce useful meanings and experiences. People are not machines that produce a consistent output given a constant input. The output changes depending on the meanings the person needs to generate, even if the environment is constant. Thus, in the sculpture and construction metaphors, it is the variability in meaning, and the events that encourage a person to strive for each of the varied meanings, that is the focus of inquiry.

A number of views have been advanced about the meaning creation process and how it relates to behavior. For example, it has been argued that people are interpretive beings that are guided by meaning, as opposed to rational beings that are guided by information (Bruner, 1990; DeGrandpre, 2000). Culture dictates relevant meanings and people learn how to assign these meanings to events and objects so that these meanings can be reexperienced at a later time. People communicate, behave, and consume in an effort to experience the meanings that they have been trained are culturally relevant and rewarding. Stimuli become associated with behaviors and these stimuli acquire meaning because of the outcomes these behaviors generate (i.e., experiences they afford). With experience, stimuli come to represent an opportunity to experience meaning. The actions performed with these stimuli lead to outcomes that reinforce the meaning of the stimulus.

The idea that meaning is in the perception of a stimulus, and that behavior with the stimulus allows a person to experience or unlock the meaning, is an implicit assumption of ideomotor action theory (Bargh, Chen, & Burrows, 1996) and the theory of event coding (Hommel, Musseler, Aschersleban, & Prinz, 2001). Ideomotor action theory assumes that behavioral responses can be associated with situational (stimulus) features. The mere perception of these features results in a behavior (e.g., mimicry). For example, people will mindlessly eat more food when it is easily accessible (Painter, Wansink, & Hieggelke, 2002; Wansink, 2005), engage in helping behaviors or aggressive behaviors when the environment supports the behavior (Carver, Ganellen, Froming, & Chambers, 1983; Macrae & Johnston, 1998), and speak more softly in the presence of stimuli associated with quietness (Aarts & Dijksterhuis, 2003). The claim that people behave in accordance with environmental cues, as opposed to reasoned action plans, has generated considerable debate (Chartrand, 2005; Dijksterhuis, Smith, van Baaren, & Wigboldus, 2005; Janiszewski & van Osselaer, 2005; Simonson, 2005).

An alternative view is that the perception of features provides opportunities for behaviors that will result in intended outcomes (Knuf, Aschersleben, & Prinz, 2001). Stimuli represent the potential to experience an outcome (i.e., the meaning of the stimulus is the outcome) and the behaviors that unlock the outcome are associated with the stimuli. The unlocking of the meaning through behavior is itself reinforcing, even if the behavior is stereotypic and/or the outcome of the behavior is undesirable. Hence, people engage in the behaviors with stimuli that reinforce the previously experienced meanings of the stimuli. The theory of event coding formalizes this idea by proposing that the cognitive codes for perception (e.g., meaning, memory, reasoning) and action (e.g., behavior) are represented in a common neural architecture. It is the actions that are performed with a stimulus that define its meaning, thus perceptual representation cannot be independent of active behavior.

The sculpture and construction metaphors have the potential to alter the way in which we view attention, perception, and comprehension. Let's assume for the moment that the construction metaphor is consistent with strategic, planned behavior and that the sculpture metaphor is consistent with intuitive, reactive behavior. Attention is a collection tool in the strategic behavior and attention is a chiseling tool in intuitive behavior. Although one process involves addition and one process involves subtraction, each process is being used to help confirm a meaning hypothesis. Perception is the experience of the most useful meaning experience among those that are available. We build (sculpt) perceptions that the environment affords and that are useful in the moment. Comprehension is the experienced meaning. It is multidimensional, varied in perspective, and nuanced. Similar to a structure (sculpture), the same meaning can be experienced from different perspectives. Wherein the core meaning may be the same, there are ancillary dimensions that differ.

The usefulness of the sculpture and construction metaphors can be illustrated through a discussion of how advertising influences behavior. In the computer metaphor, advertising provides information. The goal of the advertiser is to present the inputs as unambiguously as possible. This insures that the inputs, and outputs, will be consistent across viewers. In the sculpture and construction metaphors, the goal of the advertiser is to present the advertisements as flexibly as possible. The advertisement should allow the individual to construct a myriad of meanings that are useful for future experiences (i.e., the ad is easily personalized). To the extent the product becomes part of these meanings, its likelihood of future purchase and consumption increase. Products that can mean many things to the same person, while supported by a core meaning, have the potential to become iconic for that individual.

These ideas can be illustrated with an example. Consider the imagery that accompanies perfume advertising. The imagery can suggest elegance, playfulness, sexiness, power, or a host of other experiences. The computer metaphor assumes that these meanings become inputs into a processing system, support the production of a set of outputs (i.e., beliefs), and that these outputs become associated with the brand name or product category. In the sculpture and construction metaphors, the meanings suggested by the ad are experiences. These meanings become linked to the product so that product presence or use can create the same experiences. Thus, wherein the computer metaphor assumes that product categories and brands are associated with beliefs, the sculpture and construction metaphors assume that meanings are experienced in the presence of product categories and brands. The goal of the advertiser is to communicate the possible experiences.

The sculpture and construction metaphors implicitly assume that products in general, and brands in specific, help us experience meaning. This view is quite similar to the claim that brands are carriers of meaning (Aaker, Benet-Martínez, & Garolera, 2001; McCracken, 1986). The difference is that the product or brand is not a meaning unit and it is not an input into a processing system. The product and brand are the experience. They are the end-state.

Although it is useful to suggest alternative cognitive metaphors, it is even more useful to pose research questions. What follows is an attempt to set a research agenda, as defined by the sculpture and construction metaphors:

1. *Meaning Expansion.* A common goal of marketers is to increase market penetration by increasing the usage rate. The Coca-Cola *Always* campaign is a commonly cited example of an attempt to increase usage (consider Arm & Hammer Baking Soda for an alternative execution of this strategy). Coca-Cola used advertising to illustrate Coca-Cola consumption in a variety of situations. Yet, each of the illustrated consumption situations also provided different meanings and experiences. Thus, the research issue is how to increase the breadth of a brand's meanings (experiences) without diluting the core experiences (i.e., the experiences the consumer most often seeks when consuming the brand). What types of experienced meanings should be added and in what order should this occur?
2. *Meaning Flexibility.* How can advertisers create a positioning with core clarity and surface ambiguity? The core clarity of a positioning should be consistent across people (e.g., you are special if you use this product), but there should be ambiguity in the support for the position ("This product makes me special because…"). For example, Marlboro signifies independence and rebellion, but the instantiation of these concepts varies widely across culture. Somehow, the brand is ambiguous enough to allow for integration into very different lifestyles. The issue is not the consistency of the interpretation of the image across people, but the flexibility of the image for different interpretations. Why are certain meanings more flexible? How does imagery support this flexibility?
3. *Meaning Breadth.* How should a marketer manage the breadth of experienced meanings associated with a brand? Should the breadth of experienced meanings be defined by the specific meanings, the

affective tone of the meanings, the similarity of the meanings, the consistency of the benefits linked to the meanings, or some other factor? What types of breadth are good (i.e., increase satisfaction, increase loyalty, increase consumption, increase equity) and what types of breadth are bad?

4. *Meaning/Product Line Interface.* When should a brand's product line be extended (i.e., different blends of coffee create different experienced meanings) and when should it be limited (i.e., Coca-Cola expects a consumer will use one product from its line to experience refreshment, reward, relaxation, fun, etc.)? What is the most effective method of linking alternative experienced meanings to different products in the line? When should experienced meanings be constant across products in a line (i.e., benefits, not meanings, differentiate the line)?
5. *Advertising.* Advertising is one source of meaning creation. Advertising uses imagery to help the consumer experience the meanings that can result from brand possession or consumption. How do images promote experienced meaning (i.e., what makes one image so much more effective than another)?
6. *Imagery.* An image has the potential to create a variety of levels of meaning. There is content (e.g., it is a beach scene), tone (e.g., relaxing, quiet), affect (e.g., pleasant, unpleasant), meaning persistence (e.g., changing, perpetual), and orientation (e.g., participant, observer). What is the contribution of each of these factors to meaning creation? How should the imagery be varied to create a persistent meaning (i.e., one the person is likely to generate in the future)?
7. *Integration.* How does a marketer encourage the consumer to integrate the product category or the brand into experienced meaning so that (a) the product subsequently enters the consumers consideration set or (b) the product is used to achieve meaning?
8. *Reinforcement.* Products are used to experience meaning, but many of the meanings are not inherent to the product (e.g., nothing in the act of smoking delivers "coolness"). What reinforces, or fails to reinforce, experienced meaning? In all likelihood, it is not consumption itself because the meaning is independent of the consumption. Should prior imagery allow a person to experience the meanings associated with preconsumption, consumption, and postconsumption? Is one stage of experienced meaning more important for different types of products?
9. *Behavior.* Ideomotor action theory and the theory of event coding explicitly assume that perception (meaning) and behavior are linked. In some cases, the link is so strong, the person does stop

to consider alternative behaviors. In other cases, the link is not strong and the person always considers alternative behaviors. What determines whether meaning–behavior links will be weak or strong? Is it the type of meaning, the exclusivity of the behavior with respect to that meaning, the breadth of circumstances in which the behavior has generated the meaning, experience, or some other factor?

10. *Measurement.* Traditional measures of advertising effectiveness have been recall and recognition. A more relevant measure may be the experienced meaning suggested by the product category or brand. Effective advertising encourages a person to experience useful meanings in the presence of the product or brand. Meaning could be measured in the presence of the ad or in the absence of the ad but the presence of the product. In this view, advertising becomes a tool of meaning creation and meaning evolution. Research issues concern the development of instruments that can measure and track meaning over time.

Summary

The goal of this chapter has been to provide ideas that may spur additional research on visual communication. Some of the ideas are admittedly quirky, whereas others might seem rather mundane, especially to researchers who are well versed in the postpositivist consumer behavior literature. Regardless of the orientation, my goal has been to illustrate the usefulness of reconsidering the role of key constructs in the information processing nomological net, reorienting the focus of inquiry from information analysis to meaning and experience creation, and changing the metaphor used to guide research on visual communication. My hope is that adopting an alternative perspective may encourage the generation of novel research agendas.

References

Aaker, J. L., Benet-Martínez, V., & Garolera, J. (2001). Consumption symbols as carriers of culture: A study of Japanese and Spanish brand personality constructs. *Journal of Personality and Social Psychology, 81*, 492–508.

Aarts, H., & Dijksterhuis, A. (2003). The silence of the library: Environment, situational norm, and social behavior. *Journal of Personality and Social Psychology, 84*, 18–28.

Bargh, J. A., Chen, M., & Burrows, L. (1996). The automaticity of social behavior: Direct effects of trait concept and stereotype activation on action. *Journal of Personality and Social Psychology, 71*, 230–244.

Belk, R. W. (1988). Possessions and the extended self. *Journal of Consumer Research, 15*, 139–168.

Bruner, J. S. (1990). *Acts of meaning.* Cambridge, MA: Harvard University Press.

Bryce, W., & Olney, T. J. (1988). Modality effects in television advertising: A methodology for isolating message structure from message content effects. *Advances in Consumer Research, 15*, 174–177.

Carver, C. S., Ganellen, R. J., Froming, W. J., & Chambers, W. (1983). Modeling: An analysis of terms of category accessibility. *Journal of Experimental Social Psychology, 19*, 403–421.

Cesario, J., Plaks, J., & Higgins, E. T. (2006). Automatic social behavior as motivated preparation to interact. *Journal of Personality and Social Psychology, 90*, 893–910.

Chartrand, T. L. (2005). The role of conscious awareness in consumer behavior. *Journal of Consumer Psychology, 15*, 203–210.

Crowther-Heyck, H. (1999). George A. Miller, language, and the computer metaphor of the mind. *History of Psychology, 2*, 37–64.

DeGrandpre, R. J. (2000). A science of meaning: Can behaviorism bring meaning to psychological science. *American Psychologist, 55*, 721–739.

Deighton, J. (1984). The interaction of advertising and evidence. *Journal of Consumer Research, 11*, 763–770.

Dijksterhuis, A., Smith, P. K., van Baaren, R. B., & Wigboldus, D. H. J. (2005). The unconscious consumer: Effects of environment on consumer behavior. *Journal of Consumer Psychology, 15*, 193–202.

Fernandez-Duque, D., & Johnson, M. L. (2002). Cause and effect theories of attention: The role of conceptual metaphors. *Review of General Psychology, 6*, 153–165.

Fournier, S. (1998). Consumers and their brands: Developing relationship theory in consumer research. *Journal of Consumer Research, 24*, 343–373.

Hommel, B., Musseler, J., Aschersleben, G., & Prinz, W. (2001). The theory of event coding (TEC): A framework for perception and action planning. *Behavioral and Brain Sciences, 24*, 849–937.

Janiszewski, C. (forthcoming). Goal-directed perception. In C. Haugtvedt, P. Herr, & F. Kardes (Eds.). *Handbook of Consumer Psychology.* Mahwah, NJ: Lawrence Erlbaum Associates.

Janiszewski, C., & van Osselaer, S. M. J. (2005). Behavior activation is not enough, *Journal of Consumer Psychology, 15*, 218–224.
Johnston, W. A., & Heinz, S. P. (1979). Depth of nontarget processing in an attention task. *Journal of Experimental Psychology: Human Perception and Performance, 5*, 168–175.
Johnston, W. A., & Wilson, J. (1980). Perceptual processing of nontargets in an attention task. *Memory & Cognition, 8*, 372–377.
Knuf, L., Aschersleben, G., & Prinz, W. (2001). An analysis of ideomotor action. *Journal of Experimental Psychology: General, 130*, 779–798.
Macrae, C. N., & Johnston, L. (1998). Help, I need somebody: Automatic action and inaction. *Social Cognition, 16*, 400–417.
Marcel, A. (1983). Conscious and unconscious perception: An approach to the relations between phenomenal experience and perceptual processes. *Cognitive Psychology, 15*, 138–300.
McCracken, G. (1986). Culture and consumption: A theoretical account of the structure and movement of the cultural meaning of consumer goods. *Journal of Consumer Research, 13*, 71–84.
McQuarrie, E. F. (2007). Differentiating the pictorial elements in advertising: A rhetorical perspective. In M. Wedel & R. Pieters (Eds.), *Visual marketing: From attention to action*. Mahwah, NJ: Lawrence Erlbaum Associates.
Mick, D. G. (1992). Levels of subjective comprehension in advertising processing and their relations to ad perceptions, attitudes, and memory. *Journal of Consumer Research, 18*, 411–424.
Mick, D. G., & Buhl, C. (1992). A meaning based model of advertising experiences. *Journal of Consumer Research, 19*, 317–338.
Painter, J. E., Wansink, B., & Hieggelke, J. B. (2002). How visibility and convenience influence candy consumption. *Appetite, 38*, 237–238.
Pieters, R., & Wedel, M. (2007). The informativeness of eye-movements for visual marketing: Six cornerstones. In M. Wedel & R. Pieters (Eds.), *Visual marketing: From attention to action*. Mahwah, NJ: Lawrence Erlbaum Associates.
Pollay, R. W. (1985). The subsiding sizzle: A descriptive history of print advertising, 1900–1980. *Journal of Marketing, 49*, 24–37.
Rayner, K., & Castelhano, M. S. (2007). Eye movements during reading, scene perception, visual search, and while looking at print advertisements. In M. Wedel & R. Pieters (Eds.), *Visual marketing: From attention to action*. Mahwah, NJ: Lawrence Erlbaum Associates.
Simonson, I. (2005). In defense of consciousness: The role of conscious and unconscious inputs in consumer choice. *Journal of Consumer Psychology, 15*, 211–217.
Stephens, M. (1998). *The rise of the image, the fall of the word*. Oxford: Oxford University Press.

Tomasello, M. (1999). *The cultural origins of human cognition*. Cambridge, MA: Harvard University Press.

Turley, L. W., & Milliman, R. E. (2000). Atmospheric effects on shopping behavior: A review of the experimental evidence. *Journal of Business Research*, *49*, 193–211.

Wansink, B. (2005). *Marketing nutrition: Soy, functional foods, biotechnology, and obesity*. Urbana, IL: University of Illinois Press.

Index

A

D

E

F

G

J

K

L

M

N

O

P

T

U

V

W

CPSIA information can be obtained
at www.ICGtesting.com
Printed in the USA
BVHW042343080120
569005BV00017B/357/P